Into the Mountain Stream

Into the Mountain Stream

Psychotherapy and Buddhist Experience

Edited by Paul C. Cooper

JASON ARONSON
Lanham • Boulder • New York • Toronto • Plymouth, UK

Published in the United States of America
by Jason Aronson
An imprint of Rowman & Littlefield Publishers, Inc.

A wholly owned subsidiary of
The Rowman & Littlefield Publishing Group, Inc.
4501 Forbes Boulevard, Suite 200, Lanham, Maryland 20706
www.rowmanlittlefield.com

Estover Road
Plymouth PL6 7PY
United Kingdom

British Library Cataloguing in Publication Information Available

Library of Congress Cataloging-in-Publication Data

Into the mountain stream : psychotherapy and Buddhist experience / edited by Paul C.
Cooper.
    p. cm.
Includes bibliographical references and index.
ISBN-13: 978-0-7657-0464-1 (cloth : alk. paper)
ISBN-10: 0-7657-0464-1 (cloth : alk. paper)
ISBN-13: 978-0-7657-0465-8 (pbk. : alk. paper)
ISBN-10: 0-7657-0465-X (pbk. : alk. paper)
1. Buddhism and psychoanalysis. 2. Psychotherapy—Religious aspects—Buddhism.

BQ4570.P755I68 2007
294.3'36150195—dc22   2006027482

Printed in the United States of America

⊗™ The paper used in this publication meets the minimum requirements of American
National Standard for Information Sciences—Permanence of Paper for Printed Library
Materials, ANSI/NISO Z39.48-1992.

To Dr. Sonia Ragir and Dr. Gerald Sider, my two professors in the Department of Anthropology at the College of Staten Island of the City University of New York (formerly Richmond College).

In very different and unique ways, you both guided, supported, and encouraged my initial forays into human consciousness, relations, and self-awareness. The seeds you planted have penetrated deeply. Your inestimable influences continue to endure.

Contents

Acknowledgments

This collection is truly a dependent-arising with valuable suggestions, support, and encouragement deriving from countless individuals. The seeds of this project were first germinated and consciously conceived by me while attending a retreat in February, 2001, at Dai Bosatsu Zendo in the Catskill region of New York State. I am deeply grateful to Eido Shimano Roshi for his influence and teachings and for encouraging my exploration of the impact of Zen practice on my work as a psychoanalyst and as a psychoanalytic teacher. I am extremely grateful to Karen Morris for her abiding strength, support, and encouragement during the final phases of this project. I am also profoundly grateful to my friends and colleagues who provided me with generous encouragement, support, and constructive criticism. I appreciate their many suggestions regarding developing a creative approach to this project. I am indebted to Joe Bobrow, Michael Eigen, Mark Finn, Robert Gunn, Merle Molofsky, James Ogilvie, Ken Porter, Arthur Robbins, Alan Roland, Susan Rudnick, and Thomas Wagner for our valuable and encouraging conversations. I would like to thank all of the members of the Buddhism & Psychoanalysis study group. Our ongoing dialogue during the eight years that we met monthly continues to be deeply enriching. Polly Berends, Jeffrey Rubin, Tony Stern, and Marcella Bakur Weiner contributed their time and energy freely and generously. Their initial readings and response to the first drafts of my proposal and sample chapter were extremely useful. Many thanks to my students, teachers, and colleagues who have all contributed to my thinking and practice, and who continue to inspire me immensely. Many thanks to Maggie Brenner for encouraging me and creating the opportunity to develop a formal course on the subject of Buddhism and psychoanalysis for the Institute for Expressive Analysis in New York City;

to Eric Rhode for his response to my writing; to Jeffrey Eaton for his ongoing and stimulating e-mail correspondence.

I am also deeply grateful to Art Pomponio, Editorial Director for Rowman
& Littlefield, for his warmth, enthusiastic reception, and support in facilitating the publication of this collection. Many thanks to my production editor,
Melissa McNitt, and Lee Y. Miaio for their skillful and expedient copyediting
and production and also to the three anonymous readers at Jason Aronson for
their honest and insightful suggestions and constructive critiques of the original proposal. Many thanks to all of the contributing authors. Your commitment and willingness to contribute deeply heartfelt writings truly have
brought this collection into fruition. Thank for your abiding patience and confidence in my editorship.

I gratefully acknowledge permission to reprint the following material:

Chapter 9, "Oscillations," by Paul C. Cooper, was originally published in an
    earlier version as "Oscillations: Zen and Psychoanalytic Versions," in the
    Journal of Religion and Health 43 (3): 233–43. Used by permission of
    Springer Science and Business Media.
Chapter 11, "Bringing Practice Home," by Joan Hogetsu Hoeberichts, was
    originally published in an earlier version as "Bringing Zen Practice Home"
    in the *Journal of Religion and Health,* 43 (3): 201–16, reprinted by per-
    mission of Springer Science and Business Media.
Excerpt from the poem "Sunday Morning" from *The Palm at the End of the
    Mind* by Wallace Stevens (1971, 7) is reprinted in Chapter 12 by permis-
    sion of Random House, Inc., and by permission of Faber and Faber.
The translated poem "No Reliance on Words or Letters" from: *The Zen Po-
    etry of Dogen: Verses from the Mountain of Eternal Peace* by S. Heine, Tut-
    tle Publishing (1997, 103) is reprinted in the Introduction with the kind per-
    mission of Dr. Steven Heine.
Excerpt from "Poem: 10" from: *The Kabir Book*, by Robert Bly, Beacon Press
    (1971, 11) is reprinted in Chapter 9. Used by permission of Beacon Press.
The translated poem that begins "Vainly I dug," by Muso, that is reprinted in
    Chapter 9 is from: *Zen Poetry: Let the Spring Breeze Enter*, by L. Stryk and
    T. Ikemoto (1995, 176). Copyright © 1995 by Lucien Stryk. Used by per-
    mission of Grove/Atlantic, Inc.
The translated poem that begins "Life's as we find it," by Date Soko, that is
    reprinted in Chapter 9 is from: *Zen Poetry: Let the Spring Breeze Enter*, by
    L. Stryk and T. Ikemoto (1995, 189–90). Copyright © 1995 by Lucien
    Stryk. Used by permission of Grove/Atlantic, Inc.

Introduction:
Into the Mountain Stream

Paul C. Cooper

Not limited
By language
It is ceaselessly expressed;
So, too, the way of letters
Can display but not exhaust it.

(Dogen Zenji)[1]

In ancient China, legend has it that a C'han [Zen] Buddhist master and his student, on a pilgrimage during the summer, stopped by a mountain stream to rest and to escape the heat of the day. After resting, the master dived into the stream for a swim.

Meanwhile, the student wandered up to the footbridge that spanned the stream to take in the view. The master, upon finishing his swim, dressed himself and joined the student on the bridge to continue their journey. As the master approached, the student asked "Master, was the water refreshing?" The master suddenly grabbed his student by the collar and threw him off the bridge, shouting "See for yourself!" The student became instantly enlightened. At that moment, the master facilitated an existential leap that every sincere seeker must take. This leap, as the poet and translator Lucien Stryk notes, "is immediate, and no amount of pondering or philosophizing in itself can produce it" (Stryk and Ikemoto 1973, xviii). Such teaching stories dramatically exemplify the experiential nature that Buddhist practice and the chapters in this collection share.

In his influential *Essays in Zen Buddhism* (1961, 41), D.T. Suzuki asks "Is not the life of Buddhism the unfolding of the inner spiritual life of the Buddha himself rather than his exposition of it?" From this experiential and subjective

1

basis he asserts "The history of religion thus becomes the history of our own spiritual unfolding" (49). Suzuki thus concludes that "Buddhism is the structure erected around the inmost consciousness of its founder" (53).

Similarly, psychoanalysis derives from Sigmund Freud's direct experiences with hypnosis, hysteria, and through interpreting his own dreams. These creative forays into the elusive realm of the psyche contributed to his groundbreaking discovery of an active, dynamic unconscious. In both disciplines, theory, philosophy, and religious structures have developed secondarily from such foundational experiences.

If we think of the mountain stream as the stream of life, then remaining on the bridge keeps one safely removed from life and from the impact of life. Daido John Loori, the Zen master and abbot of Zen Mountain Monastery in Mt. Tremper, New York, frequently asserts that the student "must come down from the mountain and go into the market place." The stream of life must be engaged fully. Learning about Buddhism and/or psychoanalysis and being a Buddhist practitioner and/or a practicing psychoanalyst, as the chapters in this collection attest to, are two very different things, although the two are not by any means mutually exclusive.

During an interview early in my Zen training with Zen master Eido Shimano, Roshi, I asked about the role of study and reading in Zen training. He said "read all you want, but remember, whatever happens in your life just keep practicing!" Similarly, the British psychoanalyst Wilfred Bion, speaks about the distinction between talking *about* psychoanalysis and *being* psychoanalysis. He writes that "The *experience* of psycho-analysis affords material impossible to equal from any other source." Training analysis, he asserts, ". . . is necessary because it removes obstacles to participation in the psychoanalytic experience . . . " (1970, 26). Recently, Barry Magid (2002) has argued cogently and convincingly that practice forms the basic experiential nodal point between Buddhism and psychoanalysis.

Of course, from the nondualistic perspective embraced by Buddhism, the student, the master, the stream and the bridge are all aspects of this one life. However, what might be questioned is the quality of a life stuck, removed from the dynamic flow of full emersion in lived experience, as exemplified by the master's disrobing and immersion in the stream. Thus one becomes alienated from the possibility that Freud describes, as a reasonable outcome of psychoanalysis, as the ability to live and to work well. As Jeffrey Hopkins, the Tibetan Buddhist scholar notes in his comments on enlightenment "One who knows emptiness is aware, more perceptive, more awake, more conscientious . . . more into objects . . . more familiar . . . brilliant . . . clear" (1983, 197).

Despite differences regarding the structure and function of realization, it is clear that both Buddhist and psychoanalytic realization derive through one's direct experience. The master in the above teaching story can witness his student's understanding of the true nature of existence, but he cannot teach the student anything. He can take his own plunge into the river, but the student must make his own leap. One can stand on the bridge, safely removed from life's turbulence and movement and fail to suffer life. Alternatively, one can dive into life, suffering one's terrors, one's delights, one's pains, and one's pleasures.

One question pertinent to this collection becomes: As psychoanalysts, can we immerse ourselves in the lives of our patients and facilitate their existential leaps, as Bion (1970, 39) notes while "being submerged, but not drowning?" As Buddhists, can we immerse ourselves fully in the pulse of life, in the "marketplace" of our daily work in our consultation rooms beyond the seclusion of the mountain retreat?

What both Buddhism and psychoanalysis have to teach, as the chapters in this collection demonstrate, is how to suffer life as we find it. Both systems teach this through direct experience, such as through meditation, dialogues with the teacher, psychoanalysis, and psychoanalytic supervision. It is through these experiences that both disciplines exert the potential for a life-transforming impact; however, that impact is defined, understood, articulated, or envisioned.

Similarly, as one forms a meaningful relationship with the practices of both Buddhism and psychoanalysis in an impactful way, we might ask, "can one form a relationship with how these disciplines are talked or written about that can also exert an impact?" Can the text reflect what the thirteenth century Japanese Zen master Dogen alludes to in his poem above when he writes "Words express but do not exhaust Truth?" Can the reader form a fluid and living relationship with the text? What would such a text look and feel like? Can a text be both informational and rhetorical? If the text is informational, will the information oversaturate the reader's psychic space and stifle the text's dialogical potential, or will the text contribute to the reader's knowledge in a way that leaves room for creative thinking? Similarly, can the creative, rhetorical aspects of the text remain structured enough for a relationship to form with the reader? In a way what I am asking here is whether or not the mystical and scientific models can coexist and thrive together as the British psychoanalyst Eric Rhode suggests when he discusses the coexistence of the need for intuition of Truth through experiencing "the infinite" and the need for "specificity of configuration"(1998). Buddhism and psychoanalysis both offer different advantages; both have their limitations, an issue that I address in chapter 9.

One might talk *about* the integration of psychoanalysis and Buddhism or write more directly from one's personal experience. All of the contributors to this collection have immersed themselves deeply in both processes. Any theoretical peregrinations derive secondarily from such experiences. Both traditions are alive and vital and so must the conversation be for it to have a meaningful impact. Can linear and circular elements coexist, or are they mutually exclusive? Can the need to know coexist with the need to remain open to the unknown ineffable? If such coexistences are possible, how do different practitioners who are engaged in both Buddhism and psychoanalysis approach this task? How do internal integrations occur and how are they then reflected in our theories and technique? How can they be communicated in a way that maintains both structure and openness? More importantly, how do they influence the practitioner's mode of being in the world? So many questions! Perhaps one of the important purposes of this conversation is to keep the conversation alive and fresh by continuously raising questions, possible answers, and new questions. The many currents in the stream continue. The waters remain fresh, not stagnant. There is no place for complacency, an issue Mark Finn addresses in chapter 1, as he reflects from what he views as a "marginal space" on why we should want to "integrate" or in any way bring together Buddhism and psychoanalysis. Finn understands this matter as both deeply personal and as a reflection of a wider dynamic cultural process.

The contributors to this collection view the integration of Buddhism and psychoanalysis as a highly personal and internal process. Internal integration influences both the psychotherapist's perception and relation with patients, and our general mode of being in the world. For example, in chapter 2 Susan Rudnick elaborates how the experience of coming into the present moment informs and suffuses her work that has become her own way of strengthening and maintaining the capacity for affirmation and hopefulness about life. From this vantage point, she explores her relationship with her developmentally disabled sister and how this affected her sense of self as a professional, a Zen practitioner, and as a sibling. Beginning with the death of a close friend, Jeffrey Eaton chronicles many personal and professional relationships that evolved during his Buddhist training and through his work as a psychoanalytic candidate in chapter 3. Barry Magid describes the intertwining of his dual role as a psychoanalyst and Zen master in chapter 4. He elaborates the reality that everyone coming to either therapy or to meditation practice wants something. This is both unavoidable and natural. We come seeking a relief of suffering; however, we may conceive of that "suffering" and that "relief." From the perspective of personal experience, he explores how we can reconcile the paradox of relieving suffering while leaving everything just as it is and of discovering the "truth" that nothing is hidden. Tony Stern chronicles shifts in his relationship to his sense of self in his initial encounters with a spiritual master in chapter 5. He describes a multidimensional process that still persists, a process that he describes as a "light of faithful awareness" that unfolds more and more fully, exposing and cleansing layers of tension and self-rejection, freeing him to listen more deeply and fully to his patients and to be present to their whole situation in a visceral way, where past and present meet, and where self and other make true contact. Marjorie Schuman takes the narrative more deeply within into the shifting inner world of her own thought processes in chapter 6 as she interweaves narrative strands of what she has learned in her own psychoanalysis, her work as a psychotherapist, and from her experiences of Buddhist meditation. Jeffrey Rubin demonstrates the confluence of psychological and spiritual insight and awakening in the competitive and exhilarating world of basketball in chapter 7. He draws from these experiences to demonstrate the cross-pollination between Buddhism and psychoanalysis. In chapter 8, Robert Jonas shares a healing experience from his own life that he describes as a "perfect storm of healing" in which Buddhist meditation, Christian prayer, and Object Relations psychotherapy each provided resources for a new life. In chapter 10, Dorothy Yang addresses the potential for grandiosity and how psychoanalysis can dismantle such false claims, thus facilitating deeper and more authentic involvements in Buddhist practice. She then demonstrates the clinical implications of her insights in her own personal struggle for authenticity as a Buddhist practitioner and with her patients. Joan Hoeberichts takes up the issue of personal relatedness with regard to her own relationship and in her work with couples in chapter 11.

No discussion of any religious tradition would be complete without an explication of how the issue of death and dying are addressed. While references to personal loss are present in many of the chapters in this collection, Susan Flynn provides a detailed account of her shifting relationship to herself and to her family with regard to the death of her sister in chapter 12. From the point of view of the centrality of meditation practice, she describes how bearing personal experience becomes a way of speaking of staying with a process from beginning to end, as "staying with the process" of being both psychoanalysed and psychoanalyzing. This "staying with the process" is central to learning how to meditate and maintaining a meditation practice, and it was essential to her capacity and desire to stay with the process of her sister's death.

Experience has taught all of the contributors to this collection that engagement in both processes contains conflicting and mutually facilitating aspects that contribute to deepening Buddhist practice and understanding in relation to clinical theory and technique. The various issues and concerns that led each individual to his or her unique search for meaning within the Buddhist/psychoanalytic context result in creative living and an eventual integration with sound psychoanalytic theory and technique that is consistent with Buddhist beliefs and practices, despite diverging aspects.

In planning this collection, no attempt was made to arrive at a common definition of Buddhism or psychoanalysis that would be accepted by all of the contributors. The authors draw from various schools of Buddhism, including Tibetan Buddhism, Southeast Asian Theravada Buddhism, Zen Buddhism, and eclectic hybrids that are evolving into a distinctively American Buddhism. Yet, during discussions throughout the planning stage of this project, it became obvious to all of the contributors that there was a general consensus regarding the meaning and function of Buddhism and psychoanalysis. We agree that both disciplines, as noted above, are rooted in direct personal experience and both address basic human suffering in very profound, radical, yet practical ways with the potential for far-reaching impact on our personal and professional lives.

None of the authors express the view that Buddhism is unique or idiosyncratic. Rather we are offering a specific example, through our Buddhist experience, that demonstrates how a religious perspective and associated practices function in relation to psychotherapy and how religious experience results in a perspective that challenges classical psychoanalytic pathologizing notions of religion. The unique quality of this collection centers on our personal narrative/experiential approach to the subject matter.

This collection chronicles each contributor's personal journey. We begin from the feeling component of our own inner journey: pain, trauma, ecstasy, joy, terror, bliss, and digging in the dirt to the roots embracing both the thorny and rosy aspects of experience that led to finding our own unique inner voices beyond dogma. We then show how we have translated our personal experiences into our therapeutic voices and how our Buddhist practices influence our being in the world and our work.

In short, we are not confined by ideology or tradition—but build into our work with the individuals who seek our help and ourselves how both Buddhist and psychoanalytic traditions contribute to the whole person's integration. It is in this spirit that we invite the reader to enter the stream of this dynamic and living conversation.

NOTE

1. S. Heine 1997, 108.

REFERENCES

Bion, W. (1970). *Attention and interpretation*. London: Karnac Books.
Heine, S. (1997). *The Zen poetry of Dogen: Verses from the mountain of eternal peace*. Boston: Charles E. Tuttle.

Hopkins, J. (1983). *Meditation on emptiness*. Boston: Wisdom.

Dogen, E. (1994). *Shobogenzo*. Trans. G. Nishijima and C. Cross. Woods Hole, MA: Windbell.

Magid, B. (2002). *Ordinary mind: Exploring the common ground of Zen and psychotherapy*. Boston: Wisdom.

Rhode, E. (1998). *On intuition, hallucination and the becoming of "O."* Binghamton, NY: ESF.

Stryk, L., and T. Ikemoto. (1973). *Zen poems of China and Japan: The crane's bill*. New York: Grove Press.

Suzuki, D. T. (1961). *Essays in Zen Buddhism*. New York: Grove Weidenfeld.

———. (1994). *Zen koan as a means of attaining enlightenment*. Boston: Charles E. Tuttle.

Chapter One

Reflections from the Margin: Buddhism and Psychoanalysis

Mark Finn

My purpose in this short chapter is to wonder what we have been up to over the last twenty years as we have pursued a renewal of the dialogue between Buddhism and psychoanalysis. My goal is conversational, not theoretical, so I can only speak for myself and hope that my experience is not idiosyncratic. I am optimistic because I have come to know so many psychotherapists about my age with similar interests in Buddhism and psychoanalysis. It leads me to think that we may be a small sociocultural cohort. If so, some candor on my part may be evocative of more general themes.

In some sense wanting to live in a world of Buddhism and psychoanalysis has been a deep desire on my part to have my cake and eat it too. Put concretely, I didn't become a Buddhist monk or even make dramatic sacrifices during my training in meditation. True, I spent many vacations meditating, but I was, and have to admit, determined not only to help people but also to achieve a reasonably high level of professional attainment. I also struggled, not at all very successfully or even kindly at times, to get to married life and a family. Career and family life are exactly what the Buddha left behind. In a similar way, I admired many of the leftist radicals of the sixties and I very much wanted to be of service and have spent most of my career in the public mental health system in various roles; but again, to be candid, I wanted a certain bourgeois stability. I didn't seek wealth necessarily, but I was clear, even if I wasn't honest with myself, that I wasn't going to be poor if I could help it. So this Buddhist-psychoanalytic identity is a complex compromise, and compromises can always be expressions of weakness or failures of will. I read an interview with Ken Wilber, the self-styled grand theoretician of all psychospiritual matters, decrying this watered down dharma of which I am a clear example. Wilber went so far as to characterize psychotherapists as "pimps for samsara." It is tempting to respond in kind to remarks like that, but I shall refrain except to say that for both the spiritual warrior and the revolutionary, the therapist is always a liberal apologist. A few years ago I was invited to a conference on Buddhism and psychotherapy, which was well organized and quite sincere. However, by the time all the individual presentations were over and all the speakers had gathered for panel discussion with questions from the audience, I found myself uneasy. On the surface, it felt like an atmosphere of self-congratulation had taken hold. We were by the sea, and all the amenities were exemplary. Filled with these and other conflicted feelings I remarked that we as successful (I didn't even bother to say white) shrinks are, in fact, parasites on the body of a bloated empire. My comment was badly timed and not at all thought over. Most of the panelists seemed embarrassed and ignored my little outburst. One woman analyst skillfully countered by looking at me directly and asking, "Do you feel like a parasite?"

At that moment I realized my feelings were all mixed up with all my conflicts about my own worthiness and entitlement to success and the whole sad story of my narcissistic wounds. But still, I sputtered, the situation is more complex. Fortunately, the momentum of the conference moved past this painful point. I remained disturbed, displeased with my performance, and embarrassed at having been so revealed. One well-intentioned friend picked up on my psychodynamics and engaged me in a conversation about my persistent self-deprecating stance. There was no shortage of painful truth in our exploration of my problems, but I was left again feeling that our bourgeois success as therapists is a blessing and a problem. We are lucky to be prosperous and useful. We get the lives of intellectuals, the meaningful work of physicians, and the chance for creativity like artists. But we are also at risk for the self-satisfied smugness of self-congratulatory elites. Wilber's contempt for our profession is not, and I am sad to say, entirely mistaken. I was relieved when, at the end of the conference, several people came up to me and thanked me for taking the risk, which helped a little.

So much of my involvement with Buddhism and psychotherapy has been connected to ideas about the wisdom that comes from the margins outside of established power. Buddhism is a gesture among many to subvert a judgmental authoritarian psychoanalysis disconnected from its soul. Psychoanalysis so often presented itself as critical and condescending toward the counterculture, which despite its many self-delusions, contained for me much genuine inspiration. Richard Alpert, the Harvard psychology professor who became the spiritual teacher Ram Das was a hero for me. His public talks gave me the feeling that psychedelic wonder could grow into something real. I also saw him as a kind of verbal rock star. His talks were like Gerry Garcia's guitar solos. His more recent comments suggest he too was carried away by his own image. I remember Cary Grant once saying that even he wanted to be Cary Grant.

Psychoanalysis is a corrective critical discourse to more skeptically evaluate our involvement with Buddhism. I would argue that this is especially important in the light of abuses of authority by so many dharma teachers. I recalled the writer and critic John Berger's sadness considering the failures of the rebellions in Europe in 1968. He said "now we can say and do anything as long as nothing really changes." Part of getting involved with Buddhism at all had to do with keeping the spiritual vitality of the sixties counterculture alive without succumbing to descents into revolutionary violence, chemical self-destruction, or religious paths that seemed too zealous or flaky. A project that has been very successful for very many people, including myself, and I am very grateful to those American Buddhists who went the whole way; those who didn't compromise but built the practice centers we now all take for granted. Yet, there is in me a lingering sadness for the utopian yearnings of truth. I remember reading the poet Robert Bly in the mid-seventies that the very success of the Buddhist College Naropa Institute concerned him. He thought many students at Naropa were seeking some respite from conventional models of achievement and status. Utopian wishes are probably always unrealistic, yet they contain some space for hope if one can refrain from violence. American Buddhism seems very healthy to me, less sectarian and more truly ordinary in every sense. American psychoanalysis also seems to me much saner: psychiatric hegemony is finished and a lively pluralism has emerged. No longer imprisoned by anxious orthodoxy, psychoanalysis is bursting with lively questions. The wider culture looks dreadful. The boom in materialism is truly disheartening if not revolting. Much of this is unavoidable: history teaches us empires rise and fall; science and the dharma teach that worlds come and go. So, is this alienation a persistent hangover of covert grandiosity, both personal and cultural? Are the Buddhist psychoanalysts going to be a brigade in an army bringing down the towers of greed and violence, with the thunder of mantra and deep ironic empathy? Probably not. But to rescue mysticism from the right wing is a worthy and important purpose. Martin Luther King and Malcolm X were mystics of a sort, I believe, and their love still vibrates in this dark age. Thinking of them just reminds me of how white Buddhism and psychoanalysis are. My life and the lives of most of my progressive friends are still painfully racially segregated. It is a banality of sad observation but needs to be included since cultural change is so much at the heart of our organized efforts to bring Buddhism and psychoanalysis higher.

At this point I stand accused, by myself, of being compromised, self-interested, adolescent, and burdened with my fair share of neurotic sore points. Yet cheerfulness and confidence continue. This marginal space between Buddhism and psychoanalysis remains heartening despite self-criticism and the disparagement of the Ken Wilbers of the world. The most sustaining aspects are the practices of meditation or prayer and psychotherapy. They remain neither the same nor different and as Suzuki Roshi said, not one, not two. I am very lucky in that I have many serious spiritual practitioners in my analytic practice. The complexity and richness of these analytic partnerships combust any positions of disparagement. Buddhist practice is a daily reminder that spiritual life is not a set of ideas but ongoing experience as real as food. I am also comforted that after almost twenty years of conferences, edited books, and other professional activities, the Buddhist-psychoanalytic community has not, thank God, organized itself into formal societies with the typical madness of membership dynamics, no journal has emerged, and no standards of practice were produced. The Buddhist-psychoanalytic dialogue has remained only a space: not a thing or a product. Even this present volume with its emphasis on personal reflections moves us away from commodification and back to practice, conversation, and experience.

Chapter Two

Coming Home to Wholeness

Susan Rudnick

For Edna,
who has always held me in wholeness.

"As surely as there is a voyage away, there is a journey home."

(Kornfield 2000, 4)

Throughout my whole life I have struggled with a sense of myself as being handicapped. The word "handicapped" has a very particular meaning and resonance for me. Deriving from my childhood, it was the word used to describe my younger sister, who had physical and developmental issues for which, at that time, there seemed to be no clear diagnosis.

My way of experiencing myself became profoundly intertwined with how I saw and felt the world perceiving my sister. Handicapped was a label given to her both by the experts of that time, and by our whole community, which in turn informed and defined the ways I, and my parents, experienced her. This experience of feeling handicapped included a sense of "differentness," something wrong, feeling like an outcast, being a burden, and feeling burdened, and feeling not acceptable, inadequate, and deficient.

Looking back now, I realize that my whole family internalized an identity as a "handicapped family." We measured the world by how they treated my sister. People who were kind to her could enter our domain; those who were indifferent or mean could not. I always had my antenna out, whenever we met anyone new. I lived in a polarized world of either normal or abnormal, in which the first task was to protect the sanctity of our little family from those who judged us. At that time it could include children who made fun of her, parents who didn't make any effort to help, and even teachers who didn't want to be bothered.

In this polarized world of those who were normal and those who were not, and those who were understanding and those who were not, I was split in two ways. On the one hand by identification with her, I was definitely in the "not normal" camp. I felt embarrassment, shame, and anger but was inextricably bound to her. On the other hand I was the normal sister, who could do all the things she couldn't: have friends, run, play, skip, and jump. This was a complicated, thorny experience, which involved feelings of guilt and confusion that I had what she didn't. There was a not knowing what I was really entitled to do, be and claim for myself, and what did I owe her. In either case, into whichever camp I placed myself, I was immersed in a bifurcated, either or, okay, not okay world.

My path through this maze led me from becoming a psychotherapy patient to becoming a therapist to the spiritual path of Buddhism, and now to the process of integrating what is useful in both the Western and Eastern models of healing. I came to Buddhism because the more traditional psychotherapeutic model was not able to address the depth of my need to heal this incredible divide within myself. This was not possible, partially because the Western model of treatment, as useful as it has been, contains inherently within it, the medical model, which is rooted in diagnosing pathology, seeing the world through the same lens that was so painful for me. When I became a therapist, in part, I inadvertently reinforced the system I was trying to find my way through. I needed to find another way to address and hold my issues, and Buddhism, with its emphasis on the wholeness that is always there for everyone when we practice coming into the present, offered another perspective and opened my world. In a profound way, finding Buddhism has brought me back full circle to my sister, and the way she has always held me, and the rest of the world in wholeness. It is my hope that writing in a personal way in some detail about my relationship with my sister will highlight and illuminate both some of the limitations of the psychoanalytic model and the ways that bringing a Buddhist perspective to it can transform it. I will conclude with describing some work I did with the mother of a "handicapped" child in which I drew on the strength of my Zen practice to inform my way of being with her.

Turning back again to my life, my very earliest memories of my sister had nothing to do with the split I described. She was simply my constant companion and first love. In fact, if anything, I relied on her in new situations. She was warm and friendly in contrast to my shy, retiring self. She was cuddly and comforting, and we often cuddled in bed together at night. In that time there were no distinctions, judgments, or differences, but just a living of life and being together. But by the time I was six and had started school, an inexorable process was set in motion in which I slowly moved away from the purer experience of my sister as friend and companion to the awareness of all she couldn't do. It was like standing with one foot on either side of a piece of ice floating down the river that is slowly cracking into two pieces. I had to jump to one side or be pulled apart. And jump I did, creating the sense of a great divide and a feeling of separateness.

At the same time as this process was moving along, I know that I was also trying to understand and make sense of what was happening. I have a distinct memory of being in first or second grade, and the funny look on a librarian's face when I asked if there were any books about handicapped children. I know she found one with a picture of a crippled boy on the cover, and I remember being glad she found it. I also remember that I was not able to connect to that because my sister didn't have anything obviously physically wrong with her at that time. But at least a book existed; something in the outside world addressed the idea that there were people who had something wrong with them.

As we got older, one of the main and more painful ways we were so different was my capacity to make friends and her difficulties with that. While I had a best friend with whom I was inseparable, she was always going up to children trying to connect, which always ended with rejection. My parents found a Saturday "club" for handicapped children to which I would sometimes accompany her. Here the children ranged from those that were ambulatory to those who could barely talk and sat in wheelchairs. It was sometimes excruciating to think that here was where she had to go, and I would comfort myself with the thought that she was one of the "better, high level" ones.

Two important memories from the club stand out as pivotal in my development. One was that I idolized the social worker, who had polio herself, running the program. It was dawning on me that I could ease something inside of myself if I, too, became a helper. I could help people and make it better for them. I could make sense of all this by organizing myself around an identity of heroine who is adored by many and in some way, equalizing what is unequal. This was an important root leading me toward my career as a therapist.

The second and more complicated one, so disturbing to me at the time but which I now understand as a seed in my movement toward a spiritual path, was the fact that when my sister moved into friendships in the club, she chose one of the most severely handicapped girls there. This was a wheelchair-bound girl, very overweight, who spoke, but not clearly. I remember our whole family going to visit this girl's family, and my feeling so reluctant to go. Why did she have to pick that one, I thought? Couldn't she find someone a little less obvious? Looking back now, I realize that my sister never looked at people in the polarized ways that I did and still sometimes do now. This was just someone she liked and enjoyed playing records with. They both liked show tunes. There were no layers of "handicappedness" for her. She connected to the essential personhood of this friend and loved her, as she did me, unconditionally.

As she got older and moved into adolescence, my parents had to let go of the dream that with lots of help my sister would find a way to live in mainstream society. As they were casting about, feeling quite helpless to find some kind of viable solution, they heard about a spiritual community based on the teaching of Rudolph Steiner that was being formed in upstate New York. The idea was to form a community with, rather than for, the developmentally challenged people that would live there. Those who formed this community would choose to make their lives with handicapped people as a spiritual path and source of growth for themselves. There had already been several communities like this that had been successful in Europe. My open-minded parents arranged an interview and brought my sister and all the diagnostic reports and psychological evaluations that had been done about her. When they arrived, the people who met them didn't even glance at the reports but simply took my sister for a walk. When they returned, they said "we think the village needs Edna." This became a famous sentence in our family lore, and when my parents heard it, they knew instantly this was the place for her. Nobody before had ever spoken to my parents about her from the vantage point that she could be valuable and useful to others.

That she was needed, and therefore could live a useful productive life, was for me profound new information that reverberated on a cellular level. It meant that she was being seen, being recognized by others, in a new way. Somehow, although her handicap was certainly more obvious on the physical level by that time, there was a way in which her being or essence was being valued. Rather than being labeled or judged by her deficits, she was being welcomed as the whole person she was. At that time, wrapped up in my own adolescence, and just beginning college, I had no way to process or integrate much of this; nevertheless, another seed had been planted.

My sister spent almost forty years living at Camphill Village, and I have also spent that many years visiting her there, coming to know her in the context in which she has lived and worked and been part of a community family life. But as I look back now on these years to explain my relationship to this experience, I come back to the image of standing on the two pieces of ice going down the river. On the one hand, I could live for short periods in the world of the Camphill community, which also welcomed me, and even included workshops and discussions for family members on topics such as "what is the spiritual significance of a handicapped sibling?" When I visited there I could relax in a way that I never would anywhere else when I would be with her. But then I would leave and go back to my "real" life, where I went from college, to graduate school, and analytic training, and I would forget this life and this way of experiencing. Her life and community remained for me a separate, encapsulated reality.

In a way there was even more of a chasm between us because in addition to her handicap, she was now involved in this rural way of life, permeated by what seemed to me to be a strange, spiritual view largely unknown to most people. It was almost impossible to articulate to others the quality of life to be found at Camphill and the lens through which she was being seen. When she came home to visit us, I was left with some of the same old feelings I always had. I could still feel embarrassed, ashamed, or just plain tense.

At that time, in my twenties, the gap felt unbridgeable. There was no way for me to connect the information I was learning on a spiritual level with the rest of my life. Pushing that world aside, I chose to try to understand myself, to heal, to gain mastery, to fix it all by becoming a therapist. I plunged whole-heartedly first through social work school and then analytic training into the worlds of diagnosis, understanding personality, and psychoanalytic theories of treatment. I do still live in that world and draw on the wisdom I gained from deep immersion in it both for my life and the clients I work with.

It feels important to say that because what follows next is a discussion of my growing awareness of the profound dissonance and difficulties I have experienced with the psychoanalytic model. These difficulties became the impetus to grope my way toward Buddhism, the spiritual perspective that I have been able to integrate with my analytic work that finally allows me to move down the river of my life with a greater sense of wholeness.

Psychoanalysis has evolved in many directions over the last hundred years since Freud first introduced his theories, but in my experience its foundation is still embedded in a scientific/medical model based on understanding and curing what is perceived as pathological. It is beyond the scope of this chapter to look at all the ways we have attempted to move beyond the medical model. Rather, I am needing to underscore both for clients and therapists, in particular myself as a therapist, how this distinct flavor remains and the effects it has on the work.

In this model, which was certainly emphasized in my training, the analyst is the expert, the healer, the sane person to whom the patient, who is sick, troubled, and riddled with problems and pains turns to get help solving problems. There are two major difficulties for me with this model, which permeate the theory and practice of psychoanalysis. One is the basic dualistic assumption of health versus pathology. There is a continuum in this model, with some people healthier than others, allowing for the possibility of moving up or down the scale. People are also seen as complex, with healthy, constructive aspects or selves, within a matrix of more neurotic parts. But even in its complexity, basically we are still slicing the pie into two parts, healthy and sick.

The analyst is expected to be well analyzed and to uphold the standard for normalcy in her own personality. Further, the analyst is trained to listen for symptoms or specific kinds of behaviors and to root out and understand the pathology of the person sitting before her. The foundation of the concept of diagnosis, which can be helpful in understanding something specific, is based on looking for what is wrong. What I am bringing out here is an issue of emphasis.

Of course we are also listening to find the health in someone. However, the stronger pull, weighted down by the diagnostic manuals and also perhaps by our own fascination, is toward the sickness. For example, a young woman I am seeing tells me that her relationship with her boyfriend, whom she loves, is going well, and he has told her he would like to have a baby with her, something she also wants. In the next sentence she reveals that she is fantasizing intensely about a man whom she knew years ago, who seems to embody some of the qualities that she finds missing in her current relationship. She has kept an idealized fantasy about this man going for many years. She doesn't know why she is doing this. Is there something constructive about her need to put a wedge in here? Perhaps there are some important qualities missing, and she should be listening to that. Or perhaps this is a way of telling herself that she is not yet ready to make this shift in her relationship. On the other hand, is she afraid of intimacy, needing to live in fantasy so she doesn't have to confront her own vulnerabilities? She does tend to be perfectionistic about herself and sometimes critical of others. In my earlier years I would have focused on the latter, whereas now, while I am aware of these issues, I also am curious about and wonder about the former.

Adding to this is the second difficulty, which is the method or technique used in this process of understanding pathology. In my experience, the psychoanalytic community, while struggling to open up its understanding of technique, is still adhering to remnants of the scientific model in which the therapist is attempting to be as objective as possible. The effect of this is a tendency to observe, stand apart from, and scrutinize the patient. I have found myself moving into and relying on this stance, especially in moments when I am confronted with either great suffering or I feel confused or overwhelmed by the complicated nature of what someone is bringing. The training emphasizes this standing back and examining as the way to gain mastery by bringing intellectual understanding to the situation. Sometimes this can yield useful information, but it also moves me away from the patient. The patient inevitably has a sense of this and may experience feeling scrutinized, abandoned, or judged.

I feel it is so important to emphasize that to be a therapist is to enter into relationships with people who are at low points in their lives, in crisis, and feeling immobilized. At the points when it would seem that what is needed is to be able to really find ways to move close or to be with someone, we are trained to move away and gain control through objectifying. Using this technique we work hard to find our way back to the more comfortable place where we are again the expert in control. For example, I remember working with a woman who had been severely traumatized as a child with both physical and verbal abuse. She came in for a session and recounted to me that she had just been on a bus where a fight broke about between two disheveled people who had gotten on the bus. She was wedged between them. They were shouting and screaming, and at first the bus driver did nothing. As she told me this she began rocking, and moaning, and withdrawing from me. She grabbed a pillow and held it up in front of her eyes and continued to rock back and forth. I started to feel anxious and noticed myself distancing into my head with labels, such as this is regressed, repetitive, and autistic behavior. When I realized how I was withdrawing, I could come back for a moment to attend to my anxiety, make a space for that, let go of the labels, and return to being more present to her.

This way of distancing becomes magnified when combined with labeling people in terms of their deficits. When we use these labels they define and greatly narrow our perceptions, which then inform how we envision the treatment and interact with the person sitting across from us. When I refer to a patient as "borderline" or "bipolar," the label itself has an alienating impact and supports the tendency to move away from the person living life in a complicated, problematic way. Furthermore, this way of thinking subtly tips the balance, for me, of how I experience myself in relation to the patient. It becomes almost impossible not to put myself in a comparable mode. Either I'm glad I'm not as sick as this person, or perhaps I'm feeling, in the moment, even more mixed up than my patient. It is easy to find myself caught, together with my patient, in this polarized perspective.

Two other brief examples of the effects of this kind of labeling follow.

One way to get a glimpse of how unaware we tend to be of the profound alienation that occurs with deficit labels is the shift in recent years from the old label "developmentally disabled" to the new label "developmentally challenged." The feeling of the newer label allows for the possibility of moving toward such a person with some hope and possibility. There is some openness; after all, challenges can be met and overcome. It is only in beginning to use the new label that one may first come into contact with and realize the limiting effects of the old label. At one point in my life I ran a recreational program for the developmentally disabled. It never even occurred to me to question this label before the newer one came into being.

The second example occurred recently in my practice when a woman I see was telling me about the results of an MRI done on her son who has a neurological weakness on the right side of his body. He had already been receiving extensive therapies for this, but the MRI was suggested just to find out if more could be learned. She came in feeling rather depressed after the results were given to her, even though nothing new had been discovered. When we explored it, she realized that the results had stated that her son is "brain damaged." It was this phrase that got to her. Did she know this already? Yes. But defining him in this way, with an edict coming down from the experts, sent her spiraling down a limiting path in which she found it difficult to stay in touch with the wonderful being that is her son.

These examples illustrate how any therapist can feel limited, depressed, or hopeless when faced with diagnoses like borderline or bipolar. With my sensitivities to deficits, not only have I felt feelings like depression, but my intense needs to fix and rescue become activated. This particular issue is the crux of what has been difficult for me in working with the psychoanalytic model. I have realized that there is an inherent paradox, or double message, being conveyed in psychoanalytic training. On the one hand we are taught not to problem solve, fix, or rescue anyone. In the best psychoanalytic traditions, different theories articulate the work as being there to listen, to make the unconscious conscious, or to resolve or open up impasses in the psychoanalytic relationship. In any case, the patient is there to find his own way. But in placing all that training into the context of the tradition of the medical model, the analyst is faced with a quandary. How can I not want to help get someone out of a jam when I am asked, as an expert, to diagnose the deficit? In addition, the person sitting in front of me is often asking me to fix them. There is something that needs to be fixed not only because there is so much pain and suffering, but because we have labeled it as something that needs fixing.

What I learned about my need to fix and rescue people has been key in gravitating toward Buddhism. On the one hand, it has become clearer to me that there is wisdom in the analytic model. It really is not possible to "fix" people. Rather than doing or trying to solve people's lives, it is far more important to listen and just be with someone. But in a profound way I came to realize that the technique that was offered was insufficient to help me work on these issues. In my training, my "rescue needs" were labeled as neurotic. My task was to analyze these feelings, understand how they came from my past, and find my way back to the more objective analytic stance. I emerged from this with a sense of inadequacy, alienation from those feelings and parts of myself that would wish to heal, and a sense that I just didn't quite "cut the analytic mustard."

Without clearly articulating it, there was something inside me that needed to find another way to be with all these deep feelings: the patient who is suffering, my suffering by identifying and feeling empathic toward the patient, and the suffering of knowing that I cannot rescue anyone. Something more like the way Edna would be with her friend.

The practice of Zen Buddhism, a path based on experiencing the wholeness of the present moment, offered me a way to be with suffering that allows me to move toward my patient. It provides a process that enables me to stay open to myself, letting go of the need to "fix" and do, by allowing in whatever comes, right now, right here.

In the Buddhist perspective we are all intrinsically whole, perfect, lacking nothing. Our conditioning and belief systems may keep us from experiencing this truth, but this is our true nature, and it is true for everybody. It is possible for everyone to cultivate this experience through the practice of meditation. But even without this, most of us at some points in our lives have had some glimpses of this, maybe while seeing something beautiful in nature, witnessing the birth of a child, or in an ordinary moment, such as walking the dog or looking out a window. At these moments, there is a quality of fullness and a sense of being fully engaged. There is a dropping away of self-consciousness and an opening to just what is, rather than a need to do or change anything. When I bring this perspective to bear on my work with anyone, I have given myself a larger framework to contain all the "diagnostic truths" that might also be useful. It begins to permeate and inform the way I am listening. I am not only asking what is wrong and what is the problem, but the larger question is how do I experience the wholeness of the person in front of me? How can I be more like my sister with her friend playing records together?

When I work with Zen practice that involves a moment-to-moment way of coming into the present, by staying open to whatever thoughts and sensations arise, I begin to experience the wholeness of just this moment, the way it is. By coming into the present, I emerge into being with my feelings, thoughts, and sensations; and when I do this sitting across from my patient, this enlarges to my sensing of her feelings and thoughts and a sensing of how we are together in the room. When I move into this mode, I am not separating myself by observing and trying to gain mastery by figuring something out, but rather I am engaged in a process of opening myself to the uncertainty of not knowing and being and resonating with whatever emerges and however we are.

What emerges from this practice for me has been the experience; over and over again, that healing does occur. It happens by moving toward someone to touch pain by opening to it, by giving it space and allowing it to be there in this moment, this presentness. I learn and relearn that I can let go of my need to fix and do because I can experience the power of the shifting that happens when we allow whatever is there to be there. It is the awareness that "oh, there is nothing to do about this, I can just experience this, and from this experiencing, there is room to breathe." There is a sense of space and spaciousness; there is the possibility of possibility.

When I open to what is there, I am not avoiding any of the pain of a particular situation, but now I have a way to feel it without having to fix it. Healing occurs out of making space for, out of relaxing toward, out of acceptance of whatever is. That creates the possibility of a next step. When we move toward pain in this way, we are not isolating, tensing up, defending against, or avoiding. We are reverberating and responding with it. As I develop this capacity, there is strength and courage in this moving toward that is communicated and informs the next moment. I am able to be more with myself, which in turn creates the possibility of being more intimate with my patient. I call this way of being "holding in wholeness."

The ability to call on this practice with Sandy, whose life situation triggered both an intense desire to help and fix and an equal desire to run from it all, was essential in our work together. In our first session, I moved into this way of being as a way to be open to and navigate the intense and complex web of my feelings and thoughts.

She is sitting on the edge of her chair, a middle-aged woman, hair pulled straight back, her face taut. Speaking in a quiet controlled way, she tells me her teenage son, an honor student and rock climber, has been seriously injured in a car accident and is wheelchair bound with little or no chance of being able to walk again. She is not someone who would ordinarily avail herself of therapy but has come on the advice of a friend. In a beseeching way she asks me "how can I help my son feel better?"

I feel immediately pulled in, almost swimming in this devastation with her. My mind is spinning. A number of thoughts and feelings emerge, not necessarily in sequence or fully articulated but which form a sticky matrix that I sink in and out of. "Your son was normal, now he's handicapped" is an echo of my life with my sister. I hear my client asking me to help her fix her son. I want to, but I know I can't. I think that now my client will experience what I've been through, and she'll have no idea what she's in for. "Now you will be in my world." Then a memory of trying to teach my little sister how to walk up stairs floats up. Then I feel some shame about the way I am almost glad that, just as I suffered, my client is now suffering.

I find myself withdrawing to a safer, more distant, stance. I think, "get a grip, find out more." I ask her more questions, and details emerge, but her voice remains flat. I become aware of the part of me that doesn't want to touch any of this. I don't want to face the pain, hers or mine. The facts are so undeniable. In the beginning of his senior year in high school, just about to apply to college, everything has shifted for this young man and his family. It all feels so grim.

As a therapist I know I'm supposed to help her "accept her reality," but at this moment I neither want to nor think I can. I am trying to push it away as I often did in my own life. For a moment I become aware that I feel identified with her. We both don't want to accept this reality, and now I want to move closer to her.

I realize my work needs to be finding the way to hold all of this. I start to become aware of my breath, which is a way to slow myself down so I can be with whatever comes in a less frantic, less judgmental way. I become aware of the way I am twisting and turning away from her and away from all that is unacceptable in me. Rather than trying to analyze or even understand any of it, I just allow all the feelings and thoughts to be there, resting in it. It is this resting in it that allows me to become more present; present to the truthfulness of who I am at this moment. I don't have to deny anything, and I don't have to fix anything. Embedded in this experience of truthfulness is a moment of deep self-acceptance. In the relief, release, and strength that comes from this, I can now open to her. Perhaps, from my way of being with all of this, I can convey to her a sense of how she could begin to be with her suffering.

When I begin to speak from this place, I am able to move toward the pain without tightening. I move toward all of it: hers, mine, and ours. I say, "you would do anything to help your son, and it seems there is nothing you really can do." She nods. I continue. "How is it to be in this terrible place?" We take each other in as she beings to cry.

In this moment we are connected, kindred spirits. I do not know where the next moment will take us. But this moment where we touch is healing for both of us.

By articulating my inner process in this example, I hope I've shown that the matrix from which we live our lives and do our work is intricate and complex. Our histories continue to live within us, shaping the rhythm and rhyme of what we say and do. No matter how much work I have done to understand and become self aware, there will always be a need for me to open to the truth of the present moment.

Just recently, in my own life, it became medically necessary for my sister to move to a nursing home. Her roommate suffers from Alzheimer's. When I visited, as we walked down the hall, she ran over to her roommate, hugged her, and said "I love you." I had a moment of backing off, but she placed her roommate's hand on mine. "I'm happy to meet you," I said, smiling to her and myself.

REFERENCES

Christensen, A., and S. Rudnick. (1999). A glimpse of Zen practice within the realm of countertransference. *American journal of psychoanalysis*, 59:1, 59–69.

Gendlin, E. (1996). *Focusing oriented psychotherapy: A manual of the experiential method*. New York: Guilford Press.

Kornfield, J. (2000). *After the ecstasy, the laundry*. New York: Bantam.

Suzuki, S. (1970). *Zen mind, beginner's mind*. New York: Weatherhill.

Chapter Three

From Nowhere to Now-here: Reflections on Buddhism and Psychotherapy

Jeffrey L. Eaton

Anything looked at with love and attention becomes very interesting.

(Snyder 1999, 209)

Buddha was a man who became "awakened" to what are described as the Four Noble Truths, the underlying "laws" of experience and reality. To accomplish his awakening, Buddha took his own mind and experience as the basic objects of investigation. The deeper he penetrated into the causes and conditions of suffering, generated by the habits of his mind and by his conditioned perceptions, the more freedom he experienced emotionally. This freedom opened into a vast view of human experience characterized by a great compassion for the suffering of all sentient beings.

Buddhism begins with the recognition that suffering is real. Suffering touches *every* life in some form with some intensity. This is a difficult recognition to accept though the evidence for it is everywhere. The truth of suffering is intimidating. We are often so ill prepared to face suffering directly that we create "nowhere" states of mind to dull our mental pain. Alienated nowhere states of mind help evade the now-here experience of painful emotional reality, including the ubiquity of psychic and physical violence.

Buddha taught that the causes of suffering *can* be investigated. These causes *can* be identified in each of our lives. Investigating the causes of suffering requires courage, compassion, and sustained commitment. Meditation is one of the main tools used to prepare the mind for such a task.

Once the causes of suffering have been learned about, Buddha taught that one can decrease, even bring to an end, the unskillful habits of mind that give rise to and perpetuate suffering. By discovering the ways that we create and prolong suffering in others, and ourselves, we can gradually deconstruct the *styles of suffering* woven into character and identity.

I have been studying Buddhism since 1991, seriously practicing daily meditation since 1995. I have been influenced by many Buddhist teachers, but my primary inspiration comes from H. H. Dalai Lama, the lineage of H. H. Dudjom Rinpoche, and the kindness of my teacher Lama Yeshe Wangmo. My interest in Buddhism is very personal, not academic. I want to emphasize this point at the beginning. For me, Buddhist practice brings into the foreground the central importance of the fate of attention in daily living. My teachers have instructed me to concentrate on actual practice and meditation. They assert that, in the long run, practical experience in mindfully investigating the fate of attention is much more important than intellectual knowledge. This emphasis has become increasingly helpful to me. I endeavor to remember to continuously return my attention to the details, textures, and shapes of my own constantly arising experience.

During this same period of time, I have been training to be a psychoanalyst working with children and adults. My training has a particular focus in British Object Relations, especially the pioneering work of the English psychoanalysts Melanie Klein, Wilfred Bion, and Donald Winnicott. Sigmund Freud discovered the lasting emotional influence of the child within the adult. Melanie Klein, and those who followed her, exposed the central importance of the experiences of the very first weeks and months of the infant's life. Our earliest emotional experiences, Klein asserts, exert a lifelong influence on the developing structure of the mind through the experiences of unconscious phantasy.[1] For Klein, it is the fate of anxiety that matters most in how we come to perceive the world and ourselves.

Contemporary psychoanalysis, like Buddhism, investigates the complex conditions that generate and influence subjective experience. In our perceptions of ourselves and of others, and in our views of what is possible in personal and group relationships, there is an important link between anxiety and attention that I will begin to describe in this chapter. Psychoanalysis creates the special conditions that make possible an intimate interpersonal investigation of the ways our choices are shaped, mostly unconsciously, by our reactions to and means of coping with varying degrees of emotional pain and anxiety. Developing the capacity to bring compassionate attention to the experience of anxiety and mental pain is a task shared in different ways by both Buddhism and psychoanalysis. What follows, then, are several short "sketches" of experience, informed by both Buddhist and psychoanalytic points of view, loosely held together by the themes and variations of pain and attention.

KNOWING

Human beings are emotional creatures. Faced with the ordinary complexity of daily life that often generates frustration, uncertainty, anxiety, fear, anger, and even feelings of helplessness, we unconsciously seek, like small children naturally do, the safety and refuge of an apparently all-knowing (parental) figure. The wish to be with someone who knows perfectly defends against the terrors of uncertainty. Knowing, at a deep level, is equated with survival. Not knowing is equated with doom.

The idea of the unconscious as a powerful influence in how we live out our lives has become trivialized in popular culture today. What Freud asserted, in fact, remains both deeply relevant and troubling. Freud's vision of the human subject is that of a person *unknowingly* trapped between past and future, unable to inhabit the present moment, always somehow incompletely aware. In Freud's scheme, desire and reality clash at the intersection of personal experience. The experience of "I" is constellated in this perpetual collision and must mediate between impersonal instincts seeking satisfaction, the demands of the family and the larger group, the processes of dreaming and wish fulfillment, and the accidents and existential variables introduced by the contexts of daily life. In Freud's sobering view of human life, we can not only never completely master the external environment with our will to know, we are also faced with the reality of an internal world, a psychical emotional environment created by a lifetime of experience that is largely unexplored and always at least partially unknown to us.

What makes it so difficult for us to know ourselves and others more completely? Freud answered that almost any object can be invested with some form of what he named transference. We transfer both our desires and their frustrations from childhood relationships and modes of being into the emotional experiences of our adult lives. It is not just that there is too much detail, information, or emotion for us to cope with moment to moment; transference clouds our relationship to the now-here heart of experience with the thick shadows of the past. The subjective benefit of this transference process is the illusion of certainty and familiarity that it sponsors. The cost of this habit of mind is that we repeatedly alienate ourselves, sometimes profoundly, from some smaller or larger part of our now-here experience.

The analytic experience is a learning process. The psychoanalyst creates the conditions to investigate both how we learn, emotionally, and how we fail to learn from our experience. She does this by inviting the patient to enter into a special kind of intimate conversation. To facilitate this special conversation, the analyst requests that the patient agree to regular frequent meetings, sometimes three, four, or five times per week. These meetings occur in the same place, at the same time, and for the same fixed duration. The analyst's office is often more like a comfortable room in a home than a sterile doctor's office. The patient may choose to recline on a couch with the analyst seated behind or he may choose to sit in a comfortable chair, facing the analyst. Reclining on the couch has the benefit of allowing the patient to experience his own spontaneous inner wanderings, anxieties, and image-life without the intrusion of the social conventions of ordinary conversation. The purpose of this carefully constructed and protected setting is to promote an emotional atmosphere of openness and to encourage the possibility for expression.

In the initial sessions, the instruction is given that the patient should say whatever comes to mind. After that, the sessions are left radically open. Often people find this invitation to openness much more nerve-racking than one might have anticipated. It is, of course, a slightly bizarre situation; one, I think, of radical generosity when compared to many other conventional settings of everyday life. A patient's first attempts at free association are often frustrating. There is an obvious parallel to the person beginning to experiment with meditation. We are often surprised by our own mental worlds and frustrated that our capacity to attend to ourselves is so underdeveloped. Much patience is needed to begin both these kinds of explorations. Endurance is a valued quality that grows with patience.

The British psychoanalyst Wilfred Bion once wrote that when two individuals meet, an emotional storm is created. The patient often crosses the threshold of the analyst's doorstep bringing a storm with him. When we stop to look at the life of the mind, whether in solitary meditation or in the analytic conversation we find a simple truth: our minds are often very stormy! Many patients come seeking shelter or refuge from the storm's gaining force. Over time the storm gathers in the consulting room and, though he or she may fear its emergence and intensity, the patient experiences the darkly gathered clouds parting, session after session. From this sometimes long period of testing each other, the patient and analyst may experience an emerging new space, one where both individuals share the risk of surrendering to the opportunity of free association and creative exploration. Rather than be the knower, a temptation she must eschew, the analyst becomes observer and describer. Optimally, the patient shares this task over time. Each individual participates in observing in his or her own unique way the development of a shared emotional relationship that becomes both trusted and deeply valued over time.

Psychoanalysis is not meditation, but it may aspire to a similar level of attention. As sessions unfold, storms are not the only things that arise. Bits of dreams arise. Currents of memory trickle forth. There is a tale of hatred to be told; a story of desire to be felt; a realization of ignorance to face. The pang of sadness and regret gradually emerges. The entire Buddhist Wheel of Life may be partially glimpsed. Demons and gods and hungry ghosts trouble the conversation. Grasping, aversion, delusion, and the energy of perpetual wishing unfold to view. All of the 10,000 things seem to exist not only outside but inside. Sometimes the session has the atmosphere of a dream, sometimes the vivid concreteness of a nightmare. Throughout it all the task of the analyst and the patient is to observe experience, to lend words to emotions, and to bring attention to that which may never have been lovingly attended to ever before.

I sought psychoanalysis with a powerful semiconscious wish to become some kind of expert, to become someone who *knows*. People often seek a similar intense sense of knowing from the guru and hope that Buddhism will be a direct path to omniscience. Instead of becoming The Knower, redeemed by omniscience, psychoanalysis gave me the opportunity to discover myself in emotional ways I could not have achieved on my own. My analyst helped me to begin to become familiar with rage, shame, fear, and intense anxieties I had never been encouraged to know about before. This meant learning to identify, tolerate, and work directly with the many ways my own emotional history had never become part of my past. My past experiences had remained so alive that they continuously intruded into the present, shaping my future in many unintended ways.

Psychoanalysis, in my view, seeks to sponsor a realization of mental freedom that grows into an attitude of resilient openness toward experience. For a long time the "I" engaged in analysis must tolerate being riddled with questions. A basic and perplexing question that arises is the location of experience in relationship to the categories past, present, and future. Contrary to popular images of psychoanalysis as interminably digging up the past, what analysis investigates is the immense difficulty we all seem to have of living consciously in the present moment. In my view, the task of psychoanalysis is to *reclaim the future*, particularly from the intrusive hegemony of our unconscious transferences and our unintentional repetitions of the disowned pain of the past.

HATE

The symbolism of the Tibetan Wheel of Life is beautiful, and, with a little explanation, fairly straightforward. The Wheel of Life symbolizes the nature and causes of cyclic existence. Three figures at the very center of the Wheel represent what are called the three poisons: hatred, possessiveness, and ignorance.

Hatred, pictured as a snake, symbolizes one of the main obstacles to healing and liberation. In order to heal, difficult realities like hate must be faced. The examination of hate makes possible the lessening of the ways that we unconsciously perpetuate such poisons and their consequences through our thoughts and fantasies, interpersonal speech, and concrete actions. Hate is a pervasive and powerful state of mind. It is a state that is often enacted, rather than acknowledged. I seek to lend words to the experience.

What does hate feel like? Some people hate their parents, some their lovers. Some people hate their children, some the circumstances of their birth or class. People hate differences that they endow with toxic significance. People hate ideas or they hate feelings. Some people hate particular emotions, like intense sadness. Hatred of powerlessness, helplessness, and vulnerability are common and understandable. Some people hate time and its passing. Other people hate death or sickness or old age. Hatred, it seems, always has an object. It is frightening indeed to meet someone who simply hates, without an object to focus this energy. Hate, then, is commonplace. People dip into hate and reemerge. But some people swim in hate the way fish swim in water.

I think there is a difference between ordinary hate and malignant hate. Melanie Klein spoke about the splitting of the self and the object in order to preserve feelings of goodness and wholeness and to disown experiences of distress and fragmentation. Normal hate gets worked through as one of many kinds of emotional experience a person can gradually learn to transform (especially with the caring help of others). Malignant hate is something else. People can become (totally) identified with the power of destructive hating. People can come to depend upon hate for an illusion of invincibility and belonging. Hate organizes their egos and even, bizarrely, makes them feel safer. Sometimes hatred traps aliveness within it and acts as a wall against collapse into terrible deadness and despair. The world becomes upside down. Hate is good and peacemaking bad, a sign of weakness, a lack of resolve.

The result of chronic and intense experiences of frustration and pain and the repeated failure to interpersonally transform distress into comfort leads individuals to feel intense toxic shame. Toxic shame is ego destructive rather than constructive and the root of much hating phenomena. Toxic shame involves the chronic feeling of threat to the psychophysical survival of the "self." One schizophrenic patient told me "I have no mandate for life." For patients living with an internal atmosphere of toxic ego destructive shame, even the smallest details of daily life can become distorted evidence of obstructive intentions on the part of others or even of the world itself. Saturated by experiences of toxic shame, one feels the passive object of an active hatred. The feeling of being hated may grow so large that the person feels that living itself is equated with the experience of hating and being hated.

Malignant hatred poses serious immediate risks. People can be so immersed in their distorted perceptions that they will kill without apparent conflict. I remember a former gang member I once worked with briefly. He had witnessed a murder as a young teen in his neighborhood. It had deeply frightened him. As a young man he became a murderer himself. He hated the person he killed, and, at the same time, knew almost nothing about him. He rationalized his premeditated attack as self-defense. When he came out of prison, he started to change because he became a father. Somehow, being in the protective role of a parent to his new baby son made him reconsider his commitment to violence as a value system.

Several angry men have described to me how hate functions according to rules of intensity and amplification. Hate smolders until some detail triggers it. Hate and shame seem to go together. The awful intensity of shame requires some kind of container. Hate serves as a kind of second skin or armor. The irony is that the surface of violence, belligerence, and ruthless provocation only engages more hating reactions from the world around. The mental pain such men feel is often aggressively evacuated through violent speech or violent action. People become addicted to hating. Hating can intoxicate you.

But hatred numbs the capacity to think. People have described the literal narrowing and darkening of vision in states of hate as if one were entering a tunnel. I have experienced this too when overwhelmingly angry. But it was a transient feeling. One can go dead to hate, or, be swept up in its swirling energy. When inundated with feelings of shame and hate, people seek any relief they can find. Some groups provide an organized discourse of hate. The experience of hate groups seems to be like going inside a special world, leaving the toxic stuff outside. The logic of purity and decay (splitting, idealization, and denigration) organize such groups. It is possible to live inside hate itself.

Hate, then, can become woven into the identity. Underneath hate for others is terror of the self being destroyed. People who hate malignantly idealize the protective force of hate but unconsciously don't believe that protection can be real. Hate serves as a kind of thin insulation from the terror of all that can never be controlled. Hate fills the space where love should be. Hate fills the space where terror was and organizes a world that is too chaotic, too unpredictable, and too uncontrollable. Some kids are unfortunate enough to find people who help them to cultivate their hate. They have coaches in hating and violent perception. Their attention becomes captured by hate. Hate creates fascination that can be used for brainwashing. Hate exploits evidence of real problems that need solutions and fuels destructive reactions against the pain of so much unfinished work.

Freud's and Klein's approaches to hate have been developed by Bion in a direction that bridges biological, intrapsychic, and interpersonal dimensions.

Bion described what he called an obstructive object relationship. He felt that some patients with catastrophically vulnerable backgrounds come to anticipate almost everyone they have contact with as being inevitably rejecting of their needs. Bion asserts that a phenomenology of violent rejection suggests a background of catastrophe that the person lives within and unconsciously perpetuates as part of the legacy of early traumatic experiences. Practically speaking, an obstructive object is experienced as someone or something actively hostile toward emotional experience. Rejection generates hatred. Such people inhabit pervasive states of mind that Buddhists symbolize as the energies of the hell realms populated by hell beings and the hungry ghosts.

CULTIVATING NOT-KNOWING AND GETTING-TO-KNOW

After some years of analysis I had almost talked myself into the idea that my projections had at least diminished if not more or less ceased to obstruct my perceptions. I remember having this naive view corrected when I visited my Buddhist teacher. I had asked to see her for advice about my meditation practice. Sitting face-to-face on the floor she asked me why I had requested the meeting, and I was suddenly helplessly tongue-tied. When I started to speak, all that came out was gibberish. I felt like I was cracking up. She did not immediately rescue me from this mounting discomfort. She sat quietly, relaxed, meeting my gaze, and finally asked me, gently, to describe my daily practice. Doing so grounded me, and I was able to complete the interview.

Now, I can wonder why I had this powerful reaction to my teacher. I think I transferred my desire to know from analysis to Buddhism and made my Buddhist teacher an even more idealized figure than my analyst. My analyst helped me to become open enough to allow others to teach me. He helped me to face my terror of dependence and my belief that depending on others can only bring catastrophe. My Buddhist teachers have helped me to work with another dimension of idealizing and transference. They have shown me that what my mind generates is nothing to be intimidated by. It is as thin or as thick as I make it. Ultimately, they say, I will realize my thoughts are empty. They are no more or less real than a dream.

My teachers encourage me to repeatedly question the concreteness of my experience. They continuously remind me to simply become aware of what I am feeling, thinking, and doing in the moment. This kind of repeated reclaiming of attention is, they argue, the only practice I need to deepen and perfect in order to dwell in the now-here vividness of reality.

In a similar way, Bion advised the analyst when entering each session to eschew memory, desire, and understanding. This advice is commonly misinterpreted to mean that the analyst should try to make his or her mind a blank slate. Anyone who has ever tried meditation knows what frustration follows from such an intention. What Bion encouraged was not to try and become an empty consciousness but rather to bracket those thoughts that focused on what the analyst thinks he or she already knows (memory), hopes to know (desire), and intends to interpret (understanding). In recognizing these categories of intention, and in learning to let them fall away into the background of consciousness, Bion felt the analyst had a better chance to become more receptive, more capable of being surprised by new evolutions of experience as they arise within a session. Bion, following and reviving Freud's advice to listen with free-floating attention was, I believe, trying to define and expand the conditions that would allow the analyst to better learn to listen to himself or herself listening to the patient.

The deeper purpose of this task is, like it is in Buddhism, to realize a choiceless attention capable of recognizing and dwelling in spontaneous presence in the "suchness" of the emergent moment. The realization of spontaneous presence eludes description. It does not last, for most of us, but, having felt it to be real, it fosters a respect for attention and its relationship to O. Realizing presence opens the possibility of perceiving a basic goodness that exists and can be recognized amidst the realities of violence, death, and horror. Our task is to learn to dwell in this awareness as a background presence of primary identification. Bion emphasized the need to repeatedly open up to a process of getting-to-know. Willingness to explore is everything, to continuously risk the turbulence of turning toward the new.

THE NECESSITY OF COMPASSION

What Buddhism describes in that analysis, I think insufficiently considers, is how much compassion is needed to proceed down this path of getting to know. In Buddhism, one explicitly practices developing compassion for the hard task of learning to be more open to painful emotional experience.

There is nothing theoretical or sticky sweet about real compassion. Bringing compassion to pain helps. The Buddhist teacher Stephen Levine gives the following example. Imagine you are pounding a nail and you accidentally hit your finger. What is your first response? It is probably *not* an instant recognition that at this very moment you would benefit from a sense of calm, patient, loving kindness in order to care for your injury. Levine's point is obvious. We meet pain with aversion and with harsh condemnation. When people feel vulnerable, they harden their hearts against exposure to pain. We expect rejection, intrusion, denigration, and shame as the order of things. So we hide our pain. We all know this attitude of hatred toward sometimes intense and shocking pain. Hatred seems to be part of having a mind that registers pain.

Levine (1989) speaks of moving beyond the ownership of pain (my pain, your pain) through investigating the experience of "the pain." Pain is a given, he says. Suffering can be thought of as our habitually unskillful reactions to pain. Suffering equals pain multiplied by our resistance to pain (Young 1997). Compassion, in this context, makes common sense. Why amplify your pain by fighting it and condemning it? Why not learn how to soften to pain? Why not learn to kindly offer attention to pain? Why not begin to investigate pain? To learn its shape, its texture, its rising and ebbing intensities, its shifting locations, its sticking and melting points? To train the mind to do this would be to create the conditions for the transformation of pain, from moment to moment.

I remember an experience with my analyst. I was very angry, and I had the feeling he didn't appreciate the depth of my anger. I was in a great deal of mental pain, and it seemed to just keep growing and amplifying. Finally, I told him that the only way I could get my point across would be to buy a gun, bring it to my next session, and fill him full of bullets. This outburst frightened me. I had the feeling I was halfway stuck in a nightmare. His reply was direct, clear, and clarifying. It even had a note of humor. Had he reacted with violent aversion to my pain, our work might have faltered badly. It takes a great deal of trust to risk being honest with others and ourselves about the intensities generated by pain. My analyst's compassion contained the pain and helped to deepen our work. It sponsored a feeling of sincere gratitude and new possibility for strengths of mind I had never really imagined, much less realized.

Pema Chodron, a nun in the Tibetan Buddhist tradition, writes:

> To stay with the shakiness—to stay with a broken heart, with a rumbling stomach, with the feeling of hopelessness and wanting to get revenge—that is the path of true awakening. Sticking with the uncertainty, getting the knack for relaxing in the midst of chaos, learning not to panic—this is the spiritual path. Getting the knack for catching ourselves, of gently and compassionately catching ourselves, is the path of a warrior. We catch ourselves one zillion times as once again, whether we like it or not, we harden into resentment, bitterness, righteous indignation—harden in any way, even into a sense of relief, a sense of inspiration. . . . Every day, at the moment when things get edgy, we can ask ourselves, "Am I going to practice peace, or am I going to practice war?" (1997, 10–11)

THE FATE OF ATTENTION

Attention to the topic of attention has seemed sparse in my analytic training. This is odd because the fate of attention has an important place in psychoanalysis. It was of particular concern to Freud, Sullivan, and Bion, to name a few. Paying attention to attention is, for me, at the heart of what it means to be a psychoanalyst and to work psychoanalytically.

The late British psychoanalyst Nina Coltart, also a Buddhist, has written:

> It is in the early stages of learning to be analysts and therapists when we are de-
> veloping our technique, our confidence and our clinical acumen . . . that the use
> of "bare attention" absolutely has to be the scaffolding of everything else we do.
> Even when we are doing nothing (or appear to be), sitting in silence, testing our
> faith in the process—our constant, perhaps I should say our only attitude is one
> of bare attention. In this we try to teach ourselves so continuously to observe,
> and watch, and listen, and feel, in silence, that this kind of attention becomes, in
> the end, second nature. It is the bedrock of the day's work. And it is as this
> bedrock that it becomes forgotten and overlooked. (1992, 181)

What do I mean by attention? There is nothing mysterious or mystical about
attention. We are all familiar with it. We pay attention in many different ways
to many different things throughout an ordinary day. Indeed, unless we are
significantly impaired in some way, we are so familiar with attention that we
fail to notice how much a part of ordinary perception attention really is.

Greenberg and Snell, quoting Sylwester, define the tasks of attention:

> . . . a well functioning attentional system must fulfill several tasks, including
> identification of important elements in the environment, the ability to ignore ir-
> relevant stimuli while sustaining attention to the primary focus, the ability to ac-
> cess inactive memories, and the capacity to shift attention rapidly as the result
> of new information. (1999, 108).

Buddhism explicitly advises us to pay attention to attention. Meditation is
the vehicle for experimenting with attention. By learning to develop skills of
attention, we can investigate the various habits of perception that shape our
sense of self and other. Over time, we become familiar with the constantly
changing fate of our attention. Rob Nairn, an instructor in the Tibetan Kagyu
tradition writes:

> . . . in meditation, we are not working with the success/failure paradigm at all.
> We are simply training ourselves to be present in the moment with exactly what
> is there. For most people the big surprise is that what is there is a bewildering
> stranger." (1999, 4)

I once kept a meditation journal. A few excerpts briefly illustrate how meditation helps one practice paying attention to attention.

April
   I bring my attention gently to my breath, to the sensation of the breath entering my nose and leaving. My breath is shallow. I tell myself to let go of my tension. I feel there are layers upon layers of tension blocking relaxation. I begin to
concentrate more, to "gather in" my scattered attention, to focus only on my

breath, according to my teacher's instructions. Quickly, however, my mind begins to stray. I note "wandering" or "worrying," "planning," "anger," "have to do this right." I feel, as I often do, a concentration of anxious tension in my lower middle back. This time, however, I do not allow it to take over my attention. I don't try to shake it off. Just to observe it. I note "tension, middle back" and move on. My mind wanders again. I pull back the focus to my breath.

July
    There is a prideful mind. A mind that says, "I'm doing this right" and "I'm going to be better for it." I try to meet these feelings with attention and loving kindness. I try neither to judge them nor to make them go away. There is an angry mind. "I'm not feeling well; I don't have the energy for this." I try to meet this mind with attention and loving kindness. There is a helpless mind, a mind that desires to be taken care of, like a baby, rocked to sleep. I try to meet this mind with loving kindness. There is a rushing mind, an intellectual mind. There is an aggressive mind, an impatient mind. There is a desiring mind, the grasping mind. There is, most of all, a controlling mind. I try to meet all these attitudes with attention and loving kindness.

September
    The moment, this instant, can feel so expansive. The moment seems to open up. To just be here, now, my bare feet on the wood floor, the bitter taste of this morning's cup of coffee still in my mouth. I hear the fan in the background and the sound of a sea plane's engine as it descends. I look out at the tree tops and deep blue sky. Francisco Varela says somewhere that we teach our children to read and write and do arithmetic but we do not teach them the skills to play the instrument of their own being.

As you become familiar with the practice of meditation you can see and feel that there are different *qualities* of attention. Attention can be focused, or dispersed. It can be split and divided. It can be alternating or fixed. It can be full or depleted. One can also speak of the objects of attention. Attention can be directed to both material and immaterial objects. Consider this passage from William James:

When we take a general view of the wonderful stream of our consciousness, what strikes us first is the different pace of its parts. Like a bird's life, it seems to be an alternation of flights and perchings. The rhythm of language expresses this, where every thought is expressed in a sentence and every sentence is closed by a period. The resting places are usually occupied by sensorial imaginations, whose peculiarity is that they can be held before the mind for an indefinite time, and contemplated without changing; the places of flight are filled with thoughts of relations, static or dynamic, that for the most part obtain between the matters contemplated in the periods of comparative rest. (Rowe 1996, 115–16)

James has a keen grasp of inner experience. Through his own keen powers of observation, he shows how saturated mental experience can be. He suggests that the structure of language itself creates the possibility of a space between two thoughts. However, that space is immediately unconsciously filled by "sensorial imaginations" that capture attention. The Buddhist student immediately recognizes this description. The goal for meditation is to allow the mind to become quiet, so quiet that one can recognize the emptiness (the opportunity) of a space between two thoughts. It is in between this space that we can fleetingly recognize the nature of awareness itself. Thoughts are immaterial objects that so easily capture our attention that we may even find our attention held hostage by them. Indeed, so much of our attention seems habitually captured by thinking, that we may become alienated from more basic bodily experiences: what it feels like to sit, to breathe, to chew, to notice the reliability of our own hearts beating. Where was the thought the moment before it arises?

ATTENTION AND PAIN

Donald Meltzer, an Oxford psychoanalyst, asserts that the basic question in every treatment is: who shall have the pain? To this question I would add: What is the fate of pain? The details of how one copes with pain, whether physical or emotional, are important to investigate. Intense emotional pain gives rise to numerous conscious and unconscious strategies that all have in common the goal of ridding pain from awareness. One can fight pain, deny it, grow numb to it, rage against it, dissociate from it, or mask it (temporarily) with substances like alcohol, cocaine, or heroin. In extremes, such as schizophrenia, Bion theorized that one could even attack and dismantle the ego and its modes of perception in order not to register pain. All these strategies, obviously, tend to increase pain in the long run rather than to lessen it.

In this culture there is a deep sense of personal isolation and social alienation arising, at least in part, from how we fail to skillfully relate to pain. We are not trained to bring our attention consciously and compassionately to investigate the experience of pain. Because experiencing pain in many forms is an inevitable part of being alive in the world, we need a method for relating to, thinking about, and working with pain.

When too much pain comes too fast or too early (we are never really prepared for pain), our minds and bodies can feel overwhelmed and shut down. The experience of shock impacts both mind and body. As shock fades, pain tends to capture our attention. We can feel hostage to the sensations of pain. Thresholds of tolerance vary in both physical and mental pain. Our fear is that pain will grow bigger and bigger until it is equated with the whole of reality and perception. The terror of a feeling of "no escape" adds to the fear of pain. It is the intensity of fear that generates a hatred of pain.

Captured Attention

We are all familiar at some level with how attention can become captured by an object, whether that object is an emotion, a sensation, an image, a thought (or train of thoughts), or a wish. Attention can be captured by pleasure or pain. Desire captures attention until satisfaction arrives. The pain of yearning is bittersweet compared to the pain of raw frustration. Intense pain (mental or physical) tends to capture attention and give rise to the phenomena Buddhists call *aversion*. Freud wrote about this very early in his work. In his 1911 paper "Formulations Regarding the Two Principles in Mental Functioning," Freud writes "We have long observed that every neurosis has the result, and therefore probably the purpose, of forcing the patient out of real life, of alienating him from actuality" (13). He continues:

> The neurotic turns away from reality because he finds it unbearable—either whole or parts of it. The most extreme type of this alienation from reality is shown in certain cases of hallucinatory psychosis, which aim at denying the existence of the particular event that occasioned the outbreak of insanity. But actually every neurotic does the same with some fragment of reality. (13)

The need to control awareness of what painfully impinges upon us begins at birth, if not before. The means an infant has for filtering painful sensory experiences are quite limited in the beginning. Since infants cannot think about or reflect upon their experiences and they are highly limited in their ability to sooth themselves physically, they must rely upon the care and mediating attention of others. Often, the infant's own nascent attention is split between pain and pleasure and pressed into service *as a defense against distress*. The tradition of infant observation in England, pioneered by Esther Bick and John Bowlby, has produced many detailed descriptions of the role of attention, particularly captured attention, in responding to pain even in the newborn's earliest experiences. In this essay there is space only to gesture toward how important this phenomenon of attention's fate can be both clinically and from a developmental point of view.

  The development of the attentional system in infancy unfolds interdependently with the emotional relationships between an infant and its caregivers. When distress rises chronically, above a level beyond which soothing can be provided interpersonally, the infant relies upon its own idiosyncratic solutions. The psychoanalyst Joan Symington writes:

The baby holds himself together in a variety of ways. He may focus his attention on a sensory stimulus—visual, auditory, tactile, or olfactory. When his attention is held by this stimulus he feels held together. He may engage in constant bodily movement which then feels like a continuous holding skin: if the movement stops, this may feel like a gap, a hole in the skin through which the self may spill out. An adult's pacing up and down to help contain anxiety is a remnant of this continuous movement. A third method consists of muscular tightening, a clenching together of particular muscle groups and maintaining them in this rigid position. This is an attempt physically to hold everything so tightly together that there can be no gap through which the spilling might occur." (1985, 481)

Symington's observations help to show a potential continuity from infancy to adulthood. The infantile origins of some of the unconscious ways of coping with unmentalized pain probably arise through the defensive deployment of attention.

From a Buddhist point of view, captured attention is an ordinary part of everyday experience. At any point during any day our attention is to some degree captured. The Buddhist view of captured attention suggests that we are never fully present to our experiences. Captured attention is ordinarily benign because when necessary we can shift and reclaim our attention in order to take in new information and adjust to new demands or opportunities of the moment.

The Vietnamese master Thich Nhat Hanh writes:

We drink a cup of tea, but we do not know we are drinking a cup of tea. We sit with the person we love, but we do not know that she is sitting there. We walk, but we are not really walking. We are someplace else, thinking about the past or the future. The horse of our habit energy is carrying us along, and we are its captive. (1998, 25)

These words convey, in a condensed way, a basic but profound point. It is a constant challenge to recognize and repeatedly recover a state of presence and awareness, to shift from nowhere, to now-here. I suggest that both psychoanalysis and meditation sponsor a continual movement back and forth between nowhere and now-here. We are constantly engaged in freeing attention from habits and intensities that trap or capture it.

Both psychotherapy and meditation can help to train the mind, to practice bringing attention to how we process pain. In psychotherapy pain is investigated interpersonally. We strive to find an *emotional* language to describe and transform the experience of pain. We hope to free people from both subjective and actual isolation and to help them stop hiding from and hating their pain. As this skillful attitude of investigating pain is internalized, it can be relied upon as an attitude, a skillful way of relating to experience, one that, with enough mindfulness and intention, can be called upon at any moment. A brief vignette illustrates this point.

Investigating Anger

A patient with a history of violent anger was also a serious Buddhist practitioner. I'll call him Brian. During one of his psychotherapy sessions, Brian told me a story involving an incident from the previous weekend. He had gone to a party where he was aggressively insulted by another man and nearly provoked into a fistfight. Having been in many violent fights over the span of his life, Brian was not afraid of physical violence. However, he could, he reported, in that heated moment, question the wisdom of giving into the impulse to fight. He described deciding to leave the event and returning home where he sat down to meditate in order to try to calm himself. Brian described how he could consciously feel the hatred pulsing through him and how he had imagined ridding himself of it by pounding it into the man who provoked him. His body was literally shaking with rage, he said, something I had also seen in some of our sessions together. The atmosphere of violence is electric, even when merely being recalled. Brian reported sitting in the rage until gradually his body began to soften. He began to breathe more deeply, to unclench his jaws and fists until his shoulders, legs, and back became relaxed.

Later during the same night Brian was startled awake by a disturbing telephone call from the same individual who had provoked him at the party. The caller again insulted Brian and dared him to meet him at an empty parking lot early in the morning to settle their score. His rage ignited again by the intrusive telephone call and the intense aggressive insults, my patient agreed to the meeting. He dressed, and, powered by a sense of righteous indignation, went to his driveway to start his car. He fully intended to confront the individual and perhaps to kill him. Then he paused. It is this split second, the space between two thoughts that sometimes makes the difference in the path of a lifetime. Sitting in the car, my patient said he thought about me and about the Buddhist teachings he was struggling so sincerely to live by. He sat in the car and considered the years of suffering his own rage had rained down upon him and others. He thought, too, about how much rage and suffering his enemy must feel without any insight into it or any way of working directly with it. He went back inside his house and again began to meditate, this time chanting a compassion mantra until his hatred again began to fade. As he told this story to me, I felt the tangible presence of this man's already deep and expanding realization of loving kindness toward himself and toward his enemy. I felt close to tears with pride and inspiration at how he had turned his own rage through attention into an active act of peacemaking. In an instant Brian had traveled from nowhere to now-here. This is a journey we must learn to make again and again.

FROM NOWHERE TO NOW-HERE

When pain cannot be successfully transformed from distress into comfort, it captures attention creating what I call the need for nowhere states of mind. Nowhere states of mind tend toward isolation, sealing the individual off from relational contact protecting the person, so he imagines, from the turbulence of intense emotional experiences. Nowhere states may be vivid virtual worlds of pleasure or power or flat landscapes of psychic deadness. They offer illusory refuge from the experience of untransformed distress. Nowhere states of mind, in varying degrees of intensity, are ubiquitous. They seem to be part of the nature of having a mind that registers pain.

Irene

I was very close to my maternal grandmother, Irene. I spent much of my childhood in her presence. She was, for me, a refuge from the emotional pain and confusion of my family's complicated and difficult life. She died of cancer when I was eighteen. I helped to nurse her throughout the last year of her life. I watched her deteriorate little by little. Though busy with many activities as a senior in high school, I spent many hours at her bedside each week. I read to her as her eyes failed. I combed her thin white hair as she lost it. I changed her bedpan and held her hands when she wept from humiliation. I participated, with a kind of dazed attention, as she tried to cope with her intense frustration and fear at being sick and dying.

Like I did with much of the pain in my family life, I pretended to be stronger and more confident than I really felt inside. This is what I saw my grandmother doing. And this is what I had learned to do unconsciously from my mother and father. Much of the time I nearly fooled myself into thinking that I could handle anything. I learned to deaden my most intense feelings, fearing, I suppose, that they might frighten or overwhelm my parents. I have lived much of my life against a kind of background of mild dissociation, struggling to be present, but being, in reality, deeply alienated from the details and textures of my actual emotional experience, lost in ever more distant nowhere states of mind. So it has been as an adult that I have learned to emerge from nowhere to now-here.

That whole year my grandmother was dying I wished intensely, in such a childlike way, to be able to figure out some way to help my grandmother recover. One night, sitting in the living room while my parents silently read the newspaper, I started to cry violently and uncontrollably. The sense of helplessness I had been unconsciously denying flooded over me. There was nothing I could think, do, wish, or command that would bring my grandmother's strength back or heal her cancer. I recognized this with a kind of shattering clarity. But I had no way to process the truth of this recognition, no way to think about it or put it into words. I remember a terrible feeling of shame and loneliness as my parents tried anxiously to comfort me, telling me that things would be all right. Gradually my familiar nowhere state of mind closed in around me, to protect me, again.

I became very depressed after my grandmother died. I tried to put it all behind me as a new freshman leaving home for the first time to go to college. The next few years were very hard for me personally, though at the time I could hardly admit that. What I am calling nowhere states of mind protected me from much of the turbulence I might have experienced had I been more open to emotional development and discovery and all the new tasks that I faced at that period in my life.

RECLAIMING ATTENTION

Psychoanalysis, like Buddhism, can well be described as a process that helps to reclaim attention from a multitude of idiosyncratically sponsored nowhere states of mind. The great intimacy of psychoanalysis can come from the shared project of working together to transform pain. In order to make this possible, the therapist must somehow woo the patient into choosing attention, turning toward their fear, moving directly into the experience of pain, rather than fighting it or sealing it off. There is no formula for this delicate task except the growing conviction on the part of the analyst and the patient that such an investigation is worth attempting and can be survived over and over again by both parties as it is lived from moment to moment against the developing background of actual compassion and heart-fullness. Gradually, one learns that surprise can bring joy, which comes as a revelation.

It sounds counterintuitive to recommend learning to observe pain. Isn't that masochistic? Or sadistic, if you are watching another suffer? Won't focusing attention on the experience of pain make it worse? Actually, just the opposite is often true. Pain becomes unbearable to the degree that we actively fight against it. Denial of pain creates impasse. Hatred of the often shameful feelings that seem to arise around painful experience only compounds the sense of helplessness and fear. Psychotherapy and Buddhism provide the special conditions necessary to begin to observe pain with compassionate attention and to gradually transform the experience of it. This process, when successful, sponsors a growing confidence in the ability to relate to pain. Joy in living moment to moment punctures the long dream of yearned-for safety. There is a kind of awful poignancy and immediacy one feels subject to. Sometimes experience is momentarily so crisp, so shockingly clear, so simultaneously fierce and delicate that tears are the only natural reply. There is a momentum that grows that allows for a deeper embrace of the experience of being now-here.

THE PRECIOUSNESS OF LIFE

My experience with my grandmother demonstrated, in powerful ways, that death was an indigestible fact in my own life as a young man. Instead of helping me appreciate the preciousness of life, my initial encounters with death drove me deeply into painful, alienated, nowhere states of mind.

Teachings on the inevitability of death are an important part of Buddhism. One way of looking at Buddhist practice is as a lifelong preparation for death. Though this may sound morbid, the intent is to help a person become more fully alive in the here and now. Buddhism emphasizes the transience of all experience. Nothing lasts. This fact is called the teaching of impermanence. It is often said that without a clear and frank awareness of death, one does not feel with keenness, poignancy, and gratitude, the preciousness of life. This is not a sentimental point of view. The realization of the reality of death inspires a growing appreciation for *this very moment.*

Anita

Anita had also been a very important person to me while growing up. I remember with vivid fondness the atmosphere of her house set on a large lot near the woods. There were many books, African rugs and artifacts, two elderly Siamese cats with striking eyes, homespun wool, and the ubiquitous smell of warm freshly baked bread. Anita loved to garden as well as to cook. She would cut into a newly baked loaf of bread, and I would sit and visit and linger in the kitchen to talk while she cooked. She cared about history and politics. She loved nature and animals and ecology. She seemed very different from all the suburban mothers of my friends. When I was at Anita's house I glimpsed hints of life's wider possibilities and how interesting the world might actually be. Anita was one of the few adults I knew that made me look forward to growing up. While my grandmother had helped me to feel safe and protected, Anita enlivened my sense of possibility. I admired her.

After her children grew up and left home, Anita and her husband, a teacher, divorced and I did not see her for many years. One day she called me to tell me that she was dying. She wanted me to know, she said, how much our relationship had meant to her. She was calling all of her friends, she explained, in order to say good-bye. I responded with tears to her simple and direct message of love and caring. I think I was amazed that she had kept me in mind all those intervening years and that she would choose to include me in the intimate and painful experience of her cancer.

Buddhism had become important to Anita in the last years of her life, especially through the work of Stephen Levine. Also, Anita was working during these years with Southeast Asian refugees. She helped them to find homes and jobs and education and, in turn, was influenced by their experiences. So many people had lost nearly everything. They had no homes, no property; families had been separated or destroyed. They were living examples of what Buddha taught about the actuality of impermanence. Yet, for many, there was a strength and determination to begin again, despite their intense losses and suffering.

The experiences Anita had with her friends helped to inspire her and to prepare her for her death in an open, honest way. The brief time I was able to spend with her face-to-face at the end of her life made a deep impression on me. Unlike my grandmother, who felt helpless and humiliated by her illness, Anita had an unusual presence while facing her death. She described to me in exacting detail the progress of her illness, the course of her treatments, and the many emotions she had struggled with over the months since her diagnosis.

Her honesty and directness were at first disorienting. She gently explained that she had much to say and little time to say it in. She said she was much better at dealing with the psychological pain than with the physical pain. She said that it helped to talk about her experience with people and that she wanted me to know what she was going through. She had many friends helping her and her children supporting her. She said if I was uncomfortable with her directness she could understand that. She would stop talking about these things if I asked her to. I asked her not to. We talked about many happy memories and I told her about the changes and directions in my life. The last conversation we had was the day before she died. She was just back from the hospital again. I talked with her by phone and we said a final good-bye.

My experience with how Anita faced her cancer has become a turning point in my life. It helped me to realize how an ordinary person can face their fear, and reach out with love, even in the midst of death. I began to realize that it might be possible to investigate and to accept my own experiences much more deeply and consciously. Inertia is powerful. The habits of doubt and shame grow unless checked. Anita helped me to realize that the disturbing experiences of death and grief can be faced with courage, clarity, and openness. Over the years I have chosen to read the work of many Buddhist teachers. I doubt I would have made these choices or have been drawn to the richness of Buddhist thought without having been pointed in this direction by Anita. The seeds she helped to plant have taken root and grown. Anita instructed me to look into Buddhism. She said, "There's something there that I think you'll really get if you look." I often remind myself, thinking of Anita, "Go ahead Jeff, face your fear." Courage, I'm learning, is ordinary and a matter of how we learn to use our attention.

END PIECE

It is traditional to dedicate whatever merit an activity has to all sentient beings, with the hope that the activity will, even if in a small way, contribute to the lessening of the suffering of all beings in the universe. I dedicate this essay to Anita, to my grandmother, to my wife Kay, to my parents, and to my friends, teachers, and patients, as well as to all sentient beings.

Pema Chodron writes:

> It is never too late for us to look at our minds. We can always sit down and allow the space for anything to arise. Sometimes we have a shocking experience of ourselves. Sometimes we try to hide. Sometimes we have a surprising experience of ourselves. Often we get carried away. Without judging, without buying into the likes and dislikes, we can always encourage ourselves to just be here again and again and again. (1997, 27)

ACKNOWLEDGMENTS

I wish to thank Paul Cooper for bringing this collection of essays to fruition and for inviting me to participate. I also wish to thank Lama Yeshe Wangmo and Lama Tharchin Rinpoche for their generous spirits and inspiring instructions.

NOTE

1. Editor's Note: Melanie Klein distinguishes everyday fantasies from "phantasy," which describes unconscious phantasies that operate on the borderline between somatic and psychical processes and that are experienced both physically and mentally.

REFERENCES

Chodron, P. (1997). *When things fall apart: Heart advice for difficult times.* Boston: Shambhala.

Coltart, N. (1992). *Slouching towards Bethlehem.* New York: Guilford.

Freud, S. (1911). Formulations regarding the two principles in mental functioning. In *Selected Papers, Volume 4: Papers on Metapsychology,* E. Jones, trans. J. Riviere. (1959).

Greenberg, M., and J. Snell. (1999). Brain development and emotional development: The role of teaching in organizing the frontal lobe. In *Emotional development and emotional intelligence: Educational implications,* ed. P. Salovey et al. New York: Basic Books.

Hanh, T. (1998). *The heart of Buddha's teachings: Transforming suffering into peace, joy, and liberation.* New York: Broadway Books.

Levine, S. (1989). *A gradual awakening.* New York: Anchor/Doubleday.

Nairn, R. (1999). *Diamond mind: A psychology of meditation.* Boston: Shambhala.

Rowe, S. (1996). *The vision of James.* Rockport: Element Books.

Snyder, G. (1999). *Paris review: Beat writers at work.* London: Harvill Press.

Symington, J. (1985). The survival function of primitive omnipotence. *International Journal of Psychoanalysis,* 66, 481–88.

Young, S. (1997). *The science of enlightenment.* Boulder: Sounds True Audio.

Chapter Four

Don't Remove Delusion: Don't Even Seek the Truth

Barry Magid

The title of this chapter is taken from a line in the "Song of Enlightenment" by the seventh Zen patriarch Yung-chia (d. 713). His seemingly paradoxical admonition challenges anyone who comes to any sort of practice—whether that practice is conceived of in psychological or spiritual terms—with the master's perspective in which there is "nothing to do and nothing to master." What then becomes of the "helping professions" or "saving all beings" from suffering?

Surely everyone coming to either therapy or to mediation practice wants *something*. This is both unavoidable and natural. We come seeking a relief of suffering; however we may conceive of that "suffering" and that "relief." Yet the Zen patriarch is telling us that our search itself embodies the very imbalance we are trying to correct—only by leaving everything just as it is can we escape the dualism and false dichotomy of problems and solutions.

More than a thousand years after Yung-chia, Ludwig Wittgenstein declared that philosophy leaves everything just as it finds it. For Wittgenstein, philosophy couldn't uncover hidden truths about life for "nothing is hidden." Instead, the problem was how to get out of the grip of a fantasy of metaphysical truth that somehow was supposed to exist behind the screen of appearances, beneath the surface of language and meaning.

This chapter will explore how we can reconcile the paradox of relieving suffering while leaving everything just as it is and of discovering the "truth" that nothing is hidden. Drawing on my own experience as a Zen teacher and as a psychoanalyst, I will try to weave together clinical material from a psychoanalytic perspective of self psychology and intersubjectivity with the experiences of present-day Zen students. These new psychoanalytic theories describe the self as constituted by the ever-shifting patterns of its

relationships—a model of the mind that turns out to closely resemble the classical Buddhist picture of dependent co-origination.

Let us begin with the traditional Buddhist perspective. In monasteries
around the world, monks since the time of the historical Buddha have chanted
four vows that encapsulate the Buddhist path. The standard translation of the
first vow says "Sentient beings are numberless, I vow to save them all." What
does this mean? What exactly are we vowing to do? What kind of "saving" is
this? I'm pretty sure Buddha did not intend this vow to be a commitment to
a life of social work, but neither is it meant to be an esoteric admonition that
ignores the real needs of real people.

To understand the koan posed by this vow, we must explore in what sense
we imagine all beings need saving. We are told that Buddha's own enlightenment manifested in the realization that all beings just as they are, are already
Buddhas, whether they know it or not. "Buddhas" by definition would not
seem to be in need of "saving," though we might say that they need realize
their true nature in order to be "saved' from the delusion that they are *not*
Buddhas. Our natural tendency is to assume that Buddha-nature is some kind
of latent potential, some inner seed that we strive to develop. But our encounter with the words of Yung-chia challenges that point of view: Buddha-
nature is not a potential, it is already the way we (and all things, all dharmas)
already are. Why then don't we *feel* more like Buddhas? Yung-chia might re-
tort "What did you expect being a Buddha to feel like?"

As a way of driving home the paradox inherent in a vow to save all those
beings who are already Buddhas, I sometimes have offered my students an alternative to that traditional first vow: "Sentient beings are numberless—to
hell with them!"

Zen master Sekito told his students it didn't matter to him whether he was
reborn in hell or not. What was the difference between heaven and hell—
delusion and enlightenment anyway? Besides, if there are beings who really
need saving, where are you more likely to find them than in hell?

We are all by now familiar with the saying "If you meet the Buddha on the
road, kill him." That saying, once startling, has become a cliché, preventing
us from experiencing the full force of what was being said. We need to "kill"
any idea we have of the Buddhahood being "out there" or down the road or
in anyway outside ourselves. Yet how many people continue to practice with
the implicit goal of someday meeting Buddha? We may imagine we will
meet him in the guise of an enlightened master—a qualitatively different order of being than ourselves—or that we will one day after years and years of
hard practice, finally become whatever it is we imagine we want to turn into.
In Tolkien's *Lord of the Rings,* I first encountered the wizard Gandalf, and

his wisdom and magical powers no doubt influenced my notions of enlightenment and Zen masters years later. Inevitably all the old stories of our youth, whether taken from Tolkien or the *Mumonkan*, shape our fantasies of transcendence and enlightenment. They are the inevitable—and necessary seeds—of our aspiration, yet after they have set us on our way, we eventually have to see them for what they are. The old koans tell stories of people much like ourselves who eventually liberated themselves from their own fantasies of "Buddha." It would be a shame to become so enchanted by their example that we use it simply to renew our own dualistic fantasies of delusion and enlightenment.

We can fall into the same trap with the concept of "saving." We imagine we should always feel a certain way—compassionate, peaceful, kind, helpful—and we should always be devoting all our energies on behalf of others. Well, we don't. Not the way we think we should anyway. And so we summon up an idealistic sounding vow that seems to say we promise from now on to be good and helpful. The only problem is that this approach to the vow gets us further wedded to the attitude that there is something wrong with us and others that needs fixing. Then, we try to fix ourselves—try to make ourselves "better" people—through the practice of helping others. We become enthralled to our image of "helping." That is why I say "to hell with them!" Kill your image of the helper, and of helping, just the way you kill the image of the Buddha on the road. Both sets of images simply further entrench a dualistic way of thinking. During my training as a therapist, we had a phrase to describe that sort of "help"—the help that inflates the ego of the helper and keeps the recipient of the so-called help in a forever, needy, one-down position: "The helping hand strikes again!"

Both Zen and psychoanalysis have grappled with the paradox of nonhelping. Some therapies, some spiritual practices actively embrace the helping mode and offer step-wise techniques to relieve suffering. We train ourselves in a technique, but all too often miss the implication of a technique-oriented practice. Stephen Batchelor described the consequences this way:

> A technique is the embodiment of a logical procedure. In employing a technique, we apply a series of interconnected stages, which have been thought out beforehand. Each stage is linked causally to the next. As long as we follow correctly the various stages, we will produce a predictable result . . . Any spiritual path that speaks of a series of interconnected stages leading to awakening . . . has a technological aspect. (Batchelor 1990, 69–70)

We come to think there is a method, a rational way to get us from here to there, all the while confirming a view that where we are is somehow wrong or insufficient. Contrast this with the following quotes from two contemporary Zen teachers:

> A student who worked with learning disabled children asked Kobun Chino Roshi what the best way was to help them. Her teacher's answer was simple, "No thought of helping." (Murphy 2002, 101)

Joko Beck, when asked by an interviewer, what she wanted to share with people everywhere, replied, "Nothing. I don't want to share anything with people everywhere . . . I'm just living my life" (Beck 2003).

Whenever someone asks me to explain the difference between psychotherapy and psychoanalysis, it's this relationship to the whole notion of goal-oriented techniques and to the role of the helper that I want to point to. I like to say the difference is that psychoanalysis doesn't help anybody. Though I admit that may sound a bit facetious, I think it does point to an important distinction within the so-called helping professions. The fundamentally open-ended nature of psychoanalytic inquiry contributes to this stance of "not helping" that I've been referring to. Though patients obviously seek treatment because of problems they want solved, psychoanalysis is not a problem-solving technique. It does not aim at a particular goal or seek a particular outcome. Despite an increasing trend toward the "medicalization" of all forms of psychotherapy, driven in large part by the cost containment requirements of the managed care and insurance industries, psychoanalysis by its very nature refuses to be time-limited, symptom-focused, or outcome-oriented. At a time when psychiatry is increasingly being taking over by neurology and psychopharmacology, psychoanalysis continues to define itself in terms of such nonquantifiables as self-esteem, personal meaning, and identity. Its ancestor is not just Hippocrates, who first established the standards for the medical profession, but, more important, Socrates, who led his interlocutors into an open-ended exploration of the nature of the good life. The psychoanalytic method goes against the grain of our modern life. It is deliberately slow. It asks us to sit (or lie) still, to spend long hours immersed in our feelings, to enter into a view of life that is process rather than goal oriented. It is intimate, personal, and cannot be conducted online. It assumes that each individual's life and happiness is precious beyond any economic measure and is worth our endless care and attention. It will never be cost-efficient. All this may give psychoanalytic orientation a distinct advantage when it comes to trying to build conceptual bridges to a variety of Buddhist practices, and to Zen in particular.

For a long time, psychoanalysts, following in Freud's footsteps, were almost desperate to establish their credentials as scientists. But increasingly the profession has come to see its role more philosophically and hermeneutically. The particular psychoanalytic tradition in which I studied, called *self psychology* and based on the work of Heinz Kohut, exemplifies this distinction.

Self psychology is the study of subjective experience. It uses empathy to imaginatively enter into the subjective worldview of the other. This basic stance puts it in sharp contrast to the stance of the scientist, who by definition, views phenomena, including psychological phenomena, from the *outside*, as an independent, objective observer. As a self-psychologically oriented analyst, I acknowledge the impossibility of objectivity or complete neutrality. My view, like the patient's view, is always a view from *somewhere*, not from some position of absolute objectivity or truth. Psychotherapy—as opposed to psychoanalysis—by virtue of its problem-solving stance—puts the therapist in the position of the outside observer and judge of what the patient is doing—and in particular what they are doing *wrong*. Psychotherapy looks for what is dysfunctional, what is distorted, what isn't working, and what could be done differently. A psychoanalytic approach is more likely to explore the subjective reality of a person's experience rather than try to offer interventions designed to get them to see things another way. The impact of being empathically understood in this way can be very profound, and is, I would say, the major engine for the change and development that eventually occurs.

All this brings us to the ways in which I believe Zen and psychoanalysis share a common ground of nondirectedness, or as Buddhists would say, "no gain." Here is an example of this stance exemplified by an interchange between two modern Japanese masters:

> Uchiyama Roshi recalled that as a shy and anxious young monk he asked his teacher, the powerful and charismatic Kodo Sawaki Roshi, whether Zen practice would eventually make him a stronger person, more like his teacher. Kodo Roshi shouted back, "NO! Zazen is useless. I'm not like this because of my practice of zazen. I was like this before I began to practice. Zazen doesn't change a person. Zazen is useless." [Uchiyama, K. The Zen Teachings of "Homeless" Kodo. Libri Books on Demand]

Psychoanalysis, I would suggest, may be one of the few Western discipline that comes close to being as useless as zazen! In an age devoted to self-help and self-improvement, the "uselessness" of meditation (or analysis) is very difficult to grasp. Zazen is not a technique. It is not a means to an end. It's not a way to become calmer, more confident, or "enlightened." There are some interesting parallels in how the two practices work. Just showing up is the main requirement of both. We have to be willing to show up for each hour's experience, whether on the couch or on the cushion. Freud told his patients to "free associate," that is, to simply say whatever came into their mind. It sounds like the simplest thing in the world, but nobody can do it. Immediately we begin to organize our thoughts in our idiosyncratic ways, censuring here, emphasizing there, and trying to make one impression or another to ourselves and to the analyst. I remember when I was just starting out in my own analysis, while training as a psychiatry resident, I dutifully lay down on the couch and tried to do what I thought was free association. My analyst had helpfully arranged his office in such a way that the couch faced a wall on which was hung a drawing of a female nude. I never mentioned it. Instead I rambled on and on, "freely" flitting from subject to subject, until he finally remarked he had no idea what I was talking about.

Invariably we shape our "free" associations into distinct personas, needy or self-reliant, helpless or insightful, rivalrous or subservient. Gradually, we can learn to observe what we're doing, what we're consciously or unconsciously avoiding or choosing. We just bring our attention to the process and try to understand why it feels right to do it the way we're doing it. We don't try to change anything, just watch our minds unfold and watch our resistance to that unfolding.

In meditation, the most basic instruction is to keep our attention in the present moment, whether by following our breaths or labeling our thoughts. Again, the simplest thing in the world. How could you do it wrong? Where is there to be but in the present moment—regardless of what you're doing in or with it? This is what master Yung-chia is pointing to when he says there is "nothing to do and nothing to master"; we "neither remove delusion nor seek the truth." Yet how many years of practice does it take before we're willing to leave our minds alone?

In zazen, as in psychoanalysis, we quickly find that the last thing in the world we want is to stay present. To stay present is to become increasingly aware of what our minds and our bodies are actually doing, as opposed to the way we wish they were. We find out we're a lot less calm, compassionate, and focused than a good Buddhist is "supposed" to be. And so, like the analytic patient on the couch, meditators on the cushion begin to shape their experience, to try steering themselves in the direction they want their minds to go, rather than honestly staying with what is. My Zen teacher, Charlotte Joko Beck, repeatedly emphasized awareness of this *resistance* to moment-by-moment experience as the core of true practice. Stay with your anxiety, your anger, your confusion—in other words, stay with precisely those aspects of yourselves that you came to meditation to change! Norman Fischer, a former Abbott of the San Francisco Zen Center, also has emphasized our resistance to leaving everything alone and the temptation to turn zazen into a technique. "The problem is that we actually are incapable of seeing zazen as useless because our minds cannot accept the fundamental genuineness, the all rightness of our lives. We are actually very resistant to it, we hate it . . . we persistently think we need more" (Fischer 1999, 43).

That leaving everything just as it is, is the real practice. Just like analysis. Although both Buddhism and psychoanalysis can be said to share a common goal of relieving suffering, Kodo Sawaki Roshi's admonition that zazen is "useless" should put us on notice that the "relief" being offered may be either indirect at best, or more likely, wholly different from whatever sort of relief we had in mind when we began to practice.

We naturally expect years of meditation to change the *content* of our minds, to transform our personality. Yet, as the examples of Uchiyama and Sawaki show, we may remain the sort of person we always were. Years later, Uchiyama told Arthur Braverman that Sawaki had been right—after thirty years of practice "I'm still a wimp!" (Braverman 2003).

Some years ago, I had a student who initially came to me for psychotherapy. She was a young woman in her twenties who came to treatment because of chronic depression. Her symptoms had become quite severe in her last year of college when she was working in relative isolation on an independent research project and around the same time, she broke up with her boyfriend. She had been doing better with the help of antidepressants until recently when she lost her job and was once again on her own, without any outside support or close relationships. Her parents were divorced, and each lived in distant cities. Her father was a recovered alcoholic, and she had recently become worried about the extent of her own drinking. She drank daily, especially in the evening, and drank to the point of passing out each night as a way of getting to sleep and escaping her loneliness. Her breakup with her college boyfriend fueled her view of her parents' marriage as a legacy of failure she was doomed to repeat. Likewise, she felt afraid she had inherited her father's disease of alcoholism. To go to Alcoholics Anonymous (AA) would be a confirmation of her predetermined fate as a basically damaged human being, doomed to repeat the worst of her parents' lives.

We struggled to find a way to address her drinking that did not feed into her sense of underlying damage. We talked about whether problem drinking was a "disease" or not and what other ways of thinking about it there could be. At one point she said, with some resignation in her voice, "At least, I suppose it's better that than being all moralistic about it." I replied that actually I thought her drinking *was* a moral problem—and that was the alternative to a disease model. I explained morality was a matter of how one lived one's life—what were our values and ideals and what we did or didn't do to try to live up to them. This discussion turned a corner in the treatment. From then on she began to think in terms of her own choices and agency rather than picturing herself as the passive, resigned recipient of a flawed genetic and familial legacy. We talked about the feelings she kept at bay through her drinking and what it might be like to regularly face them sober. At some point, I raised the possibility that she try a daily meditation practice as a way to simply sit still with her feelings.

Over the next couple of years, she became a regular meditator and quit drinking without ever attending AA. However, a new problem surfaced in her meditation. Once she began attending group sittings, and especially during sesshins (intensive mediation retreats of several days duration) she found herself subject to repeated bouts of intense sleepiness. At first we tried looking at it as another sign of avoidance, but that approach didn't seem to lead anywhere useful. Gradually she found herself slipping back into her old frame of mind: there was something basically wrong with her that was interfering with her attempts to be a good Zen student. After a while she consulted a neurologist and underwent sleep studies that determined she had a form of narcolepsy. While her mind was actively thinking she could stay awake, but any period in which her thoughts quieted down seemed inevitably to lead to her falling asleep. Medication helped somewhat, but once again she was confronted with a diagnosis that seemed to undermine everything good she had come to believe about herself and her practice. The EEG seemed to be telling her she could never enter into those special states of thought-free concentration called "samadhi" that everything she read said was the goal of Zen. She seriously considered the possibility that she should quit zazen practice entirely, as it was obviously unsuited to the kind of person the neurologist said she was. Perhaps, she thought, she should take up a martial art where she could be active and concentrate in that way.

One way or another, she kept sitting. We continued to talk about sitting as sitting with our bodies and minds just as they are, without any goal other than an honest acknowledgment of what each moment brought. She was forced to sit with a true attitude of no gain—all her hopes for her practice had been thoroughly undermined by her neurological diagnosis. Yet she kept sitting, not knowing what else to do, somehow devoted to the practice even though she thought herself forever barred from what others around her would be accomplishing. Then one day, after a weekend sesshin, she went to a museum calligraphy show by old Japanese masters. Suddenly, all her sense of damage dropped away. She was who she was, and in a strange way that was nobody at all. All the old stories by which she had defined herself all those years suddenly seemed empty, just stories she no longer believed in.

After that, nothing changed. She still fell asleep sitting. But also everything had changed. Her problems were just problems, no longer evidence that proved that there was something wrong with her. She found a new boyfriend. They fell in love and then a year later, he left her. She cried but didn't feel it was her fault. It was a terribly painful experience, but she was easily able to resist casting it as a chapter in the story of how she was doomed to repeat her parents' divorce. Clearly, telling herself that old story would always be an option, but why go there?

This case highlighted for me the danger that therapy can perpetuate a person's idea that there is something basically wrong with them that will need a lifetime of work to correct—if ever. The standard AA approach to her alcoholism might have simply fed her sense of inherited damage. It doesn't matter whether that "damage" is conceptualized as biologically based or laid down in childhood traumas that are forever and irreducibly etched into who we are "deep down." So-called insights into the nature of the illness or a genetic reconstruction of childhood trauma may simply be a crutch that confirm a belief in our intrinsic infirmity rather than give rise to the strength to trust our own resiliency in the face of our life as it is.

Meditation may also fail us in characteristic ways. It too can become part of an endless self-improvement project—aimed not as therapy at the endless project of trying to erase an old flaw—but as part of endless and ultimately hopeless pursuit of perfectibility. We may enlist it in our ongoing project of becoming a special, spiritual type of person. Not only does our meditation practice prove we are a superior type of person, we may seek out groups that further convey a sense of specialness through the wearing of robes, shaving of heads, or the bestowal of dharma names. We may engage in intensive spiritual retreats that are just that—retreats from our everyday life and identity. We may pursue or cultivate "higher" states of consciousness in flight from our everyday mind and as a way of not having to come to terms with the less than pleasant aspects of our emotional reality. The more we cultivate a "spiritual" persona the more we may be secretly—or not so secretly—contemptuous of those who are involved in more earthy pursuits.

As our ideas of gain are gradually worn away, we increasingly confront the problem of motivation in practice. My patient somehow managed to keep sitting even as her ideal of ever becoming a "good" Zen student crumbled beneath her. Norman Fischer has said that eventually we come to sit "zazen simply for zazen's sake." Zazen is fundamentally a useless and pointless activity. A person is devoted to zazen not because it helps anything, or is peaceful, or interesting, or because Buddha tells one to do it—though we may imagine that it helps, or is peaceful, or interesting, or that Buddha recommended it— but simply because one is devoted to it. You cannot argue for it, or justify it, or make it into something good. You just do it because you do it (Fischer 1999, 41–42).

But that "Why practice?" keeps confronting us. Unmon said, "Look! This world is vast and wide. Why do you put on your priest's robe at the sound of the bell?" (Aitken 1991, Mumonkan Case 16). "Why" sits at the very center of Unmon's question, as crucial now as it was for him more than a thousand years ago. In the case, "Why" is like a hinge between two statements: "The world is vast and wide" and "You put on your priest's robe at the sound of the bell." As presented in his question it is as if the first challenges the second. The vastness of the world implies no foundation, no ground—this is the vastness of emptiness—in which nothing has a fixed or permanent or essential nature. Everything is empty, impermanent—why then do we follow the ritual of putting on robes at the sound of the bell?

We are confronted by versions of this "Why?" over and over again in our lives and our practice. Students ask, "Life is short! Why am I spending my precious time sitting and facing a wall?" More fundamentally we all ask, "Why do we suffer? Why do we grow old? Why must I die?" What kind of answer are we looking for questions like these? When Job asked God why he was suffering, God replied, in the manner of Unmon, that the world is vast and wide. "Why?" seeks to stand outside of life and critique it, to suggest that it can and should be other than it is. But for these big questions, there is no place outside of life to stand. In our practice, we convert these plaintive questions into simple statements of fact: We grow old. We suffer. We die. Life takes this shape and none other.

For Unmon, putting on a robe at the sound of the bell is simply who we are and what we do. Why does a bishop move diagonally in chess? That's what a bishop *is*. Though chess—or monkhood—may seem an arbitrary collection of rules, within the game, a bishop is defined by this action. Birds fly, fish swim, and bishops move diagonally. Now, of course, I'm not a monk and I don't put on a robe at the sound of the bell. As a lay teacher, the parameters of my behavior are different. There are many different kinds of birds—even flightless birds like penguins. But who I am, what I do is not a matter of any reason or explanation that answers the question, "Why?" It's who I am.

Practice gets easier over the years, but not because we get good at it. When we start out, practice is something that we choose to do. We try to decide how long to sit and how often and at which center or with which teacher. So many choices! So much effort! But as the years go by, and our practice settles down, it becomes less and less separate from who we are. We make fewer choices; we make less effort because sitting has become simply a natural expression of who we are. Sometimes I say I'm a very lazy teacher as a way of expressing how little effort it involved! Why do I sit? I simply sit.

Wittgenstein admonished us that explanations in philosophy must eventually come to an end. How do we justify a rule, like the way a bishop moves in chess? It is how the game is played. As Wittgenstein put it, "When I have exhausted the justifications I have reached bedrock, and my spade is turned.

Then I am inclined to say this is what I do" (Wittgenstein 1953, 217). We are compelled to examine what we imagine would count as an explanation or justification. "Philosophy simply puts everything before us, and neither explains nor deduces anything. Since everything lies open to view there is nothing to explain" (126).

Likewise, Zen simply lays our life as it is before us. That life includes suffering, old age, and death. The Heart Sutra tells us that there is no old age and death and no end to old age and death. To say no old age and death is precisely to say they have no separate meaning or existence outside of life. They disappear into the vast and wide expanse of life itself.

Some years ago, my wife died in a plane crash. When I told my teacher Joko Beck what happened, I said that the one thing I never want to hear from her or anybody else is that this had any meaning whatsoever. No unseen plan could justify it. No subsequent good could give it meaning. Death happens. The "Why?" simply disappears into brute fact. Yet the consequence is that disappearance is not grim resignation. It is liberation into a paradoxically problem-free life: problem-free because problems are no longer problems, no longer separate. There is just our life.

We have a life of no problems because problems simply disappear into the fabric of our life, inseparably part of its warp and woof. As part of our Buddhist service, we chant "May we exist like a lotus at home in muddy water." The lotus of enlightenment only blooms amid the nutrient mud of delusion. Yet it is so easy in our practice to become unbalanced, to focus predominantly on either the bloom of the lotus or the cloudiness of the mud. Either we become infatuated with the flower of enlightenment, forgetting its relationship to the mud of our everyday lives, or we are fixated on our problems, our inadequacies, and doubt anything could ever grow in such muck. We become either connoisseurs of the flower or launch into a water purification project! Maybe we need a new American metaphor. Perhaps we should chant "may we exist like a pig in shit!" The pig is perfectly at home in his shit-world—frolicking, flourishing in what we call waste. We're not so inclined to idealize the pig—to make him an object of veneration or spiritual symbolism like we do with the lotus . . . but really the two images are saying the same thing. We have to experience the inseparability of the delusion and enlightenment, not try to eliminate one and stay always attached to the other. I read somewhere that back in the heady days of the stock market bubble, unscrupulous stock traders had a phrase for hyping worthless Internet initial stock offerings. They called using extravagant, empty promises of riches to come from some poor, worthless Internet start-up company "Putting lipstick on this pig." But as they (Butler 1906) say, "Pigs is pigs," and no amount of lipstick is going to change that fact.

Seeking neither to eliminate delusion nor to find some transcendental liberating truth, we come back to our life as it is. Perhaps only when we forget our aspiration to become Buddhas can we really enjoy our lives as ordinary human beings. Let others decide whether we're acting like a Buddha or not. Abandoning self-improvement, we exert ourselves fully and naturally as birds that enjoy frolicking in the wind or dolphins playfully leaping in the sea. Or like a pig in shit.

ACKNOWLEDGMENT

Portions of this chapter were published in a different form in *Ordinary Mind*, Boston: Wisdom, 2004.

REFERENCES

Aitken, R. (1991). *The gateless barrier: The wu-men kuan (mumonkan)*. New York: North Point Press.

Batchelor, S. (1990). *The faith to doubt*. Berkeley: Parallax Press.

Beck, C. (2003). Interview with Donna Rockwell: *Shambhala sun*, March, 2003. www.shambhalasun.com/Archives/Features/2003/200303mar/200303.htm (accessed February 20, 2004).

Braverman, A. (2003). *Living and dying in zazen*. Trumbull, CT: Weatherhill.

Butler, E. P. (1906). *Pigs is pigs*. New York: Doubleday.

Fischer, N. (1999). In *The Gethsemani encounter*, ed. D. Mitchell and J. Wiseman. New York: Continuum.

Foster, N., and J. Shoemaker. (1996). *The roaring stream*. Hopewell, NJ: Ecco.

Murphy, S. (2002). *One bird, one stone*. New York: St. Martin's Press.

Wittgenstein, L. (1953). *Philosophical investigations*. London: Basil Blackwell.

Chapter Five

The Light of Faithful Awareness

Tony Stern

From the age of twelve, I have had an interest in Buddhism, psychology, and the meeting points between these two traditions. In my early teen years, I read the writings of Krishnamurti and books of Alan Watts, like *Psychotherapy East and West,* with keen enthusiasm, and I had little doubt that they pointed toward something real and significant. Then on Christmas Eve in 1971, when I was sixteen years old, I lay down in bed as I always did, and I became aware of the sound of my own breathing. It struck me that I had never actually heard the breath until this moment. Without warning and for no discernable reason, its rhythm filled the center of my awareness in a clean, pristine, transparent way.

The sound of breathing conveyed an utter simplicity, a perfect harmony, an eternal mystery. How sweet, how effortless! This was the image of myself as this body slipped away, as did the images of things surrounding me in the room. This left behind a sense of ecstatic energy stretching without limits in all directions. This was me, not the little mind in a little body I had thought I was! How wonderful! How surprising! In short, that night I had a taste of the truth that lives at the core of Buddhism and other sacred traditions.

On three consecutive nights the following May, a similar phenomenon occurred. With each night it deepened. What complete delight filled all of my body! It was as if I fell asleep each time, yet a crystal-clear awareness remained. Or as if the body fell asleep, yet the mind stayed fully awake and alert. Two undeniable facts presented themselves: that I was in touch with the limitless source of energy that has created everything from an amoeba to a universe, and that I had been quite mistaken about who I am. As joyful and unusual as this taste of the living truth was, it also felt radically ordinary, natural, and familiar. It was as if I had come to a place of perfect meeting between a cry of hallelujah and a shrug of "nothing special."

Over the next half year, these nighttime experiences provoked a longing for spiritual practice, and by themselves, they fit reasonably well with my own worldview and direction at the time. There was a sense of safety in how private they were. It had not yet dawned on me that every moment, no matter how mundane, is intimately connected with the spiritual path.

I had had the sense of being one with an infinite ocean during the peak moments of those nights; nonetheless, it still seemed self-evident I could have a quiet spiritual life in times when I was alone and continue to lead a "normal life." I held to the notion that there is such a thing as a "normal life"—that there is a regular old reliable world "out there" and me "over here" enjoying it and dealing with it and going somewhere in it. While there may be some truth and comfort in this idea, it is largely inaccurate, and the comfort it provides is misleading. The split between self and world is itself a false dichotomy. It implies a further false dichotomy between "spirit" and "world," with the associated delusion that whole areas of one's life in the world have little if anything to do with the spirit.

Several experiences in the next few years challenged my secure distinction between "me" and a world apart from me. One of those key experiences was the time I met my first spiritual teacher.

MEETING RUDI

About a year after the series of three sacred nights, in early May of 1972, I was seventeen years old and completing my senior year in high school. Natalie Shapiro, a cousin of a friend, heard of my interest in spirituality and suggested that if I was in Rudi's neighborhood I might like to meet him.

She was an ex-student of his and spoke warmly about him. She told me he had an Oriental art store downtown in Manhattan and that it would be worth my while dropping by just to see the art. She also related that he had been born and raised in Brooklyn and had had profound contact with several teachers from the East, including Hindu swamis and Tibetan lamas.

She went on to say that he had had a number of extraordinary mystical experiences, and that he taught a form of "kundalini yoga" whose purpose was to arouse subtle spiritual energies within the body, in particular a powerful energy stored at the base of the spine known as *kundalini*. When I had read a little about this type of yoga about six months before, I realized that those four nights I described above had involved a spontaneous kundalini awakening.[1]

I had no particular plans one balmy, leisurely Saturday a week or two after talking with Natalie. So elevenish that morning I took the Lexington Avenue IRT subway down to the Astor Place stop, figuring I would go to one or two of the spiritual bookstores in the area, maybe try a macrobiotic meal at "Paradox" or "The Cauldron" . . . and before or after lunch I would drop by to meet Rudi.

I browsed at Samuel Weiser's and East/West Books, making a few purchases, then proceeded over to Rudi's Oriental art store on 10th Street and 4th Avenue. Entering the store was like going into another world, but I can't say I took much of it in at first. I could detect a fragrance of pleasing incense within a few seconds of being there. Rudi's desk was almost all the way to the back of the large interior. I walked along an aisle crammed on either side with statues of Buddhas, bodhisattvas, and various Hindu deities. The walls displayed mountainous Chinese landscapes, Japanese drawings, elaborate Tibetan *thanka* hangings, and Persian miniatures. I wasn't surprised to learn later that this was one of the premier shops for Asian art in this country.

As I made my way to the back of the store, I saw a man with a shaved head whom I guessed was Rudi. He was wearing a light orange T-shirt, khakis, and sandals. He looked to be about 5'10" and in his early or mid-forties. He had a pronounced "Buddha belly"; his face was round and kind-looking and serious, with big ears sticking out, strikingly dark eyebrows and dark brown eyes. These eyes had a calm, clear, soft quality to them. Although I know it's silly and clichéd to say, but they did twinkle. There were a few people around Rudi, including a short old lady who turned out to be his mother.

Rudi turned and looked at me as I approached. I introduced myself and explained that Natalie had spoken of him. He noticed I had bought a few books, including *Meditation in Action*, by the Tibetan Buddhist teacher Trungpa Rinpoche. A few moments later I blurted out, "You know you look like one of those old Zen masters in paintings." He replied, "Not Zen masters in particular, just Buddhas in general, because I am a Buddha."

The thought began to form in my mind, "What an egotistical idea!" But before this judgment had a chance to coalesce, Rudi had already approached a few steps; he was stroking the stubble on my chin; he had a disarmingly humorous cross-eyed look on his face as he remarked, "*You* look like a chipmunk." We both laughed.

I asked, "What's a Buddha?" "Someone who's enlightened." But of course there are degrees of enlightenment. A friend can tell you "come on over, I've just cleaned my place. For him maybe it's clean, but you go and there's three inches of dust in the corners." Rudi spoke with a casual calm and a heavy Brooklyn accent. The resulting voice was interesting and appealing.

I had been meditating for an hour or more each day for the three weeks before meeting Rudi. At times while meditating I began to feel buttery sensations in my chest, like quick little flows or spurts of a warm liquid. It was pleasant and a bit intriguing. Now standing and talking with Rudi I was feeling these same sensations. I asked him what they meant. "It's your heart opening. First you feel the ocean, and you see it, hear it, taste it, and smell it. Then you become it." Rudi smiled. After a pause he suggested I have a look at some of the art and turned his attention back to one of his other visitors.

As I walked around, the kinesthetic buttery experience in my chest intensified both in sheer activity and in how increasingly delicious it felt. Within a minute or two I was standing still, looking down, and wondering at what was happening: the delicious streaming sensations in the chest were going wild; it all but felt as if my whole chest was melting down to the floor in a big happy buttery puddle. It was almost too much; I was amazed and verged on feeling alarmed. And then I felt an arm around my shoulders. It was Rudi. As he looked at me, he smiled and stated matter-of-factly, "It's all a matter of surrender to this energy."

It would have been reasonable for me to wonder how Rudi knew what I was going through in those moments—and how much he did know. I can't say these questions came to mind at the time. I think my answer then would have been about the same as it would be now: that Rudi sensed the essence of my experience through his own highly developed intuitive awareness. The fact that I'd frozen in my tracks with who-knows-what expression on my face must've been a bit of a tip-off, too.

"It's all a matter of surrender to this energy." That had the ring of truth to it. Over the next five or ten years, I tended to debate in my own mind which was truer: that it's all a matter of surrender to this energy or that it's all a matter of being quietly aware of the present moment. I did suspect that the two more or less boiled down to the same thing. But it's taken many years to get somewhat clearer and more comfortable with the fact that these two are intimately related aspects of the same basic work.

As one direction of a two-way process, an attention to the present opens us to a deeper flow of subtle energy in the body. In the other direction, the flow of energy brings us to a fuller attention to the present. We habitually resist this flow, but we can consciously surrender our resistance and allow it. When we let it penetrate, the inner energy unearths and dissolves tensions that otherwise keep us caught in being busy—caught in agendas of past and future. The release of tensions enlarges our awareness of the present. In the West, perhaps "the Holy Spirit" is a name for the energy that dissolves these obstructions.

WHAT WE NEED TO KNOW

My meeting with Rudi was my first distinct experience of a transmission of spiritual energy between two people. I've slowly become convinced that some such transmission happens among people all the time in mild, subtle, usually imperceptible ways. But here was an unmistakable example. Something in me came alive through Rudi's presence; something in me opened through contact with a person who had worked on himself spiritually for many years. It was an unusual moment of resonance, and it changed me. It was the most striking of several incidents in this period that shifted me in the direction of a deeper joy as well as a dedication to the spirit.

I asked Rudi several more questions as my experience was subsiding, none of them noteworthy. I was clearly jabbering to protect myself from the continued sense of intensity, and Rudi stopped me after a few minutes by saying, "You ask too many questions, Tony. To stick two pieces of paper together, you only need a dab of glue. Apply any more and it creates a mess. And it's unnecessary."

Inwardly we need only know enough to apply to the next leg of the journey— this next hour, this next day. Knowing more can interfere. It is wisdom that I've often forgotten on a true gut level and then eventually remembered again. For most of us, these things can take a long time to sink in.

RUDI AND ANA MARIA RIZZUTO

Seven years ago, almost twenty-four years after my first encounter with Rudi, I had an occasion to share the story with an esteemed Boston psychiatrist named Ana Maria Rizzuto. The setting was the American Academy of Psychoanalysis winter 1995 meeting in Cambridge, Massachusetts, where I chaired a panel on psychoanalysis and spirituality. The next day Rizzuto gave an informal case discussion that I attended.

Rizzuto is famous for her pioneering book *The Birth of the Living God* (1979), which has since become a classic. It takes an in-depth look at the parallels between people's early emotional experiences with parental figures and the images they form of God. After her presentation, a few of us joined her for lunch. Rizzuto is a diminutive, pleasant-looking woman in her sixties. The fact that she has sometimes been mistaken for being a nun is not surprising; she has a bit of that air about her.

Over lunch, we got on the subject of what heals in psychoanalysis and psychotherapy. Rizzuto stated that there is a common misconception that the answer is love. But the main thing that cures, she said emphatically, is not love, but rather self-understanding. And that understanding grows out of freely speaking about all of one's fantasies in the context of therapy.

We were surprised at Rizzuto's position. She was taking a traditional stance on a long-simmering controversy in the field. In the last twenty-five years, even quite a few diehard analysts have turned away from a central focus on "insight" and "interpretation" to a fuller appreciation of "the relationship" and its intangible elements.[2] Perhaps Rizzuto's own position has also softened over the last few decades. But in this moment Rizzuto was relishing in being old-fashioned, and it appeared that she believed passionately in a somewhat outmoded view.

I don't think I was alone in wondering how this could fit with her seriousness as a Christian. I asked, "What's the saying in the Gospel of John . . . about how God is love and where there is love there is God . . . ?" "No," Rizzuto corrected, "It's the First Epistle of John, Chapter Four." She proceeded to give a precise quote: "God is love; and he who dwells in love dwells in God" (stanza 16). But she also stuck to her guns. No doubt love informs the work of the psychoanalyst or therapist, she said. But it's self-understanding, not love, which makes the real difference in someone's life. When Rizzuto spoke of understanding, she was not referring to deep spiritual insight, but rather learning about oneself in a psychological vein—about one's own unconscious wishes and fears and defenses.

I immediately thought back to the time of meeting Rudi as an especially dramatic moment that seemed to go against her view. I described my first contact with him, my inner experience after a few minutes in his store—and how it had altered me. It seemed to have nothing really to do with understanding, but much to do with relationship, contact, and love. What would she say about that?

Rizzuto responded with interest. She acknowledged that there are holy people like Mother Teresa whose very presence can be uplifting. She also pointed out that there can be very intimate and intense experiences of nonverbal dialogue between two people. This one between Rudi and me was such a dialogue, she said. You two were deeply attuned to each other. What allowed for that? She wondered. What, for one thing, led you to be so receptive?

She was bringing the focus back to the individual psychological factors at play. Of course there were such factors, as there always are. But how fully do they explain matters of the spirit? My basic reply to Rizzuto still rings true to me: at the heart of such occasions lies the mystery of grace. By "grace" I meant all the unexpected gifts we receive—all the life of blessing that cannot be controlled or explained. Grace also implies "the light of faithful awareness" that I describe later in this paper, which itself is a central blessing that is always with us but is still out of our hands. It is the essence of who we are, yet we cannot control it.

I think Rizzuto agreed, at least partially. She told us that we might be interested to know that the Catholic Church is currently revising its theology of grace to account more for such experiences—to stress the importance of the relationship between human beings as the medium of grace.

The Question of Receptivity

Clearly, my own receptivity to Rudi was crucial. The majority of folks walking into his store felt nothing unusual. At the same time, countless people did—these kinds of openings were commonplace around Rudi, suggesting that such receptivity was fairly ordinary among people of varying backgrounds. Some, like myself, became students of Rudi's. Others did not. Nonetheless, they were affected.

For example, one of these unsuspecting visitors to the store was a well-known Reichian psychiatrist named Barbara Koopman. I met with her in 1978 about a conference on chronic muscular tension in children I was trying to get off the ground. It turned out she had known Rudi. She never studied with him, but she was powerfully impressed by his presence. When the conversation turned to her describing her own first meeting with him in his shop, she was overcome with tears. I didn't expect that. Nor did she. "It's hard to believe," she commented about these unexpected tears, "that any person could be surrounded by the remarkably fresh, renewing atmosphere that was around him. I just didn't know it was possible that a human being could generate an energy like that."

An Unexpected Facial

That first day meeting Rudi, I hung around in his store for an hour or so as he went about his business of unpacking art and shmoozing with clients, friends, and students. I finally left to have lunch. It was the first time I had a whole meal of macrobiotic food. As I was eating, I had the experience of a sweet and ever-so-gentle cleansing energy streaming out of every pore in my face. It was like a divine facial. Delighted and a little perplexed, I confess that I reflected, "Boy, this macrobiotic food really is something! It's everything folks have claimed for it, and then some!"

Only after getting to know Rudi more over the next year did it completely dawn on me that the sense of cleansing energy I experienced over lunch had had little if anything to do with the food. Rather, it was one of the direct lingering effects of meeting Rudi.[3]

THE LIGHT OF FAITHFUL AWARENESS

Since the conversation with Rizzuto, I have thought about it in relation to Rudi, my own inner work, and the work I do as a psychotherapist. Like most shrinks, I am fascinated by the questions Rizzuto raised. What is "the healing factor"? Is it love? Is it insight? Or is it perhaps a source that lies behind both? Perhaps there is a light of awareness that allows for both contact and under- standing. If so, this "light" not only leads to such gifts, but also grows out of them. It grows stronger, in other words, as we let go of old assumptions and tensions; as we make real contact with others; and as we learn more deeply about ourselves.

My first meeting with Rudi, as well as those earlier nights of spiritual ex- perience, involved a letting go of old assumptions and tensions. These times of release also seemed to have relatively little to do with my personal self. Further along in this chapter, in the section entitled "My Need for Therapy," I offer a small example of a release that did have to do with my personal self. My journey as a whole, like every person's, has engaged both my individual self and the larger life of blessing underlying and transcending the self. There is a mystery of connection between each of us as individuals and the reality encompassing all.

I continue to wonder about the proper role of the personal self in the larger picture. Perhaps if I only saw matters in a Buddhist way, I would be tempted in more dogmatic or doctrinaire moments to say that such a self simply doesn't exist. Yet the main draw of therapy lies in the recognition that life isn't quite that simple. Thoughtful Buddhists would be among the first to admit that life is complex. In the last six years as well as in prior times in my life, I have been in psychotherapy as a patient. This has helped most directly with problems of being a self in the world, just as a Zen Buddhist practice for the last seventeen years has most directly aimed at an opening beyond the self.

In my own role as a psychiatrist and therapist, I am concerned with the wel- fare and growth of my patients as selves in the world. Yet to have such a fo- cus without a connection to the limitless whole is both counterproductive and impossible. It would be like asking for a foreground without a background, a cloud without a sky, or a flower without the earth from which it grows. This parallels a wish that each of us has—to be a wave, as it were, without the ocean below it.

According to Buddhism, this clinging to individual selfhood is our central problem. Buddha proposed that such clinging is the basic root of suffering. In any case, it is a fear-driven dynamic that binds us to a surface struggle with the world; it grips us in a small whirlpool of self-centered thrashing and fight- ing, of grasping and avoiding, and thus prevents us from recognizing our con- nection with the infinite ocean, the limitless whole.

What are we so driven to avoid? Loss, death, and impermanence, in a nut- shell. Buddha encouraged us to think on these matters through many of his teachings, including his first sermon expounding his Four Noble Truths.[4] In the most practical terms, being in the world means facing little losses every day. If not the loss of a friend by means of a rejection or a move out of town, then the loss of an acquaintance; or perhaps some loss of some part of a relationship—a loss of the friend we thought we knew. If not the loss of a job, then the loss of some task or project within the job; if not a full loss of face, then a small humiliation; if not a major setback in health, then at least a receding hairline.

All losses point us to the larger fact of our own eventual death and the death of all those we hold dear. To be fully a self in the world is to learn to face our own fear of the problems presented by loss and death. To be in the world of time means facing the timelessness of the whole, though most of us become sufficiently busy and distracted that we can temporarily overlook this fact. Such hiding from our basic situation is never particularly effective for very long.

In contrast to our own Western modern culture, the Buddhist tradition greatly values the recognition of loss, the awareness of impermanence, and the fear of death as entry points into wisdom. It could even be argued that Buddha's basic yardstick for mental health was an assessment of the depth with which the individual faces the fact of death and the radical fear it provokes. In any case, he saw that people could only become serious about spiritual practice when the immensity of death strikes them to their core. Furthermore, he taught that people fall on a continuum with regard to this sensitivity. At one end of this continuum are those that hear about the death of someone in a distant village and are shaken because at this point it truly dawns on them that they, too, will die someday. They are ready for the Buddhist teaching. At the other end of the continuum, there are those who open to the fact that their lives will surely end only when they themselves are about to die.[5]

To repeat, psychotherapy is concerned with self and world, whereas spiritual practice as I have known it touches a reality that transcends self and world—a reality of love and truth out of which the self and the world draw their mutual existence. These two endeavors, therapy and spiritual practice, have seemed to conflict at times. A serious focus on time-bound concerns can be an obstacle to opening to the timeless, and vice versa. But I believe these two emphases are deeply complementary, if we allow them to be. Just as the light of awareness underlies both love and insight, so does it underlie both spiritual and psychological work.

Thus Buddhist meditative practice opens me to this light of awareness—in other words, to a quality of open-hearted attentiveness—freeing me to listen more fully to my patients and to be present to their whole situations in a visceral way. I am reminded of the psychoanalyst Elvin Semrad's remark to therapists in training, "If you can't sit with the patient until he can feel it in his own body, you're in the wrong business" (Rako and Mazer 1980, 107). This sort of elemental contact, this viscerally being present to the patient, is enhanced through Buddhist practice. Once in a while it can take the form of the kind of exchange I experienced with Rudi. Buddhist meditation deepens our capacity to dwell in the present—not only with our minds and our hearts but also with our bodies. When our whole being is more awake to the present, our contact with another is more often blessed by a rich immediacy.

In any case, I discover at times something within me and beyond me dwelling with another "at the still point of the turning world," in T. S. Eliot's words. This still point is the place of meeting between time and the timeless, past and present, and self and that, which lies beyond the self. It is also where self and other can make true contact.

I would like to make two points about this kind of "event." The first is that meditative practice is not the only means of access to it. Together with the gift of a spiritual life, however one comes upon it, the other means is the discipline of being a therapist. As a therapist, one learns to listen. One learns to be curious about the full details of a person's story. At the same time, one learns to be careful both in coming to conclusions and also in sharing whatever conclusions one reaches. In contrast, most spiritual teachers I have known have been quite ready to assume what's best for others and to tell it to them. In other words, most spiritual teachers are preachers. The challenge of the therapeutic task has been a humbling privilege; it has repeatedly shown me the limits of advice-giving and has countered a strong preacher instinct in myself that I suspect would otherwise have ruled me.

Regarding the experience of dwelling with another in stillness, my second point is perhaps so obvious that it feels almost unnecessary to say it: that the majority of the time working as a therapist feels far less profound, far more in the nitty-gritty of the mud and the trenches. Yet even here, there is some recognition of the rightness in that. In other words, Buddhist practice has helped open me to a faithfulness that shines for others as much as for me, a faithfulness that both opens to a timeless joy and bears the suffering of time. This faithfulness is part of what I mean when I use phrases like "the light of awareness."

Definitions so often fall woefully short! The light of awareness is not literally a light, and "awareness" may sound just a little too neutral. It is neutral in the sense of being unconditional, nonjudgmental, and spacious, and it probably lies at the root of "analytic neutrality" in the best sense of that phrase. But such awareness involves much more, and perhaps "the light of faithful awareness" comes a little closer to it. Awareness implies everything that comes into play in being present to another. This includes letting be and letting go; an honoring of connection and difference (recognizing the other as other); and a faithful sensitivity to aliveness and blocks to aliveness. As it deepens, awareness becomes a simple medium of love and truth.

Paradoxically, "awareness" as a word may need a bit of embellishment to convey its fuller meaning, but it needs nothing added on as a reality. The plainer the awareness, the better. The faith that unfolds in "faithful awareness" is partly a recognition that the simplest attentiveness suffices; the barest awareness works its own quiet miracle. According to Nansen, a great ninth-century Zen master, "Ordinary mind is the Way."

My nights of ecstasy at age sixteen and the chest-melting experience of meeting Rudi involved opening to the Way. These and other experiences of the spirit are a part of a multidimensional process that still persists in my life and in the lives of countless seekers on the spiritual path. It is a process where the light of faithful awareness unfolds more and more fully, exposing and cleansing layers of tension and self-rejection in oneself and others.

This also occurs at the core of an otherwise normal-appearing therapeutic process, with the usual dynamics, the usual ideas, conversations, setbacks, and occasional breakthroughs. In fact, any reasonably good therapy draws on this light of faithful awareness, regardless of how dimly or clearly this fact is recognized by the therapist or the patient. I am hard-pressed to think that a therapy enlivened by Buddhism differs all that much from any other sound clinical practice.

Like the connection with my Zen teacher, the ongoing relationship with my therapist enriches and deepens the light of awareness. The relationship contributes to the sense that anything difficult can come to light. Like other meaningful relationships, time in therapy also provides a sense of contact in the here-and-now. This opens me further to the simple rightness of the here-and-now.

How thoughtful, skilled, and capable of being deeply present is any therapist? Buddhist or not, these are the important ingredients in a helper. Buddhist practice can help some clinicians along their way, as it has for me. If nothing else, it can be enormously renewing personally—perhaps even an antidote to burnout. But I believe that other therapists access similar territory in other ways.

MY NEED FOR THERAPY

In earlier years of Buddhist practice, my main effort would be to watch the flow of thoughts and feelings I call "me" and "mine." This was my way of engaging with the question "Who am I"; to see the images of myself simply as images; to see thoughts just as thoughts. This would undercut the profound power of the mind, revealing an investment in this succession of mental images and a hitherto unacknowledged belief in it as real.

In Buddhism, it is said that "The mind is an excellent servant, but a terrible master." This still sums up a good deal of wisdom for me. "The mind" in this saying is not Nansen's "ordinary mind" above, but rather our rational faculty and our whole sense of "me" and "mine," of identity, with its absolute need to feel in control.

We are all victims of our own hidden assumptions and the deep fear that feeds them. A major intent of meditation is to allow the assumptions of the mind to surface—to bring them to light and in the process be free of them. Until this occurs, we rarely catch a glimpse of these underlying fear-driven ideas about "me" and "mine," no less recognize how much they control us. Meditation works partly with the same ideas about ourselves that cognitive-behavioral therapy and other forms of therapy do, but it goes considerably deeper, challenging our basic view of being a skin-encapsulated self in the world.

As I have already pointed out, I have been freed to be present in a fuller way through such meditation. Over the years, however, I found that my focus during the practice of meditating began to feel somewhat rigid. I became more aware that at times such a practice involved a subtle avoidance of my own wishes, fears, and pain. The flow of awareness slowly felt more and more stuck in the limitations of this self-avoidance.

Awareness itself shows us what we need to see if we are honest with ourselves. In my case, I realized that I needed more work in therapy. This has been crucial in freeing the flow of awareness, though my sense is that I am still at the beginning of a process.

Meditation and psychological inquiry work together. They nudge this process along, unearthing old wounds, drives and assumptions. For instance, in the time after an hour of meditation recently, I felt an underlying tinge of loneliness and hopelessness. That night I dreamt of talking with an old friend. We were at a college reunion, yet standing near a monastery park. As I pondered the details of the dream conversation the next day, they helped me to see that the difficult feelings the meditation had stirred up sprang from early fears of failure—from the desperate feeling that I could never measure up to my father's expectations.

I also became aware that these feelings had preceded the meditation, but in a masked form. Earlier that day, I had picked up our dog from the kennel, and I had an unexpected judgment about one of the people who worked there, seeing him fleetingly as "a failure." Noticing this judgmental and irrational thought, I was surprised and curious, and I prayed for help in seeing what lay behind it. (I am far from immune from making judgments, but they usually apply to people close to me, not so often to relative strangers.) As the dream and associations to the dream later revealed, I had been projecting my own feelings of failure onto this person I hardly knew. This set of feelings was both an assumption and a tension connected to a particular experience when my father had scolded me when I was eight years old. Once I saw this, I was in a good position to let go of this sense of failure more thoroughly.

The role the meditation played was to begin to unearth and loosen the cluster of unconscious fears and Oedipal fantasies that I had defending against through judging another. In the dream, mushrooms lying in the grass nearby as I conversed with my friend were a symbol of fresh life of the earthy sort, and they also hinted at castration fears intermixed with my idea of being a failure.

As my own woundedness is more fully exposed, I can bear the wound. Only as it is exposed can I be healed, and can I be more available as an avenue of healing. The light of faithful awareness itself is the real healer.

REMAINING QUESTIONS

I have tried thus far to indicate mainly how Buddhism and therapy are both expressions of the same light, the same basic awareness. But I have also alluded to distinctions in the orientations of these two traditions. I think it's crucial that we do not gloss over such potential and actual points of conflict. One of the arenas where the two tend to diverge is around the important area of anger. According to most Buddhist thought, anger is a poison. According to most psychotherapeutic thought, anger can be a healthy and necessary part of self-respect and self-expression.

I find myself appreciating and embodying both views. I also think these attitudes make complete sense in the larger contexts of how little and how much each tradition values the individual self. In part, "Buddhism vs. therapy" is a subset of "traditional religion vs. modern secularism." In "the old days," the individual was often undervalued. In modern times, the individual is more often overglorified. We live in an age of grandiosity that reveals and conceals a deeper low self-esteem. We live in an age of entitlement that feeds this low self-esteem. Only a self-regard gratefully connected to the whole can stand strong. (There's that preacher in me I told you about! Give it an inch, and it will run for a mile!)

Needless to say, I have only momentarily touched on the topic of anger and selfhood as they relate to Buddhist and therapeutic thinking. Most important, the subject raises the question, how can we balance healthy self-assertion with the letting go of self? Similarly, how much attention shall we pay to our own desires, fantasies, and emotional life as a whole? What kind of attention shall we pay them? I don't have complete answers to these questions, but I sense that answering them involves walking a fine line—a line that is partly revealed by the spiritual and psychological paths as they work together and also as they work against each other.

I have argued that these two paths are complementary, and I believe that they are, despite their friction at times, and even because of this friction. One of the pieces of wisdom that attempts to unify psychology and spirituality is the oft-repeated idea, "You can only lose your self if you have a self." This may be of some help. But it only ushers us into the possibility of wisdom about such matters. As a beginning, it makes good sense. As the final word, it is merely glib.

At the end of the lunch with Ana Maria Rizzuto that I described earlier, I told her that I had one pressing question. Spiritual teachers like St. John of the Cross, Meister Eckhart, and many Buddhists point us in the direction of letting go of thoughts, musings, and fantasies. The purpose is to let go of oneself. Psychoanalysts beginning with Freud point in the direction of more thinking, musing, and fantasy. The purpose instead is to get to know oneself in greater depth. Both of these directions are valid. To learn both approaches is wise. But, I asked Rizzuto, when is it best to take each respective path? When is it best to let go of thoughts and fantasies, and when is it best to connect to them more completely?

Rudi had wisely rebuked me for asking so many questions. Nonetheless, a host of closely related questions present themselves now: When is thinking a defense, and when is it an opening? Is it sometimes both? When shall I direct my attention to the very fact of consciousness itself and the sense of consciousness as a whole (for example, by asking myself in all seriousness, "How do I know that I am I?"), and when, alternatively, to the detailed contents of this consciousness? When shall I aim to be crisply if gently alert, as the Zen teachings recommend, with the risk that I am suppressing something within me by this very work of alertness? In contrast, when shall I allow my mind to drift? When shall I provide a feeling or a daydream or a train of free associations a little room to breathe and grow? When shall I go further and allow it huge room, following its momentum of musings to the end, with the risk that I am avoiding the discomfort of being more quietly in the present moment, or with the risk of hiding in myself, of reinforcing the sleepy and distracted "me"? Is there a stance that is truly in the middle, that lets go of thoughts and also embraces them, all at once? What would a life balanced between these two approaches look like? How widely would it differ from person to person? How is some comprehension of these choices best conveyed to my patients? All of these questions, among others, spring up as immediate offshoots of my single question to Rizzuto.

In response to this basic question of when to let go of thoughts and when to embrace them, Rizzuto smiled and replied, "If I could answer that, I would win the Nobel Prize for Spirituality!"

Yes, it is indeed a difficult question to answer. But answer it we must. And answer it we do. Every day, without the benefit of a Nobel Prize level of understanding or attainment, each of us is faced with this question, and each of us must answer it for ourselves, however tentatively or even unknowingly.

Whether we realize it or not, the way we relate to ourselves in each hour is itself an answer to the question. Like an elephant in the living room, its challenge is unavoidable. As spiritual seekers, as therapists, or simply as people trying to live and to help others, we are constantly making subtle choices in relation to this challenge. At the same time, this vision of endless choice is only half of the story as I explain below.

LETTING THE MIND BE

At this point in my life, I feel a considerable need for both psychological and spiritual exploration. I respond to the challenge of the choice of *when* partly by falling back on tried and true matters of scheduling: set times for meditation in the morning and evening; set hours in therapy each week and retreats for longer periods of inner work one or more times each year. Such a cut-and-dried approach doesn't address the question of focus or inclination "the rest of the time," even while immersed in work tasks and other outer activities. Here my main response is experimental trial and error.

The vision of endless inner choice is incomplete in any case. To entertain such a notion as our exclusive model is an artifact of seeing inner growth only as the outcome of methods and techniques that we apply to ourselves, and it suggests a busy pursuit of interior goals that would rival our more usual pursuit of outer goals. How easily I get caught in keeping busy! In the midst of all my doing, all my diligence and enterprise, Buddha comes along with the subversive statement, "You are not the doer."

What could it mean, simply to allow the mind to be? Perhaps this question begins to answer the question I asked Rizzuto. The less we try to be anyone or to impose an agenda on the present moment, the more an answer steps forward on its own. At the same time, how often we need to exert the utmost focus to counteract the sway of old tensions! The twelfth-century Zen teacher Dogen emphasized how nothing needs to be done, yet he also said that the Way takes sweat, tears, and sometimes blood.

The answer that steps forward and meets us is the mind finding its own way. This way is natural, living, and ongoing. It includes the mind and the body and all to which they are connected. It presents and it bears with both the sense of a messy undergrowth with mushrooms sprouting and the sense of a wide-open sky with soaring vistas and absolute freedom. It encompasses ease and rigor, muddled fantasy and diamond clarity, the personal self, and the breeze of utter transcendence. When we have sufficient faith, we can *be* the mind in all of its modes, rather than always working consciously to observe it and unconsciously to limit it.

In other words, when we allow our thoughts and feelings to be, the mind is free. This is true in any case, but we are often too busy to see it.

NOTES

1. For more on kundalini, see A. Mookerjee (1982) and P. St. Romain (1991). See also the excellent annotated bibliography at the end of St. Romain's work. The book I had read prior to meeting Rudi was M. Eliade (1969). Rudi studied for twelve years with the well-known kundalini yoga teacher Swami Muktananda and had brief but significant contact with Muktananda's own teacher, Nityananda.

2. This was true for most of the psychiatrists at Cornell where I did residency training, including Dick Munich, Bob Michels, Arnold Cooper, Ted Jacobs, and probably even to some degree Otto Kernberg and Paulina Kernberg. Merton Gill and James Grotstein are two prominent psychoanalysts who have led in this shift of emphasis. But most psychoanalytic thinkers have moved at least somewhat in this direction.

3. Sadly, Rudi died in a plane crash the following February, three months after I had begun to study with him formally. See J. Mann (1987) and S. Rudrananda (1990) for a good introduction to his teaching.

4. See A. Low (1989), 26–30; M. Epstein (1995), 41–102; T. Nhat Hanh (1998), 3–44; and K. McLeod, (2001), 19–30.

5. See A. Low (1995), 206.

REFERENCES

Eliade, M. (1969). *Yoga, immortality and freedom*. Princeton, NJ: Princeton University Press.

Epstein, M. (1995). *Thoughts without a thinker*. New York: Basic Books.

Low, A. (1989). *Zen meditation plain and simple*. Boston: Charles E. Tuttle.

———. (1995). *The world: A gateway: Commentaries on the Mumonkan*. Boston: Charles E. Tuttle.

Mann, J. (1987). *Rudi: Fourteen years with my teacher*. Portland, OR: Rudra Press.

McLeod, K. (2001). *Wake up to your life*. San Francisco: Harper San Francisco.

Mookerjee, A. (1982). *Kundalini: The arousal of the inner energy*. Rochester, VT: Destiny Books.

Nhat Hanh, T. (1998). *The heart of the Buddha's teaching.* Berkeley: Parallax Press.

Rizzuto, A. M. (1979). *The birth of the living god.* Chicago: University of Chicago Press.

Rudrananda, S. (1990). *Rudi in his own words.* Portland, OR: Rudra Press.

Rako, S., and H. Mazer. (1980). *Semrad: The heart of a therapist.* Northvale, NJ: Jason Aronson.

St. Romain, P. (1991). *Kundalini energy and Christian spirituality.* New York: Crossroad.

Trungpa, C. (1985). *Meditation in action.* Boston: Shambhala.

Chapter Six

Driven to Distraction: Observations on Obsessionality

Marjorie Schuman

For me, this chapter provides an opportunity to write about my own experience as a psychoanalyst, as an analytic patient, and as a Buddhist meditator in a way that is both personal and professional. What I want to explore from these separate but interrelated points of view is my thinking about obsessionality.

Specifically, I will discuss the nature and function of obsessionality as I have come to understand it in myself and in my patients. I have spent many hours observing the obsessional behavior of my own mind both in psychoanalysis and in Buddhist meditation practice,[1] and in this chapter I attempt to conceptualize these experiences within a framework which integrates Buddhist and psychoanalytic thinking and, in addition, is informed by a psychobiological perspective.

Buddhist psychology reinforces the idea that an intrinsic tendency of the mind is cognitive activity that is continually recurring and autonomous. For example, it is said that the mind forms thoughts as water forms waves. In whatever metaphor, the mind engages in an unending (although intermittent) process of discursive thought. So what, then, is the distinction, if any, between this basic restlessness or lack of attentional focus in the mind (autonomous thinking) and obsessional thinking? Is there a seamless spectrum of activity between "normal" restless mind and clinically defined obsessionality? And, if so, how can this continuum best be understood?

OBSESSIONALITY

Obsessionality may be defined as the domination of a person's thoughts, feelings, or behavior by persistent, recurrent thoughts, ideas, or images; obsessions may involve wishes, temptations, prohibitions, or commands, or they may involve anxious rumination about a problem. Obsessions involve the effort to solve an emotional problem by thinking (Moore and Fine 1990). In classical psychoanalysis, the obsessive-compulsive dynamic was conceptualized as a defense against hostile or sexual impulses, although in a broader sense it may also be interpreted as a defense against awareness of feelings, or against thoughts that tend to produce shame, loss of pride or status, or a feeling of weakness or deficiency (i.e., narcissistic injury) (Salzman 1980). In simple terms, obsessions substitute for feelings that are unsafe to experience.

In his classic description of obsessive-compulsive character, Shapiro (1965) emphasized several interrelated features that bear repeating here:

- The obsessive's character style is one marked by rigidity in regard to thinking and intellectual activity, a rigidity that extends also to behavior generally, including body posture and social manner.
- The obsessive person's attention operates with intense, sharp focus, but in a way that is inflexibly narrow and which lacks the ability to be regulated at will. The cognitive inflexibility of the obsessive person is revealed in the inability to shift attention from one thing to another, a lack of volitional mobility of attention.
- The obsessive person is also described as "driven"; genuine motivation is replaced by the sense of necessity or requirement to do something that, in actuality, is a pressure that the person applies to himself. For example, the obsessive gives himself or herself deadlines for activities, which logically may be quite arbitrary.
- But if the obsessive is driven, he or she is equally the driver. The obsessive person's life space is structured around a sense of "should" that is quite ego syntonic, (although the person may complain about the experience of the pressure).
- "The activity—one could just as well say the life—of the obsessional person is characterized by a more or less continuous experience of tense deliberateness, a sense of effort, and of trying." The obsessive is overcontrolled, operating from a state of tense effort that restricts affect, playfulness, and spontaneity in general. There is thus little room to experience satisfaction in doing anything without a continuous sense of purpose and effort.
- Any relaxation of deliberateness or purposeful activity is felt to be improper, uncomfortable, or worse.
- The overcontrol of the obsessive is linked with a specific anxiety and discomfort over loss of control.

It is important to bear in mind that obsessional style as described by David Shapiro cannot be viewed merely as a dimension of psychopathology. The capacity to focus and to organize the *doing* of life in an obsessional manner is a very adaptive capacity in our culture. Natural intelligence may readily be channeled into obsessional activity that provides gratification and success in school and which can be of great value in the achievement of work-related goals in adult life. Too much obsessionality, however, results in a loss of cognitive flexibility.

PSYCHOBIOLOGICAL SUBSTRATES OF OBSESSIONALITY

From a neurophysiological perspective, the process of recurrent and autonomous thinking in the mind reflects a baseline level of mental or "computational" activity in the brain.[2] Salient components of such cognitive activity in normal waking consciousness include the functions of planning and problem solving, thought to be mediated by the prefrontal cortex. In turn, this baseline level of activity reflects the balance of subcortical and emotional processes.

One current theory is that dysfunctional levels of obsessionality, termed obsessive compulsive disorder (OCD), come about when the subcortical neural circuits involved in the regulation of cortical activity become dysregulated. Using PET scan[3] technology to compare the brain function of patients with OCD to normal controls, Schwartz and Begley (2002) have found that OCD patients show hypermetabolic activity in several brain areas, including orbital frontal cortex, which are involved in the regulation of cortical activity. Without belaboring the neurophysiological details, the basic idea here is that OCD involves a state of what Schwartz calls "*brain lock*." Essentially, subcortical pathways that are supposed to regulate the activity of the cortex become locked up, such as an automobile transmission that fails to shift, and thinking becomes dysregulated; as Schwartz explains it, it is as if certain brain mechanisms become stuck in the "on" position so that the brain can't move on to the next thought. The OCD patient typically experiences this being "stuck in gear" as ego-dystonic;[4] obsessional thoughts and compulsive urges are experienced passively, something that occurs with no choice and that feels beyond the patient's ability to change. Thus, in Schwartz's theory, obsessive compulsive behavior arises from chronic overactivity of the orbital frontal cortex and the resultant state of "brain lock" which ensues.

The attitude of mind cultivated in mindfulness meditation is a natural antidote to the state of "brain lock," in that mindfulness practice develops flexibility of attention. With this hypothesis, Schwartz has done research studies on the application of Buddhist mindfulness meditation to the treatment of OCD patients. His findings demonstrate that the habitual narrowing of attention, which is pervasive and encumbering in OCD patients, can be counteracted by mindfulness meditation in combination with cognitive behavioral interventions (Schwartz and Begley 2002).

From a Buddhist perspective, the understanding of obsessionality may come down simply to this: the severely obsessional person has a unique difficulty with simply *being*. He or she can only *do*, in the very restrictive manner described. The attitude of mind cultivated in Buddhist sitting meditation counteracts obsessionality by fostering receptivity in place of active effort, *being* instead of *doing*.[5]

In the remainder of the chapter, I want to try to "unpack" the psychological importance of obsessionality and attachment to *doing* in relation to psychoanalytic and Buddhist ideas about the mind.

INDWELLING PATTERNS OF AROUSAL
AND ASSOCIATED PERSONALITY TRAITS

As a starting point, I will describe phenomenologically what will be elucidated in later sections of this chapter. I will use my own experience as a "case study" to illustrate the major themes. The "case material" is divided into segments in relation to particular points.

Case Study of Self #1:

My experience of waking in the morning is typically one of "hitting the ground running." Throughout my life, even preceding my addiction to morning coffee, I have found that I become instantly busy when I wake up in the morning, actively engaged in what I want to do that day before I am even fully awake. There is an anxious, driven quality to this pattern, discernible in the experience of (literally) cold feet.[6] For years I counseled myself that it might be helpful to do my sitting practice first thing in the morning in order to counter this state of arousal. But often I would find that a half hour of meditation was no match for the strength of this pattern. In contrast to the state of tranquility that I encountered almost invariably when I sat for any length of time, morning meditation for me was completely dominated by this experience of being "driven to distraction." I concluded that it was more skillful for me to sit at the end of the day, when conditions were more conducive to stability of concentration. It is only in recent years, probably as a result of a commitment to deepen my practice through frequent attendance at meditation retreats that this intractable pattern has begun to shift.

Apart from acknowledging that I am a rather high-strung person with adrenaline-dominated habits of being, I have found that my morning arousal is a useful barometer of my level of stress. It varies from "over the top" (a label I attach to an ego-dystonic amount of early morning hype) to a more gentle form of desire to "get going." Being hyperaroused has come to feel distinctly unhealthy to me and has become increasingly ego-dystonic over time. I attribute this change in large measure to my sitting practice because the mindful experience of hyperarousal in meditation has changed my sensitivity to and awareness of my own anxiety.

I have also spent many hours in my own analysis looking at where this pattern comes from and what function it serves, one example of which is elaborated in the next section of the chapter. My analytic work with patients has given me additional opportunity to see how hyperarousal relates to personality characteristics of ambitiousness, perfectionism, and performance anxiety.

HYPERAROUSAL, PERFORMANCE, ANXIETY, AND OBSESSIONALITY

In my efforts to understand the genesis of my hyperarousal pattern, I have found it useful to consider the literature on Type A Behavior, originally described in cardiac patients by Friedman and Rosenman (1959). The classic Type A individual is characterized as intensely competitive, aggressive, and impatient, with a high time-urgency, and is described as having a persistent desire for recognition and personal advancement. The psychophysiological profile of the Type A person also has certain distinct characteristics, including high levels of sympathetic (autonomic nervous system) arousal.

I am organized psychologically in certain ways (but not all) that match the classic description of Type A. In addition to the pattern of sympathetic arousal already mentioned (including my cold feet), I have been motivated by a persistent desire for recognition and personal advancement in my professional and academic life, and the pace of my work day tends to be dominated by a sense of "time urgency." Looking at Type A traits both in myself and in patients I have treated, it is quite clear to me that they cluster with related characteristics of perfectionism, performance anxiety, and obsessionality.

In my own case, I think that all of these behaviors and personality characteristics became established in relation to the early development of my intellect and the programming connected with school. The drive for achievement and its associated performance pressure engenders stress and psychophysiological arousal. These traits are much less pronounced in me now than when I was younger, a change I attribute in large measure to my mindfulness practice and dharma study[7] over the past thirty years.

Meditation in a retreat setting has allowed me to enter into states of profound calm, a shift that represents a radical departure from the familiar baseline of my psychophysiological "self." These experiences have brought into exquisite focus the habitual nature of the "engine racing" that my mind often engages in. One way to convey this experience might be to say that meditation has heightened mindfulness of the ways I animate myself, and, concomitantly, has facilitated the emergence of an alternative experience. This has also been accompanied by the insight that, whereas prior to my meditation practice I might have been inclined to say that *I am* a Type A individual, I am now clear that Type A behavior is something that *I do*.

In addition, I have readily observed that when I am faced with a task that has performance pressure connected with it (such as the writing of this chapter), I am likely to seek out additional stimulation in the form of caffeine in an effort to "power through" this anxiety. I call this the "adrenaline junkie" syndrome because it seems to me that it has elements in common with substance abuse. As I have come to think of it (based on my own experience as well as that of patients I have worked with), I am psychologically dependent on a state of arousal that seems necessary for the performance of certain psychological tasks, especially when there is anxiety associated with them. The desired arousal state may be self-generated or may be facilitated by the ingestion of caffeine. Such "autoaddiction" to adrenaline[8] seems quite parallel to substance abuse involving exogenous stimulants. Indeed, I have worked with patients who used nicotine or cocaine in a similar manner to sustain performance.

Conceptualized psychoanalytically, the state of arousal (or hyperarousal) I have described might be thought of as a self-state. If so, we might further theorize that some people become "autoaddicted" to their own self-states, repeatedly inducing those states in themselves (albeit unconsciously). This "addiction" is a habitual way of being that rests on a platform of performance anxiety in a multifaceted way: hyperarousal is sought as a way of coping with anxiety, while at the same time it is itself a *manifestation* of anxiety and *sustains* anxiety. I hypothesize that this complex relationship between performance anxiety and hyperarousal may be one of the underpinnings of obsessional character; the chronic and repeated experience of states of anxious hyperarousal generates obsessional defenses as a way to defend against and contain them.

Case Study of Self #2:

When I am engaged in a creative project that I find stimulating, my mind tends to go into overdrive, and I experience what I affectionately call "my obsessional neurosis." A recent example is typical. I was redecorating my bedroom and was bogged down in indecisive uncertainty about what color to paint, what fabrics to choose, and so on. My mind will typically become completely preoccupied with a creative problem of this kind, aided and abetted by my perfectionism and accompanying self-doubts.[9] Once my mind gets its teeth into this kind of problem, it doesn't easily let go, to the point that it will often interfere with my getting to sleep at night. As one might expect, obsessional thoughts about these decorating decisions began to permeate my daily meditation practice. There was so much energy attached to my creative problem that thoughts about decorating even disrupted my (generally quite stable) psychoanalytic attention in the consulting room.

Sitting with this kind of experience in meditation has been instrumental in my coming to realize that obsessional thinking rests on a foundation of anxiety. When I am relaxed, my mind does not perseverate on thoughts; and, conversely, when I am in obsessional mode, I can invariably become aware of the bodily experience of being hyperaroused. At the same time, to the extent that I am obsessing, I lose touch with being grounded in my body, and it generally takes quite a bit of steady and patient effort for me to settle down from this jangle into a meditative state in which I feel more embodied.

In my sitting practice, my effort is to try to get in touch with the bodily aspects of the anxiety "underneath" my recurrent thoughts.[10] At such times, each moment in meditation that my attention returns to the present tends to find me holding my breath, shoulders tensed. I find the experience of my mind racing to be quite aversive, a condition that makes it difficult to stay present with my experience.

Although I had certainly been aware for some time that there was a lot of anxiety entangled in this "obsessional neurosis," the whole psychological structure of it came into focus for me one day after I had spent some time with a friend who was acting as a decorating consultant for me. I had put together an entire little design "presentation," including a list of the confusions that I was experiencing. My friend commented on how difficult it was for her to be with me because of the intensity of need she felt coming from me. Although she intended (and said) this to me in a very loving way, the feedback felt humiliating.

That evening in my meditation practice, I found my mind replaying the interaction with my friend. As I sat with this experience, my mind automatically examined these events in a way that is second nature after many years of psychoanalysis. It became clear to me that the psychological pressure I brought to bear on my friend derived from experiences that were common in my relationship with my mother. My mother had been a working mom and, with three children, seemed always to be in a hurry. (No question that my mother was a Type A individual). When I needed her to help me with something, she would always do her best to be there with me, but the sense that I had was that I had to be very focused and organized about what I needed. This gets quite intense at times. The humiliation I experienced with so little provocation by my friend tipped me off to the painful feelings that had been associated with the experience of dependency on my mother. Feeling anxious, needy, and vulnerable made me feel ashamed, as though I was *too needy* and fundamentally flawed.

These insights proved pivotal in the resolution of this particular episode of obsessionality. Once I realized that I had an unmet need for maternal attention in relation to my decorating process, it became evident that my obsessional thinking was functioning as a substitute for maternal care. The obsessive planning and thinking in my mind was providing a form of containment that allowed me to tolerate the anxieties associated with my decorating project. I elaborate on this idea below in connection with the psychoanalytic concept of the *mind-object.*

In response to these insights, I realized that it would be useful for me to hire a professional decorator to help me resolve my design problems. That way, I could have all the time and attention (i.e., substitutive maternal care) I required without feeling a sense that my needs were an unwelcome burden. With this resolved, my mind settled down and my obsessional decorating neurosis disappeared.

The process of insight and problem resolution that is described in this series of events illustrates the interdependence, for me, of psychoanalytic insight and meditation in penetrating obsessional processes in the mind.

PSYCHOANALYTIC FACTORS: THE GRANDIOSE EGO-IDEAL

Case Study of Self #3:

As I worked to understand the issues I am discussing in the crucible of my own psychoanalysis, I remembered an event that occurred when I was three years old and which was formative of my performance pressure and obsessionality. My father was taking piano lessons at the time, and had been practicing trills (rapid alternation of fingers on two adjacent keys of the piano). After listening for some time, I jumped up next to him on the piano seat and excitedly begged, "Let *me* try!" After banging on the piano keys experimentally (probably not the first time that I had done so), I successfully executed a trill. This mastery would have been sufficient reward unto itself, but my father then proceeded to make a major fuss over me, calling my mother and other family members into the room to see what I could do.

I believe that what happened at that moment (and, undoubtedly, on many occasions thereafter) was a co-opting of natural curiosity and play in the service of approval;[11] the nucleus of a narcissistic constellation within my psyche. In place of the mirroring that would have been matched to *my* developmental needs for mastery, my father conveyed that having a bright daughter was narcissistically gratifying to *him*. Thereafter, on a lifelong basis, I endeavored to perform in ways that would win both approval and recognition of my having exceptional intelligence. School was a perfect breeding ground for the development and elaboration of this deep-seated personality trait. I became an outstanding student and endeavored to make my parents feel that they must be wonderful parents to have such a brilliant child.

In her well-known book *Prisoners of Childhood: The Drama of the Gifted Child and the Search for the True Self,* Alice Miller (1981) wrote very insightfully about this search for admiration and its confusion with love. She understood attachment to admiration as a substitute gratification for the meeting of primary needs for respect, understanding, and being taken seriously— that is, love. Miller further explains that a self-esteem that is based on performance or on the possession of any specific qualities or traits, occludes the development of a healthy self-esteem based on the authenticity of one's own being. Benjamin (1999) echoes these ideas in her conceptualization of the need for recognition in the development of subjectivity. The search for admiration defends against the pain of nonrecognition, low self-esteem, and the loss of contact with the true (or authentic) self. In addition, the search for admiration may hide conscious and unconscious fantasies of grandiosity, functioning as a defense against an underlying depression.

THE MIND-OBJECT

Along similar lines, Corrigan and Gordon (1995) wrote about psychic development in the precocious child (which I certainly was). Following upon earlier thinking of the British psychoanalyst D.W. Winnicott and others, they describe how precocious intellectual development can become so important in the child's psychological economy that the mind itself comes to function as a mother-substitute; the cognitive mind in essence becomes an internalized parentified object that plays nursemaid in the care of the child-self. This results in a reliance on the mind at the expense of bodily experience, a fracturing of what is presumed to have been, originally, a seamless connection between psyche and soma: "when the mind takes on a life of its own, it becomes an object—separate, as it were, from the self." Corrigan and Gordon (1995) term this phenomenon the "mind-object"; the cathexis of one's own mind and intellectual function. They also describe how this mode of psychic function serves the need to feel in control.

Clinical observations reported in Corrigan and Gordon's work are quite germane to the mental processes I am focusing on here and are worth quoting. One patient, "Mr. A.," described the recognition of his effort to be in "fierce control . . . The very act of making something happen—no matter how insignificant—is what that is about for me." A second patient, "Mr. B.," tells his therapist: "My mind is like a factory, it has to produce work." "Miss C.," a profoundly depressed woman, speaks of "never being able to relax or trust her academic and career accomplishments." Despite exemplary achievement, fears of failure and exposure are ever present. "Mrs. D.," a young physician and mother, describes how "I do everything in a hurry. . . . I'm always ahead of time. . . . But I feel if I wait, it won't happen."

These examples illustrate the interrelationships among drive for achievement, obsessionality, perfectionism, and the need for control; the similarity to the Type A syndrome described above is also instructive. Corrigan and Gordon comment that the patients they describe vary in the nature and extent of their pathology as well as in personal style; some are narcissistic, some depressed, some boringly obsessive, while others are wonderfully quick and humorous. They also remark that "none of these patients are on particularly good terms with their instincts or with their bodies in general." They describe their series of patients as blocked in relation to free sexual expression, and, in many instances, as having medical conditions with significant psychosomatic components. They view these patients as "fiercely attached to their mind as an object, an object whose use is overvalued and exploited, whose existence is vigilantly protected, and whose loss is constantly dreaded. . . . The mind object promises perfection and omnipotent control, but this ceaseless search never yields satisfaction, only anxiety, depression, and threatened breakdown." Perhaps most significant, in the present Buddhist context, is their comment that these are patients who "cannot relax into just being, but must be constantly stimulated and enlivened by something or someone outside themselves."

Understood within an object relations[12] framework, mind-objects form as a distillate of experiences which the child has had in actual relationships, encoding not only the actual behavior of real others but also the affects that have colored those interactions. What is unique in the mind-object formulation is that it describes how we *relate to our minds* in object relations terms. I discuss some of the implications of this concept in the light of Buddhist thought in the final section of this chapter.

BUDDHIST MEDITATION, OBSESSIONALITY, AND THE MIND-OBJECT

Juxtaposing the characterological features of obsessionality with the experiences cultivated in Buddhist meditation, the first thing that becomes clear is that obsessional style is in some ways antithetical to the process of mindfulness meditation. An obsessional person may be able to rigidly control attention in meditation, and may be able to achieve certain altered states of consciousness in this way, but meditating with tense effort actually impedes the ability to let go and "surf the mind,"[13] which is the sine qua non of mindfulness meditation. The modus operandi of the obsessional mind is incompatible with flexible mindfulness.[14]

Mindfulness practice develops flexibility of attention. Presumably, this comes about in relation to the emergence of states of consciousness in which the mind becomes markedly more settled and obsessional thinking decreases.[15] Such experiences are fairly typical in sitting practice. What determines whether such shifts in mental experience during meditation become consolidated and stabilized over time?

In my effort to address this question, I find it useful to invoke the concept of the mind-object. As a way of illustrating my point, however, I want to turn next to some "case material" quoted at length from journalist Lawrence Shainberg's memoir *Ambivalent Zen* (1995). In this book, Shainberg narrates his attempts to use Zen sitting practice to free himself from the prison of his obsessional mind. What makes *Ambivalent Zen* especially relevant for the present discussion is the fact that its author was both a Zen practitioner and a psychoanalytic patient. Shainberg's journal expresses beautifully the complex texture that can be generated by the cross-fertilization between the two traditions. His narrative conveys the dance between spiritual (dharma-related) and psychological insight in the context of a real life experience. In reading the section that follows, it is important to bear in mind, however, that Shainberg studied meditation with a Japanese-born Roshi (Zen teacher) and that this took place during an era in American Buddhism (in the 1980s) when many people studied Buddhism with foreign-born teachers who came from a very different cultural tradition and who were not necessarily equipped to relate to the psychological difficulties of their American students.

Shainberg came to Zen practice with a life history that included a father who had been a psychoanalytic patient as well as an early follower of Krishnamurti,

Alan Watts, and others who popularized Eastern philosophical traditions in 1960s American culture. Several passages from *Ambivalent Zen* provide apt descriptions of what can happen in the collision between obsessionality, meditation practice, and the "crazy wisdom" of the dharma.

Case Study #4: Ambivalent Zen

Our "case material" begins with excerpts from Shainberg's diary, which he begins at the suggestion of a psychoanalyst, in which he records his problems and his efforts to understand them.

> I write [in the diary] only when my mood sinks, which is more and more often these days, and I feel better as soon as I pick up my pen. A typical entry begins, "feeling totally depressed, I don't know why." No matter how much one entry resembles another, I am always excited when I begin. Often, I write in my diary as soon as I wake up in the morning, hoping to organize my thoughts or at least slow them down. Away from the house, I make notes if possible for future entries, and, if I cannot write them down, make mental notes which, if I forget them, leave me bereft and obsessed to remember them. Sometimes, the thought of the diary alone can lift my spirits, and sometimes, too, it seems that I derive so much pleasure from writing in it that I cultivate my problems. . . . [often] my words seem slightly disconnected from my thoughts, and this makes it seem as if my pen is ahead of my mind, almost as if my hand is writing on its own. With the exception of masturbation, there is no other activity in which my concentration is so complete or my sense of time so absent. As often as not, I am certain that the writing is profound. Sometimes I have visions of its being posthumously published. Later, when I read it over and find it vague and muddled and embarrassing in its self-absorption, my disappointment does not discourage me but leads instead to another entry: ". . . feeling depressed that I spend so much time writing in this diary . . ." Psychological and spiritual understandings appear with equal frequency and to me seem interchangeable. I am beginning to be familiar with words like "ego," "desire," and "emptiness" . . . I see Zen and Krishnamurti as extensions of psychoanalysis, a sort of Oriental pipeline that fuels the engine of my diary. (55)

In counterpoint to his diary, Shainberg also presents anecdotes describing his interactions with his Roshi. One series of encounters revolves around Shainberg's confusion about what to do in his relationship with his girlfriend:

> "Listen, Roshi, I've come to you with a problem. I don't know what to do, OK? In America we call this 'indecision.' Are you familiar with the word?"

> "Indecision?" He pronounces it "indeeseeshun" with accent on the last syllable. "Yes, I understood, Larry-San. Cannot decide. Wandering mind. Indeeseeshuyn. Very good word."

"And yet you are telling me that the cure for it is to make a decision?"

"Yes, yes. Great decision! Never shaking! Never turn back."

"But Roshi. . . . I've just been telling you. A decision is just what I can't make. Have you never had that problem?"

"Of course I have that problem," he says. "Twice."

"Twice!"

"Yes, after high school, when I cannot decide what to do. And again before I go to monastery."

"Before the monastery! That was thirty years ago! C'mon, Roshi, admit it. You don't know anything about indecision! I'm a fool to ask you for advice. It's like I'm crawling up a mountain, and you fly past me in a helicopter."

Confused by the word, the Roshi consults his dictionary, and at last, pronouncing the Japanese word, he cries: "Yes! Yes! Hellicopper! I hellicopper! You crawling on mounting! I flying! You crawling! Ha! Ha! Ha!"

And then, turning suddenly serious again, the Roshi says: "Listen, Larry-San. I fly over you, I see what you not see."

"What's that?"

He presses his thumb against his forefinger and holds them poised together above his teacup. "You and mountingtop—only this far apart!"

Much later, leaving the Zendo after an evening sitting, Roshi asks if I've come to a decision about my girlfriend. It's a question I've been dreading.

"No, I can't decide."

"Can't decide? Ah, great decision, Larry-San! My teacher, he say, 'If you confused, do confused. Do not be confused by confusion.' Understand? Be *totally confused,* Larry-San, then I guarantee: no problem at all" (43).

This interaction between Shainberg and the Roshi has a humorous element that relates, in part, to communication across the language barrier. On the one hand, it conveys a sense of the paradox which, for Western readers, may seem to typify Zen. Examining this exchange from a clinical vantage point, however, what strikes me even more is Shainberg's psychological urgency. Perhaps he had less need for Zen guidance than for an empathic and interpretive understanding that would help to liberate him from his obsessional dilemma.

Also illuminating is Shainberg's narrative of his sitting practice. Although he is at first skeptical about whether sitting practice is good for someone who already watches his mind to excess, Shainberg decides to try it. And, predictably, despite the intellectual understanding that sitting is about being with what *is,* not about achieving some ideal concentration, Shainberg experiences great difficulty with his inability to control his mind. Agitation dominates his meditation, and he finds himself chagrined and embarrassed at his inability to tame his mind.

Before long, breath counting has incorporated itself into Shainberg's obsessional paradigm; he finds himself counting breaths when he is out for a walk or on the subway, even at times while sitting across from a friend at dinner. As he comments, he stumbled into a confusion about Buddhist practice in which sitting practice began to seem extraordinary and ordinary life felt reductive and distracting.

As his sitting practice deepens over time, Shainberg has many experiences of what feels to him like profound insight or some sort of an enlightenment experience. In the present context, what was especially fascinating to me was how experience that opened in a space of meditative insight could devolve in the next moment as it was reified and "swallowed up" by obsessional structures in Shainberg's mind. He himself was acutely aware of this, noting his observation that meditation can reverse itself, becoming fixed and rigid rather than a means of letting go: "The more I sit, the more I am aware of the impermanence of my thoughts and emotions, and the more I am seized by a need to control them" (Shainberg, 112).

At one point, Shainberg engages in a month-long period of solitary retreat. He returns from retreat feeling heroic, ecstatic, and filled with fantasies of Zen triumph. However, within a few days, his ecstasy collapses on itself, depression sets in, and his inner "Zen voice" begins a litany of self-criticism:

> "How can you imagine that you've learned anything from Zen when you turn a simple one-month retreat into an exercise in vanity and self-importance?" The inner Zen voice, which loathes nothing so much as self-loathing—is ashamed of being ashamed. "When I search[ed] for the insights I had on retreat—all those epiphanies about Beckett and time, memory and impermanence—I find nothing but hollow, intellectual fragments, like pieces of small talk overheard on the street. Within a week, I have stopped sitting altogether. My mind spins with the argument between the Zen voice and it's opposite. . . . Is Zen good for me or bad for me, a practice in humility or an exercise in narcissism?" (114)

Later, Shainberg attempts to cleanse himself of ego by destroying his diaries:

> It is punishing to read, an irrefutable confirmation of Zen's argument against self-consciousness and analytic mind. After reading just a few pages, I pile all of my steno pads into the car and take them to the dump. Three garbage bags, sixteen years of self-analysis and what I took to be revelation. A huge compactor closes on them like a set of teeth, crushes and grinds for a moment, then drops them into a dumpster parked behind the building. I feel a kind of giddiness. It's

as if the compactor has chewed up my self-consciousness. As if the I-me separation on which self-consciousness depends has been compressed into singularity. After all, what am I doing on my cushion if not destroying my diary breath by breath, uniting that which watches with that which it presumes to watch? (112)

In the end, however, Shainberg's familiar obsessional behavioral patterns prevail:

> Finally, the argument becomes *interesting*. I go to my office and write about it: my Zen attraction, my Zen resistance, Beckett and Zen, writing and Zen, everything I remember about my retreat, everything that's happened since it's ended. Fascinating! Brilliant! The best writing I've ever done! Three feverish hours at my desk, fifty five pages in a brand new notebook. . . . I tell myself this is not a "diary" but a "journal," the beginning perhaps of the book on Zen that I have been wanting to write since the first time I sat on a cushion. I am wrong, of course. It is a brand-new diary I have begun, and I have been keeping it ever since. (115)

These excerpts from Shainberg's book illustrate how experience, which is authentic and centered in the present moment, can get co-opted by an obsessional mind-object. In place of experience that flows along moment-to-moment in an unfettered manner, the mind is held hostage by a process of obsession and self-judgment. Before leaving this narrative, it is interesting to speculate on what might have been possible if Shainberg had studied Zen with a psychologically sophisticated Western teacher; or, better still, if Shainberg had discussed his meditation experience with a Buddhist-informed psychotherapist, who might have been able to help him get at the emotional issues underlying his "Zen sickness."[16]

In an earlier section of this chapter, I developed a few basic concepts about the "mind-object." To reiterate, the mind-object of precocious self-sufficiency described by Corrigan and Gordon pushes and drives the "self" with intense feelings of guilt, anxiety, and inadequacy. Such a (persecutory) mind object develops in relation to premature and rigid structuring of ego ideals. From the integrative perspective I have tried to develop in this chapter, an underlying biological disposition to OCD coupled with psychodynamic influences may be thought of as interacting to create an obsessional mind-object in a susceptible individual.

Shainberg's narrative illustrates the anxiety-based perfectionism, drive for achievement, and obsessionality that Corrigan and Gordon described in their series of patients. His relationship to his mind-object also seems typical: on the one hand, he feels frustrated by his inability to get past his obsessional thinking and feels controlled by it, but at the same time he is infatuated with his psychic productions.[17] His relationship to his mind-object is truly ambivalent.

Since I personally resonated with many of Shainberg's experiences, especially his intense yearnings to transcend the prison of his "ego" (or, as I am thinking of it now, mind-object), it was especially poignant for me to observe how the glimpses of real freedom that Shainberg experienced were so quickly co-opted by his mind-object functions. What makes the mind keep reverting to the familiar egoic structure of obsessionality? What is necessary for one's mind-object to become lastingly transformed by meditation/dharma practice?

In my own case, I have a distinct impression that meditation practice and/or psychoanalysis *have* created lasting changes in my mind-object structures. Although obsessionality, perfectionism, and drive for achievement still remain formidable challenges in my psychic life, I seem to have developed an impressive capacity to let go of those "psychological imperatives" in favor of an experience of equanimity. As I think of it, the psychic membrane of my mind-object structure has become more permeable, more receptive to change from the stimulus of insight. This leads me to the tentative but hopeful conclusion that meditative awareness *can* develop into a mind-object function in its own right, one which is healthier than the mind-object of self-sufficiency described by Corrigan and Gordon.

While there are many ways of conceptualizing the psychological function of meditation, I am struck most by the way in which meditation practice can become a container for experience. (This function has been described in the work of Joseph Bobrow (1997) and others.) Though helpful, however, the containment afforded by meditation may be insufficient for getting free of the domination of a rigid mind object. For myself, I am inclined to believe that one essential factor was my analytic treatment.

There are several ways that I credit my psychoanalysis with helping to transform my relationship to my (at times dysfunctional) mind-object. First, my analyst brought my mind-object into my conscious awareness by her interpretations of the ways it presented itself in my experience. She supported the cultivation of a more loving and beloved superego (Schafer 1960). Second, she was receptive to the insights I brought back from meditative retreat, mirroring and validating developments in my capacity to be present, to be more embodied, and to be openhearted. Third, there was an attunement in the analytic space that facilitated the development of a mode of conscious experience that I have elsewhere termed the "transcendent position" (Schuman 1998).[18] Following Melanie Klein's notion of a psychological position, the transcendent position is a space from which is possible to de-center from and disidentify with entrenched and previously unconscious habits of being and states of mind. The transcendent position represents an evolutionary development in subjectivity.

By analogy with the development of subjectivity in the infant, I believe that transcendent awareness develops in an intersubjective context. Perhaps it may even be said that such awareness is intersubjectively *communicated*, existing in potential or virtual form in one person and brought into being by another. In any case, although we never spoke about it directly, my sense is that my analyst's own dharma-awareness created transitional space in which I could develop transcendent awareness.[19] The analytic relationship together with my practice of mindfulness cofacilitated my ability to be compassionately aware of the ways that I habitually related to my mind.

My exchanges with my analyst were informed by her capacity to recognize and articulate self-states that were characterized by expanded consciousness. Perhaps these features were lacking in Shainberg's relationship to his analyst, (and in his relationship to his Zen teachers). Perhaps meditative awareness, in and of itself, is insufficient for the transformation of a mind-object; perhaps such transformation requires a working through which can happen only in the context of a good-enough relationship.

SUMMARY AND CONCLUSION: BUDDHISM AND THE INTRAPSYCHIC OBJECT RELATION

As I have tried to illustrate in this chapter, mindfulness meditation has helped to mitigate my obsessionality in several interrelated ways. First, the receptive awareness cultivated in sitting practice has been conducive to my letting go of body tension and to the relaxation of my mind's habitual and automatic obsessional thinking and efforts to be in control. Second, sitting practice has been a container for my being able to notice and be present with my obsessiveness in a new way. Third, meditative awareness—supported by a framework coconstructed by Buddhist psychology and psychoanalytic space—has helped me to become aware of the object-relational aspects of my mind's relationship to itself. Specifically, it has heightened my awareness of the fluid, constantly shifting, and nonunified experience that comprises the "mind-as-subject" and "mind-as-object," what is termed the *intrapsychic object relation*. Paying close attention to one's experience in meditation or simply noting the linguistic structure in which experiences are expressed—for example, in the narrative from *Ambivalent Zen* extensively quoted above—it is evident that there is a fluid and shifting focus of identification between the experiencing self and the mind-object.

Elaborating this point further, it should be noted that mind-object tends to be equated with "intellect" or "ego functions." To the extent that we are identified with ourselves as cognitive beings ("I think, therefore I am") there are embedded confusions between "self" and "ego" and between the subject and object of experience.[20] Moreover, if we have a developmental history that fosters the precocious and therefore premature development of the intellect, we are especially vulnerable to developing the kind of obsessional mind-object that has been discussed in this chapter.

While it is helpful to become familiar with the functioning of the mind-object within psychic reality, from a Buddhist perspective the concept of mind-object suffers from several reductive oversimplifications. Principal among these, mind-object is predicated on a dualism between one part of the mind and another; it divides the mind into subject and object. Indeed, Corrigan and Gordon (1995) acknowledged this in the way they delineated the concept of mind-object in the first place: "when the mind takes on a life of its own, it becomes an object—separate, as it were, from the self." Mind-as-object also exemplifies a dissociative split within the sense of agency. In being "driven to distraction," it is the mind-object, not *me,* which is the driver.

Even within the realm of dualistic experience, it is misguided to imply that there is a singular self, which cathects a singular mind-object. A psychoanalytic conceptualization of the mind-object more compatible with Buddhist thought might emphasize, instead, the existence of multiple mind-objects and the complex and fluid psychodynamics that govern our relating to them. The concept of mind-object tends to reify what is in reality a set of complex and dynamic *processes* in the mind. Do we attempt to live up to the performance standards of our mind-objects? Do our minds boss us around, drive us to distraction? Do we ignore the imperatives of our mind-objects in favor of sensory pleasure or impulsive acting out? Alternatively, can we become aware of and learn to *be with* the mind-object in a way that begins to heal the split between psyche and soma? Can practice with *being* begin to inform and transform our relationship to *doing?* In psychoanalytic terms, can we develop an intrapsychic object relation that transcends old self-structures, including obsessional mind-objects?

As may be said of "ego" generally, mind-object bears the stamp of defense. The engaging of mind-object functions, including obsessionality and planning mind, seeks to protect us and create the illusion of control in a world which otherwise threatens us with a free-fall of groundlessness. Attachment to doing, to staying busy, defends against anxiety; it blocks both awareness of *being* and the (co-arising) fear of *nonbeing.*

Psychoanalysis and Buddhist mindfulness meditation in tandem provide a unique opportunity for subjectivity to evolve beyond blind domination by our mind-objects. As I understand it, this transformation of intrapsychic object relations may develop in several stages. Initially, meditation cultivates a (non-pathological) splitting of mind through development of the observing ego. Supported by the culture of dharma, experiences arise in meditation that transcend old self-structure[21] and promote new ways of being. Deep experiences of awareness, presence, and clarity promote insight that potentially may transform our relationship to our minds (intrapsychic object relations). However, in order for this transformation to be consolidated and worked through, it is necessary to have an intersubjective context supporting that transformation. Otherwise, new experience rapidly devolves (as it did for Shainberg) into old paradigms.

Ultimately, of course, the real "goal" of meditation is to go beyond subject and object to the realization of nonduality. As I have conceptualized the process in this chapter, meditation helps to make such realization possible by establishing a new, meditative mind-object, thereby transcending old self-structures, including the structure of obsessionality. In this way, it is possible for the very conception of the mind and of the subject who is experiencing his or her mind to change as the web of representations in which the self is entangled is slowly penetrated.

NOTES

The title of this chapter was created without knowledge of the existence of a book by the same title, on the subject of Attention Deficit Disorder, written by Edward Hallowell.

1. Vipassana mindfulness meditation.

2. Computational mind is a term taken from cognitive science and is based on a model of the brain as a computer-like device that embodies logical principles in its component elements or neurons. This assumptive model is not essential to the discussion at hand.

3. Positron emission tomography.

4. An unwanted and noncongruent aspect of the self.

5. Notwithstanding this distinction, there is a certain kind of effort involved in the practice of mindfulness.

6. Peripheral vasoconstriction mediated by the sympathetic branch of the autonomic nervous system.

7. "Dharma" is a comprehensive term in Buddhism that refers both to the universal truths which underlie human existence and to the Buddha's teachings about these truths.

8. More accurately, the pattern of psychophysiological arousal under discussion is probably mediated by norepinephrine (noradrenaline) or a combination of epinephrine (adrenaline) and norepinephrine.

9. This dualistic construction exemplifies a split between the observing ego and the functions of the mind that are being observed. I elaborate on the significance of this split in a later section of the chapter.

10. An important insight in this regard was facilitated by a meditation teacher who pointed out to me that I was using the Vipassana technique of noting "thinking" in response to my obsessional thoughts as a subtle way of *pushing away* the *experience* of them. This allowed me to put attention on the bodily experience that accompanies obsessional thoughts.

11. This example shows how authentic experience or "true self" in Winnicott's sense can be dominated and replaced by another mental function, described and elaborated in the next section of the chapter ("The Mind-Object").

12. Object relations is the school of psychoanalytic thinking based on the premise that the mind is formed of elements taken in from the outside, primarily aspects of the functioning of others with whom we have significant relationships (such as our parents).

13. The surfing metaphor comes from Jason Siff's book, *Unlearning Meditation* (2000).

14. It should be noted that the early stages of meditation experience will likely tend to be driven by a perfectionistic mind-object in someone who is organized psychologically in this way. Although meditating with tense effort is less than optimal, this may perhaps be a necessary stage in the development of meditation that ultimately helps to develop mindfulness of one's obsessionality. In my own case, like many meditators my natural tendency for a long time was to try to discipline my mind in a manner that unconsciously reflected the (obsessional) habits of overcontrol that were second nature to me. As Siff has noted, right understanding of meditation instructions may be subverted when the meditator (unconsciously) employs them within a context of *should* infused with self-judgment (Siff 2000).

15. See J. Holroyd (2003) for a systematic discussion of the role of attentional processes in altered states of consciousness induced through meditation and hypnosis.

16. P. Kapleau (1965).

17. Patients with OCD typically experience their symptoms as ego-alien or even malignant, and feel controlled by them. They are often less aware of positive feelings they have about other features of their obsessionality or may not even recognize them to be obsessional in nature.

18. C. Alfano (2005) has developed a similar concept, "transcendent attunement."

19. I do not mean to suggest, however, that an analyst necessarily needs to be a Buddhist or a meditator in order to facilitate this type of transformation.

20. See M. Schuman (1991) for a further discussion of the relevant issues.

21. See F. Summers (1997) for an elaboration of this concept of transcendence.

REFERENCES

Alfano, C. (2005). Traversing the caesura: Transcendent attunement in Buddhism and psychoanalysis, *Contemporary Psychoanalysis*, 41(2), 223–48.

Batchelor, S. (1983). *Alone with others*. New York: Grove Weidenfeld.

Benjamin, J. (1999). Recognition and destruction: An outline of intersubjectivity. In *Relational psychoanalysis: The emergence of a tradition*, ed. S. A. Mitchell and L. Aron. New York: Analytic Press.

Bobrow, J. (1997). Coming to life: the creative intercourse of psychoanalysis and Zen Buddhism. In *Soul on the Couch,* ed. C. Spezzano and G. J. Gargiulo. Hillsdale, NJ: Analytic Press.

Corrigan, E. G., and P. E. Gordon. (1995). *The mind object: Precocity and pathology of self sufficiency.* Northvale, NJ: Jason Aronson.

Friedman, M., and R. H. Rosenman. (1959). Association of specific overt behavior pattern with blood and cardiovascular findings. *Journal of the American Medical Association,* 169, 1085–96.

Holroyd, J. (2003). The science of meditation and the state of hypnosis. *American Journal of Clinical Hypnosis*, 46(2), 109–28.

Kapleau, P., ed. (1965). *The three pillars of Zen*. Boston: Beacon Press.

Miller, A. (1981). *Prisoners of childhood: The drama of the gifted child and the search for the true self*, trans. R. Ward. New York: Basic Books.

Moore, B. E., and B. D. Fine. (1990). *Psychoanalytic terms & concepts.* New Haven: American Psychoanalytic Association and Yale University Press.

Salzman, L. (1980). *Treatment of the obsessive personality*. New York: Jason Aronson.

Schafer, R. (1960). Loving and beloved superego in Freud's structural theory. *Psychoanalytic Study of the Child,* 15,163–88.

Schuman, M. (1981). The psychophysiological model of meditation and altered states of consciousness. In *The Psychobiology of Consciousness*, ed. R. J. Davidson and J. M. Davidson. New York: Plenum Press.

———. (1991). The problem of self in psychoanalysis: Lessons from Eastern philosophy. *Psychoanalysis and Contemporary Thought,* 14(4), 595–624.

———. (1998). Suffering and the evolution of subjectivity. Paper presented at a conference on *Psychotherapy, Spirituality, and the Evolution of Mind*, May 1998, in Santa Monica, CA.

Schwartz, J. M., and S. Begley. (2002). *The mind and the brain: Neuroplasticity and the power of mental force.* New York: HarperCollins Publishers/ Regan Books.

Shainberg, L. (1995). *Ambivalent Zen*. New York: Pantheon Books.

Shapiro, D. (1965). *Neurotic styles*. New York: Basic Books.

Siff, J. (2000). *Unlearning meditation*. Skillful Meditation Project, Idyllwild: CA.

Summers, F. (1997). Transcending the self: An object relations model of the therapeutic action of psychoanalysis. *Contemporary Psychoanalysis*, 33(3), 411–28.

Chapter Seven

Through the Net:
A Journey from Basketball to
Psychoanalysis and Buddhism

Jeffrey B. Rubin

It happens when you least expect it — walking on a country road, listening to music, playing sports, doing yoga. You are taken by surprise. When I experienced it in a basketball game when I was eighteen, I didn't even know it existed.

Sometimes it comes out of pain. Other times silence or beauty. Whatever its source, it is unusually intense and compelling. Heightened awareness, intensity, and aliveness. You are catapulted out of (or into) your self. You feel intimate with the universe. The world is more vast and wondrous than you knew or imagined. You see glory in the flower, poetry in the birds frolicking in the sky. You feel graced, as if a gift had been given from the universe. Life has a deeper meaning.

Happiness or peace are inadequate ways of expressing what you feel because it is radiant and luminous. You feel suffused with aliveness. Spiritual experiences give *life* to life. The sacred is all around us. We can experience it anytime, anywhere: in our daily activities, at work, in our homes, and in our relationships. I experienced it playing basketball. And it changed my life.

The memory, almost three decades later, remains vivid. February 1971. Riverdale, New York. My team was playing an away league game against The Fieldston School, a team we were favored to beat. In order to remain in contention for the league title, we had to win.

It was a close, heart-throbbing, hotly contested, roller-coaster battle, with no clear winner. When we scored a basket with ten seconds left, our one-point lead appeared, like our youth, to be invincible. Victory was sealed. But with six seconds to go they scored. Suddenly we were down by one point. My teammates looked devastated, shell-shocked.

Suddenly a great calm descended upon me, and I called time out. Five seconds remained on the clock. I can still see the panic on my teammates' faces as we huddled closely, sweat dripping, wrung out. They had given up. In their minds the game was over.

I moved next to my coach and put my hand on his shoulder. I asked him to tell my teammates to stay calm and get me the ball. "Spread the floor, move without the ball and let Jeffrey take the last shot," he said. "If Jeffrey is double-teamed be ready for a pass from him." ("Double-teamed" means two players guarding one player).

Look at your watch. Count out five seconds. It is over in an instant. I had little time to try to do whatever I was going to do. We took the ball out underneath their basket, ninety-four feet from our goal. The other team lined up down the court near our basket. They were playing a "box-and-one." That is, four of their players played a zone defense, guarding the specific area they were assigned, and one of them, who was 6'2", shadowed me wherever I went. I was 5'7". A teammate rolled the ball to me near mid-court—the clock wouldn't start until I touched the ball—approximately forty-five feet from the hoop.

I am sure there was noise in the gym, but when I scooped the ball up and dribbled up the left side of the court, the gym was as quiet as a monastery. I couldn't hear the crowd, the squeaking of sneakers, or the thumping of the basketball. I was in a cocoon of concentration—alert, focused, undistracted, fully and effortlessly in the present, with no thoughts or feelings. My mind was as quiet as it had ever been. Grand Canyon quiet. And clear. Like the open sky.

Time seemed to slow down and elongate. I floated up court with no sense of exertion. I felt no pressure, no fear. The hope of victory, the dread of losing, did not exist. My opponent didn't faze me. There wasn't really any opponent. Oh, there was someone guarding me, but he had no impact because at that moment, he was like a cardboard cutout of a defender standing between me and the basket, with no real power to influence me. There was just me, the ball, and the basket. And we were one. I felt harmonized with the game. If maintaining that state of grace meant giving up everything I owned, I wouldn't have hesitated.

As I approached the top of the key, my defender picked me up. I sensed it was time to shoot. I wrapped my left hand around the middle of the ball, my fingertips touching its seams, my right hand cradling the top right-hand corner the way I had practiced for thousands of solitary hours since the fifth grade until it was grooved into my soul. I squared my shoulders to the basket, bent my knees, and jumped in the air. My opponent jumped toward me. I scanned the basket like an archer measuring the target, then released the ball.

My left arm was extended, right through the fingertips, straight and true. The palm of my left hand waved to the rim and then faced downward, the way Nat Holman, Clair Bee, Bill Bradley, and countless coaches and players have recommended before the game went airborne away from the fundamental ground from which it was born.

Just as I released the ball, the arms of my 6'2" defender enveloped me and blocked my vision so that I could no longer see the rim. As my feet touched the wooden gym floor, there was a cavernous silence. I looked at the basket and saw the net raised skyward, the way it does when a high-arching shot drops cleanly through the net. I looked at the scoreboard and saw that my shot had gone in, and we had won the game. A teammate recently told me my left hand punched the air downward like I had beaten death. A deafening roar broke my spell as our fans mobbed the court.

The locker room was noisy, but I was strangely quiet, unmoved by the dramatic win and my personal heroics. I wasn't numb. Nor was I indifferent to winning; as a highly competitive teenage athlete, victory was very important to me. The victory did not lose its luster because I was upset by the transience of its sweetness. No, I was unemotional about our comeback because victory paled compared to what I had experienced.

I remember standing alone in the locker room after my teammates had showered and dressed, completely motionless, replaying what I had experienced during the last five seconds of the game: the heightened attentiveness, focus, and clarity; the way time seemed to expand; the absence of thought, pressure, and fear. The ecstasy and serenity more joyous than victory or acclaim.

Before the last five seconds of this game, I would have called my childhood—which was devoid of religious training or spiritual experiences—nonreligious. But now, I had entered a space I can only call the sacred—a nameless Vastness in which I was open to the moment without a sense of time, unselfconscious but acutely aware, highly focused and engaged, yet relaxed and without fear.

"There is another world and it is in this one," writes the surrealist poet Paul Eluard (Dunn 2001, 38). While my teammates were celebrating our narrow victory, I was preoccupied with the tantalizing glimpse I had of another dimension of being, what I would later term spirituality and the mystical.

What I experienced in the waning moments of the game in the Fieldston gym became a defining moment in my life. If I hadn't glimpsed that other world, my life would have been greatly diminished for I would have remained forever asleep to potentials of the human spirit I had never known. I don't know if astrophysicists feel a radical transformation and expansion of their own world when they discover alternative universes. I do know that after that game, I knew directly and viscerally that there was a radically different way of experiencing myself and relating to the world than I had previously been exposed to. The vice grip of ambition, competitiveness, and victory—the divinities I had worshiped—was loosened.

All of a sudden I saw them as false idols. While winning still felt better than losing, the joy of just playing the game became as important as victory. Zero-sum games, in which to have a winner you must have a loser, were less interesting.

As an American male I had been taught that willful effort was one of the highest virtues. I still valued focus and determination. But what I experienced at the end of that game is the way self-forgetfulness, as well as self-assertion, is crucial to a human life. She plays the piano best who is not concentrating on her fingers. In that state of grace you respond wholeheartedly without thinking. It was now clear to me that surrendering to and flowing with life was no less important than planning and goal-directed behavior.

As I slowly dressed, I thought of the gift and the lecture my father gave me on my tenth birthday: "Don't play too much basketball," he warned me solemnly as he handed me a leather Spalding basketball. "You'll never earn a living playing a game." His warning was a compromise between my mother's belief that school and sports didn't mix and my father's memory of the joy he and his brother, my uncle Hank, felt playing ball on the sandlot fields of Far Rockaway, New York. Three weeks later my low black Converse sneakers had holes in the toes the size of silver dollars. And it wasn't from running errands.

That gift fueled a single, secret dream: to become the very best basketball player I could possibly be, squeezing as much ability out of my not immensely gifted, now 5'7" body as was humanly possible. Little did I know my life would be forever transformed.

In the locker room of the Fieldston gym, that cold winter afternoon when I was eighteen, I recalled my father's lecture as well as his present. Basketball would never provide a livelihood. But it was more than just a game. The poet William Blake had found the universe in a grain of sand. In a basketball game I had caught a tantalizing glimpse of the other world—the one that mystics know—that is within this one. Sports writers and academics claim that sports provide an opportunity to build character and a laboratory to discover the best within yourself. For me, basketball was both of those things, but it was also a raft to another shore.

To give you a picture of how the last five seconds of that game when I was eighteen affected my spiritual quest, I'd have to take you back to the gym in the Bronx when my adolescence ended and intimations of something more eternal emerged.

If I were a painter I might try to depict the afternoon light streaming through the windows high above the gymnasium floor that winter afternoon in the Fieldston gym in 1971 when my world was turned upside down. But I'm not. And even if I could take you back to that gym and make you feel what happens when you are hyperalert, intensely aware, with mind and body working together in harmony, or what it's like to be graced by a breeze of divine vitality and rapture, I'm not sure I'd want to because I'd still be leaving something out. Because none of that would help you understand where it took me—the journey it inspired and the worlds it gave birth to—and how it shaped the man I would become. I didn't realize then, as my adolescence ended and I lay suspended between the not-yet of the future, and the no-longer of the past, that I would be launched on a passionate quest and become an astronaut of inner space.

THE SEARCH

It started with three questions in the locker room of the Fieldston gym. "What happened the last five seconds of that game? "What is this new universe I glimpsed?"And, "What did it all mean?"

The questions led to the search. "The search is what anyone would undertake if he were not sunk in the everydayness of his own life," the narrator of Walker Percy's *The Moviegoer* says, "To become aware of the possibility of the search is to be onto something. Not to be onto something is to be in despair" (1960, 13).

I wasn't feeling despair as a teenager, but I was very alienated from the world I inhabited. I felt deeply at odds with my subculture, in which material success was the highest value and profits all too often trumped people. Conformity was demanded. Questioning was not tolerated. Be like the rest of the herd. Join the pack and do something useful and profitable. At whatever cost to yourself. One could—many did—drown in the enveloping seas of conventionality. I resisted. Fought back. Challenged the pressure to give up the dreams and the search. I felt the weight of conventionality, of stepping into line and giving up and handing over my life, and I often doubted the wisdom of my alternative path but walking toward my own trivialization and diminishment by subscribing to someone else's prescribed identity was something that felt deadly. Glimpsing the vibrant and alive world the last five seconds of that game made it easier to live outside the usual tyrannies. But I paid a stiff price to keep my soul. I felt alone, estranged, and disconnected. Basketball was one of my only sanctuaries.

For someone who came of age in the 1960s—in the midst of pervasive skepticism and disillusionment and the moral and spiritual upheaval of Western civilization—commitment to a cause, to a direction was a challenge. The conventional image of success was one option; radical social change was another. The older, wealthier men I met growing up didn't seem happy or content. Nothing ever seemed enough to quench their thirst for the "more." and I don't mean wisdom or spirituality. Each "success" only drove them to strive for more. It seemed like an endless treadmill, with no one ever getting off. Nor did I feel moved by the more rebellious or politicized path of my younger compatriots. Politics—even when radical—seemed a cesspool, and even the most well-intentioned and idealistic people were polluted by compromise and hypocrisy. Fundamental social change—psychological and spiritual—was the path I chose.

I spent the better part of the 1970s and 1980s voraciously reading the classics of Eastern and Western psychology and spirituality, playing basketball regularly, training to be a therapist, and studying meditation and yoga. I now realize that I was trying to understand what happened when I was eighteen. Many of my peers seemed to view life as a survivor's game, with achievement the highest virtue. Existence became, for me, a question, and I became immersed in plumbing its depths and fathoming its secrets.

Buddha and Freud, Lao Tzu and Jung, and Patanjali and Krishnamurti were my guides and mentors in my quest to illuminate that glimpse I had had of something more in the Fieldston gym. I was most drawn to psychoanalysis, Buddhism, and yoga. They seemed to offer me the greatest potential enlightenment.

Psychoanalysis and Buddhism, an unlikely pair, each adopt diametrically opposed assumptions about human beings and a sane life. But each gave me priceless gifts including a new way of looking into my self. And each helped me see.

Worrying about a future that has never happened, replaying old hurts and wounds, cascading like a pinball from memories to fantasies to fears, the mind has a mind of its own. Even when we think we see clearly, we often observe life through a distorted lens. A mirror wiped clean—the world of Zen. Meditation, the training of moment-to-moment attention, helped me begin to watch the workings of my own mind and curb its wayward flights. By teaching me to hear what I listened to and taste what I ate, meditation showed me how asleep I was, how much life I had missed. I began to glimpse greater possibilities for awareness and clarity, freedom and compassion.

The influence of yoga was no less powerful. I thought yoga would stretch my body and calm my mind. What I didn't realize was that it would change my life. Through yoga I learned how to unite with whatever I was doing and explore and play the edge of the limits of my being.

And then there was psychoanalysis. There are still many people a hundred years after the publication of *The Interpretation of Dreams* (Freud 1900), who indiscriminately discount Freud. Now talk therapy is out; quick fixes, that is, taking drugs (Prozac, Xanax, and Viagra) are in. But in dreams (and symptoms) lie truths buried from the waking mind. For me, psychoanalysis, which I have come to think of as scuba diving into the swirling waters of one's emotional life, has been an endless source of enlightenment and inspiration for the past twenty-four years.

From psychoanalysis I learned many things: how humans have an endless capacity for self-deception; how to seek the depths and hear the unsaid; how to see feelingly; and how to respect the unconscious and trust and decipher my dreams.

Therapy, like meditation, made me more honest. Before—and even during—therapy I was an expert at hiding myself. Most people didn't really know who I was.

Over the next decade I flowered. I came out of hiding and wrote a book integrating the Eastern meditative and Western psychotherapeutic traditions (Rubin 1996). I began lecturing around the country on psychoanalysis and Buddhism and the perils and possibilities of psychoanalysis.

But I knew that as illuminating as psychoanalysis was, it did not clarify the mysteries of life, including the heightened state of consciousness I had experienced at the end of that game in the Fieldston gym. Basketball had taught me that there was a fourth state of being—the superconscious—in addition to Freud's preconscious and unconscious. In that state of being, one feels more alive and connected, awake and free.

The questions at the end of the Fieldston game led to the search. The search—which occupied my twenties, thirties, and forties—led to the quest for integration, how to make one's life a work of art. I didn't yet know how to practice or live the art of living, but I knew it was what I wanted to learn.

INTEGRATION

After the ecstasy comes the laundry.

(Jack Kornfield 2000)

I walk into a luxurious New York apartment that looks like a museum of Asian art filled with paintings, sculptures, and artifacts and greet a colleague, part of a group of captains of industry who have invited me for a consultation to help their group reach deeper levels of authenticity and intimacy. It is the spring of 2003. The group, which has been meeting regularly for close to two decades, is bogged down in dysfunctional patterns of relating. Many of the members hunger for closer and more authentic communication. I was excited and apprehensive before the meeting, the way I used to feel before a basketball game, worrying about whether I was prepared for the unexpected challenges I'd face and whether I would perform at a high enough level. The colleague I know introduces me to one of the other members of the group, a sportily dressed man in his early sixties. "Oh you're the shrink!" he says, sizing me up before he has seen me play.

"No I'm the expander," I say. They both laugh. The ice is broken. The meeting went well, and the group hired me. I remembered a session years ago when another shrink-lover in the form of a thirteen-year-old boy, also pressed me full court trying to defeat me. At the end of our first session, he stood in the doorway to my office, dwarfing his mother, with his bulk.

"All psychiatrists are assholes," the precocious teenager announced.

"There are two problems with your statement," I said. "One, I am a psychoanalyst, not a psychiatrist. Two, given your supposed intelligence — why did it take you so long to figure it out?" He is silent for a moment.

"I'm going to poison my mother," my psychiatry-loving patient said, upping the ante.

"Thank you," I said.

"You can't say thank you, you're a shrink," he said, momentarily stymied, trying for damage control. I had made my first shot in this bruising game of one-on-one.

"Well, you've given me a new strategy I can use against stubborn teenaged boys," I say.

The half-smile on the right side of his mouth conceded round two. Eight years later, the former C+ high school student whose father's suicide precipitated a dangerous slide, is an honors graduate of an Ivy League university. And more importantly, we have kept suicide at bay, and he now wants to live.

Later in thinking about where my response to the hostile man and the lost boy came from, I thought back to that game in the Fieldston gym. In all three cases I had to respond creatively and freely in order to do the unpredictable and turn the expected on its head. The mystical experience in the Fieldston gym provided a glimpse of improvisational living. When I was dribbling up the court at the end of that game, wholeheartedly immersed in what I was doing, time seemed to stand still and elongate and I accessed a different kind of awareness in which perception and response happened simultaneously.

I knew then, although I couldn't articulate it until years later, that truth lives outside of the systems and boxes we place ourselves in out of training, habit, and fear. The boundaries we ordinarily use to divide and navigate our world—boxes like "psychoanalysis" and "Buddhism," "East" and "West," and "psychology" and "spirituality"—are mostly man-made. They create "gaps" within us and between us and the outside world. Gaps between our minds and bodies, gaps between ourselves and other people. These gaps are illusions. They inhibit intimacy by creating a wall between us and ourselves and us and the world. When I walked through that gap between me and my world in the last five seconds of that game, I knew that much greater intimacy with the universe—and of course myself and other people—was possible.

I didn't yet know how to unite mind and body, self and other in the Fieldston gym, only that it could be done. My studies of meditation, yoga, and psychoanalysis in my twenties and thirties gave me tools for living the insights I had on the basketball court—and for integrating those insights into how I lived.

And this eventually changed how I lived and worked. I began seeing Life itself as a sanctuary, a kind of sacred space in which we can meet and sometimes dance together: "There is a kind of peace that is not merely the absence of war," writes Toni Morrison. "It is larger than that . . . the peace I am thinking of is the dance of an open mind when it engages another equally open mind" (1996, 7).

A patient complimented me one day: "You are disarmingly fluid and flexible," she said. "It's like being with flowing water."

"Therapy is yogic," said another. He recognized that yoga is wholehearted immersion in whatever we are doing. I now realize that basketball was my first yoga teacher. That place of greater connection that basketball, yoga, and meditation graced me with a glimpse of, has provided an unusual opportunity to explore and illuminate inner life. "Our therapy is meditative," another client said. "It slows down normal time and lessens the noise of everyday life which helps me see other aspects of the world. You stop the world in order to go into it."

Because of that mystical experience—which had no zip code and was the province of neither "East" nor "West"—I became un-American—actually not only American. I sought wisdom wherever I could taste it, usually outside the narrow and suffocating confines of single groups (spiritual or psychoanalytic), nations, or schools of thought. I became un-American in yet another way—in my values. You're supposed to keep striving, pushing, aching to be more, better, greater, if you're an American. And if you don't, you are supposed to feel guilt or shame. In my thirties and forties I embarked on a new path—the culmination of my Grail studies of meditation, yoga, and psychoanalysis in my twenties, thirties, and forties—the art of living. The art of living: pursuing my passion with discipline so that I could express and embody my unique vision, which I subjected to revision. And this consisted of trying to make my life a work of art, a life with no score, no winners or losers, no shame or fear, just the pure joy of searching and playing together with those of like-minded spirit. And the great open secret is that transcending the ordinary and experiencing the divineness of life comes in many forms and is a possibility open to any of us. I experienced it playing basketball and practicing Buddhist meditation, yoga, and psychoanalysis. Many of us have had a glimpse of this experience, but we don't know what to do with it. But you will find that when you pursue your passion with discipline so that you master the medium you are playing in—parenting, marriage, work, hobbies—and bring out your unique vision, your own particular view of the world, you can find the extraordinary within the ordinary and taste the divine. Then the everyday world is wondrous and enchanting. And since we all shape tomorrow, we all cocreate the future when we live and play with heart and soul; we assure that the evolving world is a better place.

My life would change—injuries and losses, disappointments and death would darken and complicate the landscape—but through it all what I saw and felt during that mystical experience when I was eighteen and the awakening it gave birth to has never completely left me. And while not always in the forefront of my consciousness, it has always served as a hidden resource and inspiration. The gift I received from I know-not-where showed me how miraculous and abundant life is, how much possibility it holds, how magnificent it can be.

REFERENCES

Dunn, S. (2001). *Walking light: Memoirs and essays on poetry.* Rochester, NY: BOA Editions.

Freud, S. (1900). *The Interpretation of dreams.* In the standard edition of the complete psychological works of Sigmund Freud, ed. and trans. J. Strachey, 4–5, 1–751. London: Hogarth Press. (1953–1974).

Kornfield, J. (2000). *After the ecstasy, the laundry.* New York: Bantam.

Morrison, T. (1996). *The dancing mind.* New York: Alfred Knopf.

Percy, W. (1960). *The moviegoer,* New York: The Noonday Press.

Rubin, J. (1996). *Psychotherapy and Buddhism: Toward an integration.* New York: Plenum Press.

Chapter Eight

Cigarette Smoke and Incense: A Perfect Storm of Healing

Robert A. Jonas

"And why, after all, may not the world be so complex as to consent of many interpenetrating spheres of reality, which we can approach in alternation by using different conceptions and different attitudes. . . . On this view religion and science, each verified in its own way from hour to hour and from life to life, would be co-eternal."

(William James 1958, 107)

Beneath me, the moving black water flowed around the concrete pilings that had been driven deep into the clay and sedimentary rock under the Wisconsin River. From my precarious perch, I gazed downward into the dark currents, wondering what fish or other creatures might be prowling below. Each of my ten-year old hands gripped a cool one-inch steel rod that extended from the gray spray-painted beams beneath my feet up to the iron underbelly of the concrete roadway. Sparrows and pigeons swooped through the undercarriage of the bridge as I walked carefully on the I-beams from the west side of the river to the east, a full city block away.

Eventually, I wanted to get from my maternal grandparents' house to my paternal grandparents' house, and along the way I looked for pigeon nests loaded with eggs and baby birds to throw into the river. I would not have said that I wanted to kill living things. I might have said that I merely wanted to see what was inside the eggs or merely to watch some little featherless beings sink into the deep to join whatever strange community was circulating there, where the grown-ups couldn't see. I might not have known that I was angry.

I didn't know how dangerous it was for me to be playing with life and death fifty feet above the river. Maybe I was a born adventurer, fascinated with the fragile boundary between life and death, between what I knew and

what I didn't know, between me and God. Maybe I was toying with death—
that peaceful and happy heaven that I was hearing about in our Lutheran
church. Maybe I just wanted to escape the pain or to get back at my parents.
Maybe I thought I was immortal. Strange, how often I'd head for that bridge,
my secret hiding place. How fitting that the rendezvous was beneath the road
where grown-ups rushed along to destinations that apparently meant more to
them than I did.

I spent a lot of time alone as a boy. Life at the edge of civilization lured me.
I was mesmerized by liminal movies—*Creature from the Black Lagoon*,
20,000 Leagues Under the Sea, *The Blob*, *Boys Town*, and *Rebel Without a
Cause*. They were so real to me that I found it difficult to swim or to go down
into a basement without turning on all the lights and carrying a bat. Who
knows what might emerge from the shadows or arrive from outer space? I
grew a duck-tail haircut, wore engineer boots like Marlon Brando in *The Wild
One*, and got in trouble with the law, just like Mickey Rooney and James
Dean. When I was eleven years old, I got arrested for breaking and entering.
While I waited for my mother to pick me up at the jail, I rifled through the
magistrate's desk and stole a pair of sunglasses.

My mother and father were preoccupied at the time. Dad had been a marine
in World War II and had been called up again during the Korean War. So he
was gone a lot. In 1956 he bought a tavern on the shore of Lake Wausau, a decision he later told me was the biggest mistake of his life. He shared his regret
with me on his deathbed over forty years later, after his divorces and decades
of estrangement from his three children. I shared the startling truth that after
our mother divorced him, I never went back to his parent's house again.

I was the oldest of three children and because my parents were so distracted,
I watched out for my brother and sister. Sometimes I felt sorry that I couldn't
protect them from the noise when Mom and Dad came home at 2 a.m., shouting, calling each other names, and pushing each other into the hallway walls.
I'd cover my head with a pillow and imagine being somewhere else.

I didn't know that their divorce was imminent when I tore out and threw
away the newspaper column in the district court section of the newspaper that
told the story of how Dad hit Mom in the face with a Coke bottle and that she
was pressing charges. All she told us kids was that her eyes were black because she had fallen. The swirl of dangerous passion has obliterated many
memories, but I do remember a few mornings in fifth or sixth grade when I
went to the liquor cabinet and took a swig of Crème de Menthe before walking to school.

My mother's parents—Grandma and Grandpa Radenz—were the steady
ones. My younger brother and sister and I stayed at Gram and Gramp
Radenz's a lot, and we felt safe there. They had bought a TV, and we'd often

spend the evening watching *Jack Benny*, *I Love Lucy*, or *Leave it to Beaver*. I suppose that the goal of my most consistent fantasy—hopping a train for Florida or California—was to find Beaver's family and to be welcomed and taken in.

With the help of my mother's remarriage and our move to a nearby town, the love of a girlfriend who was a straight-A student and a devout Christian, and the fatherly compassion I received from a Lutheran pastor and a high school football coach, I found myself inside a new story during my teenage years and throughout college. I became a good student, was elected the captain of the championship football team, and the president of the Luther League. I attended Luther College and then graduated from Dartmouth. But the new self in the new story was overlaid on the early, untold one. At the gates of the old story stood creatures as ugly and ferocious as the Fudo who stand guard at the doors of Japanese Buddhist temples.

My shame would never have surfaced into consciousness if I hadn't begun therapy when I was thirty-two years old, an exploration into my childhood that continued intermittently for another twelve years. I wouldn't have remained interested in my past if I hadn't been trained in Object Relations (OR) at Harvard and then practiced as a psychotherapist for most of a decade. Without the OR story, I might never have asked myself "Who? Who are my significant 'self-objects'?[1] Who was I hiding from or looking for under that bridge or in that river? With whom was I so angry? Whose love did I crave? Who was the 'you' implicit in my silent self-talk?"

During my years in the psychotherapeutic world, I was also a spiritual seeker. As I studied OR and as I myself became a therapist for others, I wondered how to integrate my longing for ultimate meaning and for the ultimate "You"—my longing for God, if you will—with my psychological work as a client and as a therapist. As an undergraduate at Dartmouth in the late 1960s I had accepted the reigning cultural story that God was dead, had left my dear Lutheran Jesus behind, and settled into Chinese Ch'an meditation, Taoism, and karate. Then, some years after graduation I met some wonderful Catholic Carmelite monks who taught me that long before Luther's Reformation, Roman Catholic and Orthodox monks had taught forms of meditation that are similar to Taoist and Buddhist practices. I welcomed this knowledge, converted to Catholicism, and took vows as a Third Order Carmelite.

The Carmelite tradition is gifted with the writings of two devout and brilliant sixteenth-century Spanish writers, St. Teresa of Avila and St. John of the Cross. In them I found teachers who artfully integrated Christ's *kenosis* (self-emptying love) with a mysterious, direct and devout I-Thou relationship with Christ. Going outside the boundaries of their own tradition, my Carmelite monk mentors also engaged me in conversations about the Trappist monk,

Thomas Merton, who was friends with the Dalai Lama and wrote skillfully about contemplative Christian prayer, Taoism, Buddhism, and the peace that arises when one discovers one's "true self." Though Merton never went into great detail about this true I, it seemed obvious to me, with my OR training that one's true "I" can only be realized in relationship with a corresponding true or ultimate You. What would be the nature and reality of such an I and such a You? Where is the meeting ground between Buber's (1958) spiritual I-Thou and the I's and thou's of the real intimate relationships we were studying in OR? Was Freud correct in his analysis that every divine Thou is merely an anthropocentric projection of the psyche?[2]

As a doctoral student at Harvard in the early 1980s I attended Catholic Mass on Sundays and became friends with Fr. Henri Nouwen, the remarkably charismatic and prophetic priest and writer who was then teaching at the Divinity School. Henri also envisioned a true self, emphasizing its essential quality of *belovedness*. For him, the summit of the spiritual quest was to realize, as Jesus did, our belovedness, our peace and our joy in God. For him, the beloved self is birthed when one establishes a relationship with his or her ultimate source in a God who is love.

Even though I had grave doubts about organized religion in general, I was drawn to the simple wisdom of Henri's teaching. Perhaps I connected with Henri so easily because his self-knowledge and his writing were so thoroughly blended with his previous psychological training at the Menninger Institute. I took his honest and straightforward descriptions of his own narcissism, despair, and depressions as a rough sketch of my own suffering. His confidence in the personal, social, and cosmic proportions of Jesus's message gained my trust.

In addition to my Christian path, I had maintained my interest in Asian spirituality. While at Harvard, I began Vipassana Buddhist training with Larry Rosenberg and other teachers of Insight Meditation. I wondered if I had an Asian gene because I felt so at home on the cushion, just following my breath. I understood immediately, and valued, the Vipassana teaching that all my ideas and theories about reality are not solid but merely temporary constructs that shimmer around a profound, clear emptiness. Very quickly I saw the truth in the Vipassana teaching that at least some of my suffering was caused by "monkey mind," my attachment to certain ideas, my pursuit of pleasure, and my avoidance of pain. Somehow I was not too troubled by the apparent contradictions in the Vipassana, psychotherapeutic, and Christian worldviews. They each illuminated different dimensions of my mind and heart.

Though I suffered severe bouts of anxiety and self-doubt while at Harvard, I did glimpse moments of peace, and I felt stimulated by the juxtaposition of Henri's passionate, personal, and prophetic declarations about Jesus's real presence with Vipassana's clarifying, stripped-down present moments on the cushion. As a client in psychotherapy, I was just at the beginning of my journey, but I did catch a peek of a world where I might be loved even though I felt worthless. With friends and colleagues, I enjoyed wrestling with ultimate questions in the interfaith conversation. Is there a God or not? Is God a mere projection or is God projecting me? Is there a self or not? Does it matter? What's the difference between the healthy ego we speak about in psychotherapy and the true self we hypothesize in spiritual paths? Are words and concepts valuable or not? Of course, what I wanted most from the psychotherapeutic, Christian and Buddhist traditions was not to engage in theoretical debate. I desperately wanted to realize an inner peace that eluded me, a way to be healed, and a path that would offer guidance about my vocation. What would heal me, and how could I help to heal others?

I could not speak about my spiritual quest at Harvard, so I lived a divided life during graduate school and in the first few years of my vocation as a psychologist and counselor. Academic psychology was only marginally interested in religious issues. As psychologists, we were more concerned with questions of life adjustment in specific relationships than with ultimate questions. Fortunately, there were exceptions in the work of Ana-Marie Rizzuto (1979), John McDargh (1983), Richard Katz (1982), and James Fowler, (1981), but these psychological investigations into religious experience seemed marginalized at Harvard.

Part of me reveled in the competitive intellectual atmosphere of Harvard and in the investigation of therapeutic concepts like "self-object," "transitional object," "projective identification," "ideal self," and "splitting."[3] But midway through the doctorate, both my mother and my marriage died, and the suppressed tumult of my inner life cried out for attention. Having only enough money for infrequent visits to a therapist at the time, I hunkered down. I did my doctoral research, wrote my dissertation, and held down three part-time jobs. Some days I could barely function and conducting academic research did not offer any healing. What I studied and what I lived did not fully connect.

In the decade after graduate school, I finally entered therapy for extended periods of time and practiced as a therapist and as a consultant in businesses and not-for-profits. I was fortunate to receive nourishing attention from some fine mentors and therapists. One of the good things about being a psychotherapist is that if you listen closely and with some empathy to your clients, you get curious about the sedimentary layers in your own life. You find yourself stuck in the muck of countertransference,[4] grandiosity, and self-defense. You pick up resonances, smells, images, and story lines that seem familiar. Sometimes you enjoy connecting with your clients and, if you are lucky, you often grow to love them. But, occasionally you squirm uncomfortably in your chair, happy to see that the hour is about done. Several times, I felt that I was thrown overboard into the same sea in which my clients languished and took on their fears and distress, even their mannerisms. In such times, I was glad to take the pain to my own therapist, to the meditation cushion, and to prayer.

At the forward edge of my learning I carried the same question every day: how to be empathetic and compassionate while simultaneously being mindful of the essential difference between my clients and me. Growing up in an alcoholic home, I had been schooled in codependency—I knew how to enter so deeply into the suffering of my clients that I could virtually *become* them. I was easily drawn to talk about spiritual oneness and nonduality, but I gradually learned that for me, oneness had a pernicious shadow side. I could too easily take my wounds and hide out in oneness. I had to learn how to keep one foot in my own world, even as I let go my boundaries sufficiently so that I could accompany my clients where they needed to go.

Having decided that Vipassana meditation was not helping me to understand myself or the problems that I was having in interpersonal relationships, I began attending Korean and Japanese Zen retreats. These forms of Mahayana Buddhist meditation seemed more relational to me, more open to the reality and importance of intimacy and generally more relevant to my everyday life. In comparison with Vipassana practice, Zen focused less on emptiness, sensations, and the generic quality of thoughts and more on the paradoxical ground of form and emptiness and on the interdependence of all beings. "No emptiness without form, no form without emptiness," the Heart Sutra said. I appreciated how, in Zen, the term "beings" could be used without deconstructing its wholeness into discreet *skandas* or packages of sensations that seemed to have nothing to do with the wholeness of other persons in community or of the natural world.

I did not want merely to investigate in a quasi-scientific way the emptiness of sensory experience but also to consider every form—every image, idea, memory, sensation, or feeling—as a possible doorway into the sacred dimensions of *dharmakaya*, ultimate reality, and of the greatest Thou, God. Perhaps I gave up on Vipassana meditation too soon, but after many retreats it seemed that Vipassana meditation was asking me to somaticize and to deconstruct all emotional and psychological experience into small, meaningless blips of impersonal energy passing by within the confines of my own skin, and to see others as mere objects of perception.

In the end, I could not accept a spiritual path that focuses so exclusively on one's inner experience, bypassing the healing power of action and speech. It is powerful to experience the emptiness within which our thoughts pass by, but it is equally powerful to speak a word of understanding or love to someone who is lonely. It is indeed powerful to see one's passions become attached to thoughts and to see directly how one's actions flow from one's thoughts, but it is also powerful to speak out in a political arena against injustice. For me, the Vipassana path was too dangerous, tempting me to become more solipsistic and emotionally isolated and less politically active than I already was.

I remember one retreat with a well-known Vipassana teacher in which I had to hold tightly onto the arms of my chair so that I did not jump up and shout, "I am not a mere object of your fucking awareness!" I began to think of Vipassana meditation, as practiced in America, as a kind of cult that can undermine the importance of I-Thou relationships and obliterate the reality of other persons as subjects in their own right who should be honored in their "otherness." It is good to face oneself on the cushion, but it is also good to connect with other people and to inquire into their experience. I resolved for myself that I would not follow a spiritual path that placed the cushion above conversation.

Of course, narcissism is a danger with any kind of meditation, but it seemed to me that Zen is more open to the power of relationship. Zen seeks to realize a larger (truer?) interdependent self that is both not separate from other people and also respectful of the subjectivity and "otherness" of others. Zen's attention to and respect for the world of form and relationships resonated well with my training in OR that held that our deepest selves are created and sustained in real embodied relationships. Perhaps Zen's teaching that our deep selves are holographic nodes in the cosmic Indra's Net, each one of us reflecting the whole, rang true because I had already been steeped in images of the community as "Christ's Body."[5] As Jesus puts it in his farewell speech in the Gospel of John,[6] "I am in my Father, and you in me, and I in you"; "Abide in me as I abide in you"; ". . . so that my joy may be in you, and that your joy may be complete"; ". . . that you love one another as I have loved you." I saw John's Jesus as an Indra's Net of God's grace, a harmonious interpenetrating mix-up of love.[7] For me, the doctrine of the Trinity was the deep archetype of the self, whereby the paradox of oneness and otherness is preserved and respected.

My Christian life remained active during and after Harvard. As my first marriage fell apart, I was fortunate to meet a woman who shared my interest in both psychology and spirituality. She was a Christian who had benefited from psychotherapy and was also interested in Buddhist meditation. Soon after we married in 1986, she became an Episcopal priest, and I began to attend Episcopal services. In 1989 I enrolled in a post-doc Masters program at the Weston Jesuit School of Theology, where I studied the history of the Christian contemplative path. By now I had integrated Christian prayer and *zazen* in my morning meditations.

During these years, I gradually became aware of some painful emotional patterns that were disrupting my relationships with loved ones. I experienced eruptions of shame, anger, and jealousy, and I felt profoundly alone. I began to meet weekly with three men for counseling—a psychologist, an Episcopal priest monk, and a Zen master. Fortunately, each one was less disturbed by my strong emotions than I was. I drank in their steady, nonjudgmental attention. Though the three approached suffering in distinctive ways, with different vocabularies and perspectives, and offered different paths to healing, they all agreed that healing was possible. I remained hopeful.

As the three healers converged on the precise locations of my inner wounds, I sometimes felt that I was experiencing a perfect storm of bad news. Zen showed me how my mind was usually engulfed in a "monkey mind" of chaotic worrying, problem solving, and imagining the worst. Silent meditation gave me a direct experience of how driven I was by habitual, repetitive thinking, and how attached I was to certain ideas about myself. Christian liturgies, reading Scripture, and prayer revealed a vision of love that illuminated my selfishness and my fear of commitment and community. Psychotherapy exposed the long trail of pain in my past intimate relationships. Bad news from every direction.

Fortunately, my mentors trusted that good would come from the bad news. And I guess I had some faith that even though I was at sea without a map or radio, eventually I'd be able to find and accept myself if I took a fix from three stars—Christian prayer, *zazen,* and psychotherapy. Each path seemed to offer a corrective balance for the other two. And after awhile, the winds of their worldviews, coming from different directions, created a perfect storm of healing.

One morning in December 1992, before my clients arrived and my workday began, I sat on a cushion in my home office to meditate and to pray. A candle flickered inside a red glass orb and a stick of incense burned in a bowl of sand on an altar in front of me. White-orange beams of morning light slanted across the carpet. Just one breath at a time, I said to myself. As usual, I entered the silence by silently reciting Psalm 139, which I had committed to memory:

> My God, you have searched me and known me;
> you know my sitting down and my rising up;
> you discern my thoughts from deep within.
> You trace my journeys and my resting places
> and are acquainted with all my ways.
> For you yourself created my inmost parts;

you knit me together in my mothers womb . . .
My body was not hidden from you,
while I was being made in secret
and woven in the depths of the earth.
I thank you for I am marvelously made;
your works are wonderful, and I know it well . . .
How deep are your thoughts, O God!

God's thoughts, not mine. God as the You who had created me, sustained me, knew me and understood me. God as the ultimate, invisible You that opens Himself, Herself to me through the persons of my mentors and loved ones and in my own depths. God, the ultimate Lover.

Vipassana meditation and *zazen* had revealed my thoughts to me in the most intimate way: I could see them and hear them in the silence. Very often they zipped through my mind like a cloud of bats in a cave, roused from their sleep. More and more, I was drawn to the spaces between the thoughts, and that is where I often looked for God, whose thoughts were beyond mine. I was gradually becoming able to tolerate the paradox of being in relationship to a You upon whom I was totally dependent and yet also a You who was beyond all my understanding.

Sometimes I found solace in the silence, but on this morning I was aware of irritation and anger in my belly, neck, and legs. My thoughts ran to a disagreement that I had had with a friend, and it was difficult to feel grateful or to trust in God. I felt a fullness in my chest. "You have searched me and known me," I repeated silently, along with a simple phrase my Zen teacher had given me, "What is this?" "Is this irritation about my friend or is it about something else?" I breathed into the search and into the question.

Then I remembered that recent conversations with my three mentors had been stirring up some childhood memories. "Is that it?" I wondered to myself. "Is this about my parents again?" Maybe I feared that I'd be inundated with painful memories. But now I was able to notice the irritation and fear with a sense of acceptance and curiosity.

As I sit in silence before the flame, a recent dream of Gram and Gramp Radenz opens into a dim memory. They were the ones who had so often rescued us kids from the alcoholic irresponsibility of our parents, so I was grateful for them, but this memory is unsettling. Should I explore it? I am uncertain. Meditation is not for remembering, analyzing, problem-solving, or following a story. My Vipassana teacher told me to treat all thoughts as boats going down the river. Just sit there on the riverbank and watch them float by. Another teacher compared thoughts to moving trains that should be watched and not boarded. But somehow it seems as if this memory train carries a special cargo. On an Ignatian retreat at a Jesuit retreat center, the priest emphasized the iconic power of the imagination to serve as a vehicle in our journey to God. God can work through memories, he suggested. Sitting here, at the doorway between the sunlit ordinary and the shadowed liminal ground of memory, I decide to breathe in the remembered smells that mix with the burning incense and candle wax.

In my mind's eye, I am walking through the kitchen door of Gram and Gramp's home in Wausau, Wisconsin. Gram and Gramp were born in the late nineteenth century, before the invention of cars, airplanes, movies, telephones, TV, and the Internet. Gramp was a quiet man, allowing his Germanic, controlling, and somewhat paranoid wife free rein to run the show at home. Gramp had built their two-story house with his own hands. He and Gram had dug out the basement by themselves and brought in landfill with a horse-drawn wagon to help dry up the wetlands.

When he was young on the farm, Gramp had played fiddle and harmonica in a polka band. Before he died in 1995, he and I would play *Amazing Grace* together in his nursing home—he on his harmonica and I on my Japanese bamboo flute—to the astonishment and joy of the nurses and residents. In some ways, I had very little in common with my grandparents, especially after my college education, but we shared a joy in Gospel and polka music, and we were ardent true-believer fans of the Green Bay Packers, who played just eighty miles away.

Sitting on the cushion as I walk through the door thirty years ago, I smell cigarette smoke, whiskey, beer, caramelized popcorn, pork chops, and the tang of newly opened cans of beets and beans that Gram packed that fall. Gram and Gramp, my four aunts and uncles, and my mom and stepdad move back and forth between the kitchen and the dining room. My cousins run up and down the stairs to the basement and second floor, and Gram yells angrily, "Now stop that running, you shysters!"

A pall of cigarette smoke hangs over the kitchen, just above the level of the children's heads. Through the far door, the dining room table is set up for another long evening of sheepshead, a card game that came with our ancestors from Germany. On one end of the kitchen table lie big platters and bowls of food—pork and beef, mashed potatoes, cranberries, red jello (with grated carrots suspended inside), bowls of candy, and mounds of sweet homemade oat cookies. On the other end stand several jugs of Christian Brothers brandy, Beefeater gin, and Kesslers whiskey; large glass bottles of "wash" (ginger ale, 7Up and sour mix); and a few six-packs of Miller High Life, Schlitz, and Blatz beer—all Milwaukee products and our family's favorites.

My belly tightens with anxiety to have such an immediate sense of my childhood world. I feel lonely and cold. I have the curious, paradoxical sense of being both a young boy and also a grown man who has learned a few things. I am aware that I've talked about scenes like this with my therapist, but now the memory seems more vivid and real than any normal memory. I don't feel the impulse to complain about what I am smelling, hearing, and seeing. I don't feel like rehearsing the same old litany of complaints: that I had a lousy, lonely childhood, that my parents were narcissistic, that they didn't have a clue about how to raise children.

Now, the loneliness is giving way to something new: my heart is open, and I am seeing everything through little Bobby's eyes. I am seeing everything with the innocence and openness of a child. I notice that no one is making eye contact with me or anyone else. Everyone is talking quickly, anxiously, with furtive glances in each other's direction. No one pauses to ask me, "How are you?" "What's new?" "What have you been up to lately?" And, most important, "Is anything bothering you?"

Here on the cushion, I see what Bobby is missing, but I'm just noticing, without judgment. I see that others aren't receiving direct attention either, and that they aren't even aware that eye contact, much less an intimate conversation of sharing and listening, is possible. The content of the adults' talk is laced with complaining and blaming others for various misdeeds. There is laughter, but there's an edge to it. As a boy, I didn't know that anything better was possible, but now, as a boy, I do. I am Bobby, but I am also someone else who is standing beside Bobby. I am watching him and listening to him as my dearly beloved, and I know that he is aware of me and receiving my love.

The adults are puffing away at their cigarettes, lifting their glasses, gesturing with their playing cards, trading a story here and there, and occasionally calling out their children's names. My aunt Lucille, the one who always said that she wanted to be buried in a mausoleum above ground because she couldn't bear to be eaten by worms, is drinking a martini, nervously biting her lip and smiling vacantly. Oh, they all smile at each other occasionally and touch each other on the shoulder, but the offered words and touches are almost thrown at the recipients, as if the giver wanted to get rid of the thing as quickly as possible. Aunt Beatrice and Uncle Earl, the Catholics in our Lutheran family, glow with a genuine love for each other, but they too seem caught up in the anxiety and nervous laughter that is in the air. As long as we kids aren't breaking anything or running up and down stairs too fast, we are ignored.

I had shared some of these images with others before, with a tinge of self-pity, but in this moment my heart is softer. It's not self-pity that I feel. It's not blame, guilt, or shame. It's gratitude—gratitude for these dear family members. The tears that wet my cheeks spring from gratitude and sorrow for the wounds we shared and the love we missed.

I reach for the white leather Bible that Grandma gave me at my high school graduation. I touch the Bible with respect for this sacred love story passed on from generation to generation, a story that reaches back across the twentieth century through the European Reformation, back through the Middle Ages, the Dark Ages, the early Councils of the Church, and Constantine's recognition of Christianity; back across the time of the Christian persecutions and the anonymous desert monasteries, then back to Jesus. My bedrock faith in Jesus, in some eternal part of him, was never fully shaken during the "God is dead" cultural shift of the late 1960s, despite my years of Buddhist sitting and the heart-crunching skepticism of a Harvard doctorate. And now here it is again, that sense of his powerful and loving presence in me.

The touch of my finger on the Bible reminds me of something. I look over at my small statue of Buddha touching the ground with his forefinger. It is the moment in which he is enlightened and embraces all truth. He touches the ground just as Jesus touched the ground while a neighborhood mob prepared to stone a woman caught in adultery. I see a flash of light radiate from Jesus's muddy fingertip, and I hear his words, "Let the one among you that is without sin cast the first stone."[8]

On my cushion, I see the acrid smoke, smell the whiskey, and sense the estrangement that hangs in the air, but something is different. Everything is as it was, but it is happening in an ambience of love. I see each person in Gram and Gramp's house as if bathed in the light of forgiveness. The card-playing scene looks exactly as before, but everyone is transparent to love. Their physical and emotional wounds are still there, but now it's as if the light of love shines through their wounds and everyone is being blessed. The wounds are like stained glass windows, transmitting a holy light.

It is as if all the memories of my childhood have come to this, a moment in which the former bitterness, complaint, shame, self-pity, and anger have dissolved in an all-pervading love, as if Christ were overseeing the whole of it. I see all the members of my extended family, no matter how wounded, as if they are icons, transmitting an image of divinity. They are too broken to know it. Back then, they loved me and I loved them, but none of us knew how to express that love well. Now, I see that Love has been here all along, holding us safely, even in the midst of darkness. Buddha is sitting down on the floor of Grandma and Grandpa's home, breathing in the suffering of my family and with each exhalation, breathing out compassion. Jesus, always ready to party with his friends, sits down at the table with us to play sheepshead.

I notice that I am smiling as the tears on my cheeks dry. I feel such love for everyone, and somehow this love seems larger than me as an individual. The love has obliterated the walls of neurotic separation with which I grew up. Not only that, it has also momentarily dissolved the passage of time. In the lovely eternity of the memory, I spoke words of blessing and forgiveness to my dear relatives. I repeated silently, "I'm sorry, I'm sorry, I'm sorry." Not the sorry that comes from guilt, but the kind that comes from love: "Sorry that we didn't see and love each other well, sorry that I made you worry, sorry that we didn't know how wounded we were, or how much we needed each other's forgiveness, and sorry that we only had that one small chance to get it right. Sorry that we can't be with each other now, knowing what we know after death has separated us."

This experience on a cushion changed my life. Afterward, I experienced less fear, envy, anger, and self-doubt. I felt more kindly toward myself, and I approached others with less judgment and more patience and compassion. I felt a greater capacity for empathy. It was a true healing occasioned by a perfect storm of three healing paths: psychotherapeutic, Buddhist, and Christian. Each one contributed particular tools for self-understanding, a measure of hope, and real live mentors who helped me to face some childhood traumas and to integrate these experiences into my adult life as a professional, a married man, and a father. After this experience, I sensed an even greater love and empathy for my own son, Sam, who was a toddler at the time. I would commit myself to father him from this larger love. A perfect storm had blown in at just the right moment, and it seemed to radiate outward to both the past and the future.

I don't understand time, how people and things can be here and then not here, not here and then here. I have blurted out the phrase so many times at home that my wife only smiles and rolls her eyes: "I don't understand time." It's a mystery that is rarely reflected upon in the world of psychology. Fortunately, Buddhism and Christianity do call attention to time and do find value in wondering about its qualities. Not all spiritual teachings about time have been valuable for me. I believe that some spiritual teachers, for example, are missing a certain richness of meaning when they tell me that past and future are an illusion. They are not illusions. They are real. But their kind of existence is a mystery, and our only access to them is through the present moment.
. In Mahayana Buddhism, such as Zen, one gets a glimpse of deep, timeless interdependency: everything that is, everything that was, and everything that will be, are at once emerging, transient, and already gone. In the West, Plato's realization in *Timeaus*, that "time is the moving image of eternity," echoes in the Judeo-Christian tradition, wherein the past and the future live in each moment in the timeless, placeless Now of God. God, who creates time, is found both beyond and within time. In Hebrew Scripture we are told that God, who created time, has set eternity in our time-bound hearts.[9] In Isaiah and Jeremiah, we read that God connects eternity and time in a relationship of love when He says, "I love you with an everlasting love."[10]

This theme of a sacred eternity that touches every moment of chronological time is abundant in Christian scriptures. When Jesus is accosted by the religious leaders, he tells them,

> Your ancestor Abraham rejoiced that he would see my day; he saw it and was glad.
>
> Then the Jews said to him, "You are not yet fifty years old, and have you seen Abraham?" Jesus said to them, "Very truly, I tell you, before Abraham was, I am."[11]

Who is this "I" who endures for eternity? Perhaps my perfect storm of healing was a glimpse into this timeless consciousness of Jesus who is present, not only to his personal past and future, but to all past and future. Perhaps I had momentarily experienced what our tradition calls Christ consciousness. Since Christians are taught that we share the mind of Christ,[12] our deep selves share common ground with the deep "I" of Christ, for whom all those who have passed away are "alive" in God.[13]

I wonder about the implications for psychotherapy. How do we as therapists understand time, and how do our assumptions affect our actual sessions with clients? Does it make a difference if we love our clients? How is an everlasting love different from an ordinary love?

For me, the therapeutic goal of coming to terms with my past and of being released from its suffering was completed by tapping into a consciousness that I can only regard as spiritual. Of course, it would be a mistake to think that I was present at my grandparent's house in the same way that I was sitting on the cushion that particular morning. I know that my parents, grandparents, and many of the adults at that evening party are dead. What has passed is gone forever. Yet those moments of seemingly timeless love, including a sense that somehow the love in my heart was "actually" reaching my family "back then," seems as real to me as the cushion that I sat upon, as real as the keyboard on which I now type.

For Jews, Christians, and some Buddhists, the psychotherapeutic project is profoundly affected by our traditions' understanding of time. If we as human persons are not bound irrevocably by the one-way directionality of time, then our "past" significant relationships continue to live within us. Of course, from the scientific and medical perspectives our past relationships may be considered to be no more than electrical reverberations in specific areas of the brain. But if we believe that our true selves are created and constituted in interdependent relationships, and if we believe in the wholeness and integrity of human persons, then we should be mindful of the critically important "I-thous" that resonate in our depths and in the holy vaults of our memories.

Perhaps the healed self is a self in which all relationships—past, present, and future—are resolved in love. When we or our clients are in the mode of remembering, we might recognize that we have crossed a liminal boundary, not only into the generic coming and going of mere "thoughts," but rather into the sacred temple of inner I-thou relationships that form the ground of our personhood vis-à-vis others.

For spiritual seekers who also follow the psychotherapeutic path to personal healing, our painful, abusive, unjust, violent, disgusting, shameful, and evil incidents in the past exist in some real way in the present. We might say that this is not good. We would prefer that painful memories be completely erased. (At this writing there is some excitement in psychiatric circles about new drugs that apparently can erase our memories of suffering.) But because our past, painful experiences and the resonance of earlier relationships continue to live in us, they can be redeemed. In any given moment, we can become aware of, and be surprised by, other "thous" whose presence bubbles up from the unconscious. We can carry the koan, "Is this remembered relationship complete and resolved in love or not."

The techniques of disciplined, moment-to-moment awareness that Buddhist meditation brings to psychotherapy are of tremendous value to both therapist and client. These techniques build upon Freud's prescriptions for the ideal analyst, as one who displays an evenly suspended awareness in relationship to the client, a kind of Buddha-like equanimity and openness to surprise. Freud envisioned the competent analyst to be so aware that he or she would actually catch new material as it emerged from his or her own unconscious. The therapist, he said, should "turn his own unconscious like a receptive organ toward the transmitting unconscious of the patient". . . and bring full awareness to his or her perceptions as a clue to what is happening in the client (Tansey and Burke 1989, 11). Buddhist meditation can deepen one's ability to "not-know" with the client, making it more likely that repressed memories, thoughts, and feelings can emerge in oneself and in the therapeutic relationship. Deep within the Mahayana tradition is perhaps its most important teaching, that when one is truly detached and present to "what is," compassion naturally arises. Out of emptiness comes compassion, a sense that our suffering is not different from that of our clients and a spontaneous inclination to help.

One should not assume that the goal of psychotherapy for both therapist and client is only the development of detachment. Here, the Christian contemplative tradition may have something a bit different to offer. Teachings about detached awareness can be traced back to desert monks such as Evagrius and Cassian in the fourth and fifth centuries CE and were developed further by the Dominican friar, Meister Eckhart, in the fourteenth century and St.

Ignatius Loyola and St. John of the Cross in the sixteenth century.[14] Like their contemplative Buddhist cousins, each of these spiritual teachers values an open awareness that is unattached to pleasure or pain, but because they, as Christians, sense that the dynamic core of a person resounds in a sacred I-Thou relationship, they are drawn to balance inward detachment with the continuous affirmation and valuing of human connection and community. Both of these orientations of awareness—detachment and healthy attachment—are essential in the quest for psychotherapeutic healing.

I wonder if the love that I felt that morning on the cushion in fact did reach my dear relatives "back then." I have imagined that in that very moment, perhaps on a cold December night in 1957, each person's spirit stood up straight like a prairie dog under an open sky and heard a voice from the future—my voice, but perhaps a voice that transcends my own—saying, "I see your shame, your guilt and your fear, and it's all OK. I love you with an everlasting love, and I will welcome you home when you die." Perhaps this voice of love is coming to me now from my own future. I honestly don't know how to square these time-shifting experiences with our usual perception that chronological time passes along in each moment from past to future with no possibility of reversal. Yet I expect that many of my fellow Christians, steeped as they are in the language of eternity, might empathize. I can only speculate that some Buddhists and seekers in other religions may have similar experiences of time's elasticity.

I don't know how one tests the validity of spiritual and psychological healing. If it is by the fruits of such experiences, then I believe that there was something authentic about the perfect storm of healing that I've described. I had been completely infused with a love, unmistakably real, that is rooted deeper than the scientistic paradigms that often govern our great universities, a love that is deeper than the cynicism and violence that can spring from suffering, deeper than the cold indifference we can see on the bloody hands of a boy who kills baby birds or in the frigid, impersonal whirling of the planets through the darkness of outer space. *The light shines in the darkness, and the darkness did not overcome it.*[15]

NOTES

1. The psychotherapeutic tradition of Object Relations (OR) has its roots in the work of Sigmund Freud (1856–1939). Freud assumed a radical distrust of everyday—including religious-consciousness. For him, a person's inner life is driven by instinctual, especially erotic, desires. Thus, he spoke of the "object" of our unconscious desires. OR therapists focus less on the biological energies of a person, and more on the

dynamic relational structure of the self. Who are the "objects" of my need for mutually loving and respectful relationships? The term "self-object" refers, e.g., to any (usually unconscious) image that I might carry of myself in relation to my mother. In OR my "self" is actually a kind of underground streaming movie of myself in relation to many significant others-parents, mentors, heroes, heroines, lovers, and teachers. According to OR theorists, this stream of memories of me in relation to others *is* what we call our "self," and it tends to imprint itself and its archetypes on all our current relationships.

2. S. Freud. *Totem and Taboo.* (1913). Trans. James Strachey. New York: W. W. Norton & Co.,1913, 1950.

3. A *transitional object* (TR) is the infant's first not-me possession, such as a doll or blanket. A TR is external to the infant, and yet he or she imbues this object with qualities shared in the mother-child fusion. *Projective identification* happens when I project part of myself onto another person and then identify with that person, thereby temporarily disowning that part. *Ideal self* refers to a fantasized best self that hides, even from myself, my true or authentic self. *Splitting* is the process whereby I unconsciously parcel out certain qualities of personhood to myself and others in such a way as to keep these qualities separate.

4. In a psychotherapeutic relationship, *transference* is the process whereby the client projects onto the therapist certain qualities of personhood whose psychic source is the client's childhood image of his or her parent. *Countertransference* is the process whereby the therapist projects some aspect of his or her own psychic experience inappropriately onto the client.

5. 1 Corinthians 10:16: "The cup of blessing that we bless, is it not a sharing in the blood of Christ? The bread that we break, is it not a sharing in the body of Christ?" 1 Corinthians 12:27: "Now you are the body of Christ and individually members of it."

6. Gospel of John, chapters 14 through 16, New Revised Standard Version.

7. This phrase connotes the symbiotic, unifying relationship of mother-and-infant, a healthy phase of psychic development. If this phase of personal development is not completed successfully, an adult person will have problems with boundaries in his or her intimate relationships. The phrase, "harmonious interpenetrating mix-up" is attributed to the OR therapist, Michael Balint. See, for example, *The Basic Fault.* London: Tavistock, 1968. P. 115. Bottom paragraph.

8. Gospel of John, chapter 8: 1 ff

9. Ecclesiastes 3:11

10. Isaiah 54:8 and Jeremiah 31:3

11. John 9:56 ff

12. Philippians 2:5

13. Luke 20:37

14. Evagrius Ponticus. *The Praktikos & Chapters On Prayer.* Trans. J. Eudes Bamberger. Cistercian Studies Series: Number Four. Kalamazoo, Michigan: Cistercian Publications, 1981. John Cassian. Conferences. Trans. Colm Luibheid and preface. *Classics of Western Spirituality.* New York. Paulist Press, 1985.

15. John 1:5

REFERENCES

Buber, M. (1958). *I and thou*. Trans. R. G. Smith. New York: Collier Books.

Fowler, J. W. (1981). *Stages of faith: The psychology of human development and the quest for meaning*. San Francisco: Harper & Row.

Freud, S. (1950). *Totem & taboo*. Trans. J. Strachey. New York: W. W. Norton & Co. (Original work published 1913.)

James, W. (1901). *The varieties of religious experience*. New York: New American Library (1958).

Katz, R. (1982). *Boiling energy: Community healing among the Kalahari Kung*. Cambridge, MA: Harvard University Press.

McDargh, J. (1983). *Psychoanalytic object relations theory and the study of religion*. New York: University Press of America.

Rizzuto, A. (1979). *The birth of the living god*. Chicago: University of Chicago.

Tansey, M., and W. Burke. (1989). *Understanding counter-transference: From projective identification to empathy*. Hillsdale, NJ: Analytic Press.

Chapter Nine

Oscillations*

Paul C. Cooper

"Between the conscious and the unconscious, the mind has put up a swing:
all earth creatures, even the supernovas, sway between these . . . "

(Kabir)[1]

Despite any clever rationalizations that I might evoke, suffering served as the prime motivational force for seeking out and for submitting to the rigors of both the path of Zen Buddhism and psychoanalysis. Given the unique demands of these respective journeys, it would be indeed naive to suggest otherwise. Both disciplines contain converging and diverging dimensions that exert unique and complimentary mutually facilitating forces on the serious practitioner. This chapter describes how Zen practice can engender experiences that can then be processed through the lens of psychoanalytic training and psychotherapy. Such processing, both individually, through self-analysis, and through the ongoing dialogue that occurs in personal psychoanalysis can contribute to deepened Zen practice. Thus both practices can operate in mutually enhancing and reinforcing ways. The concept of oscillations will help create a conceptual framework that supports and provides structure for the experiential aspects of this discussion.

---

*This chapter is an expanded and revised version of "Oscillations: Zen and Psychoanalytic Versions," which was originally presented at the International Federation for Psychoanalytic Education Conference held in Pasadena, California in November 2003 and published in the *Journal of Religion and Health* (P. Cooper 2004).

BUDDHIST EXPERIENCE

Involvement in Buddhist study and practice, for me, has been an ongoing series of oscillations occurring with variations in pitch, speed, depth, and intensity. Oscillations deriving from my Buddhist experience have become perceptible to me mainly in retrospect. Initially, like a swinging pendulum, I would touch Buddhism lightly, let it touch me, bounce away, and then bounce back again.

Looking back, these initially broadly oscillating encounters increasingly narrowed. My early involvement with Buddhism, perhaps through reading a book, then another, occurred years apart. Thus such oscillations in and out of Buddhism give the impression of straight lines, leading nowhere, like so many new interests, that one peeks into and then backs out from. Yet, like deeply planted seeds, they remain buried and germinate out of sight until they sprout and blossom as each oscillation deepens, diminishes, and repeats in its own time. With deepening involvement and experience, microoscillations appear woven into the fabric of wider arcs. For example, oscillations occur with regard to fluctuations in intensity, duration, and frequency of sitting meditation sessions. Initially, I would sit occasionally, for brief periods of time, perhaps ten to fifteen minutes at most. Over the years, I developed a daily practice of one or more forty-five minute sitting periods. These daily "sits" would intensify with visits to the zendo[2] and would further intensify on retreats. At other times I might find myself stopping this practice, or I might practice and notice a diminished intensity or a lack of clarity and focus. Enthusiasm would wax and wane. At some points during meditation sessions, I would simply notice time passing and fabricate daydreams to get through the boredom and through the sitting period. At other points of intensified sitting, states of timelessness would ensue. I am told that all of these oscillating states are valid aspects of practice, not to be judged, embraced, or dismissed. So, sitting continues.

PSYCHOANALYTIC EXPERIENCE

Psychoanalysis, on the other hand, as a process, in my experience, despite periods of turbulence, has always felt steadier than my initial forays into Buddhism. Since my first encounter, I simply stayed with the process with very few interruptions. Thus, despite their presence, psychotherapy's oscillations often remain unnoticed, unconscious, or evolve in arcs too wide to perceive close up. Yet, oscillations certainly do occur between hope and despair, fragmentation and wholeness, depression and elation, pride and shame, agitation and equipoise, to name a few. Once initiated, psychoanalysis slowly deepened over time, first, through increasing session frequencies and followed soon after by reading and then by study and formal training.

Oscillations draw momentum from both inner and outer sources. Deep longings emerge from within, become intensified and shaped through reading, visiting museums, attending lectures, conducting anthropological research, and participating in introductory meditation sessions. My initial motivation for these explorations centered on simple curiosity deriving from the desire to expand the edges of my seemingly narrow universe. Curiosity operated in combination with misguided efforts at self-healing. Most predominant were my longings that continue to consist of a bittersweet blend of wonder, doubt, passion, deadness, sadness, elation, joy, and pain. They persist, in varying degrees of intensity, to this day. When attended to over time, both painful and joyous aspects of longings begin to exert a different kind of impact than they had at first. They lose their threatening feel and paradoxically intensify, adding energy, richness, and meaning to life. They are no longer perceived as something dangerous and toxic to be discarded. Rather, whatever emerges can be accepted for what it is and for what it is not. Experience can be embraced and relinquished in endless cycles of emerging, rising, crystallizing, and dissolving. However defined, initially, my deepest longings ultimately expressed a matter of life and death urgency. With passing time, as each oscillation deepened imperceptibly, the resulting encounters began to touch an emerging gnawing desire to get at "the something" or "the no-thing" inside of myself.

SUFFERING

Clinical Perspective

From the clinical perspective, the British psychoanalyst Wilfred Bion notes that "There are patients whose contact with reality presents the most difficulty when that reality is their own mental state . . . people exist who are so intolerant of pain or frustration (or in whom pain or frustration is so intolerable) that they feel the pain but will not suffer it and so cannot be said to discover it . . . The patient who will not suffer pain fails to 'suffer' pleasure and this denies the patient the encouragement he might otherwise receive from accidental or intrinsic relief" (1970, 9).

The patients that Bion has in mind can be said to "experience pain but not suffering. They may be suffering in the eyes of the analyst because the analyst can, and indeed must, suffer. The patient may say he suffers but this is only because he does not know what suffering is and mistakes feeling pain for suffering it . . . " (19). For Bion, psychotherapy requires suffering the fact that pain exists for both self and other.

From this perspective, Vivienne Joyce writes: "If human beings are to acquire a little more respect for suffering, the demand is to be truthful about misery and catastrophe. Respect for suffering is the path to transformation and is essential to both the treatment and the cure" (2005, 110).

Buddhist Perspective

For Buddhists, the term *duhkha* acknowledges the primacy of suffering in the first of the "Four Noble Truths." The *Bodhisattva* vow, the Buddhist commitment to save all sentient beings, acknowledges the suffering of both self and other. In the context of the notion of forbearance, the Zen teacher, Robert Aitken points out that " . . . *suffering* is an ambiguous word that can also mean *permission*" (1994, 50). Quoting the New Testament, Aitken writes, "'Suffer the little children to come unto me,' Jesus said. Let it come, let it happen. The whole world is sick; the whole world suffers and its beings are constantly dying. Duhkha, on the other hand, is resistance to suffering. It is the anguish we feel when we don't want to suffer" (50).

Perhaps this constant, ambiguous "something inside" that I felt was, at the time, the best I could do to describe the nameless depths of my own suffering. "Something inside" perhaps serves as a compromise for what can and cannot be said about what might or might not be felt. We want to feel the impacts that life offers us while we simultaneously buffer ourselves from the actual force of such impacts. Thus the capacity for suffering, and even *naming* suffering, gets buried under layers of self-deception. In a misguided effort to "reclaim" this buried territory, we become "experience collectors," running from one "powerful experience" to the next. However, when viewed exclusively through a dualistic perspective that engenders a separation between "inside" and "outside," despite their initial potency, [non] suffering remains an omnipresent and vital motivating force for both the Buddhist and the psychoanalytic quest. My, by no means unique, observations find expression often enough, perhaps so often, that they reach the point of meaninglessness. Overuse can strip language of its meaning and impact. Whatever can be said about what might be numbed out and what might be felt becomes safely reduced to cliché. However, despite the many ways one might conceptualize, articulate, buffer, or neutralize experience, suffering remains real. At stake is one's capacity for experiencing suffering, which might or might not have been developed, derailed, damaged, deformed, interrupted, or stalled.

From a Sufi perspective on psychotherapy, Janet Pfunder observes that: "Psychotherapy and spiritual practice both offer the opportunity to actually suffer our suffering, offsetting the ways we have become numbly unreal to ourselves" (Pfunder 2005, 143).

BREATHING

Buddhist practices, such as sitting meditation, function to strip away our self-deceptions and to free us from the anguish of self-protection. Buddhism teaches us that we continue to crave, cling, grasp, relinquish, repel, and ignore in unending cycles of desire and aversion, compulsion and revulsion. These shifting states are basic and breathe life into oscillations. The natural rhythm of the breathing process serves as an instructive example.

While of great significance to Buddhist practice and to other Eastern wisdom traditions, until recently, virtually no attention has been given to the breath in Western psychology (Eigen 1993). However, minimal attention to the breathing process is both revealing and transformative in terms of self-perception and emotional life. I will focus on rudimentary aspects of breath awareness that relate to oscillating states. As soon as we inhale, oxygen becomes converted into carbon dioxide. The body impulse is to get rid of what was initially nourishing, now toxic, and immediately an exhalation ensues. However, no sooner is the exhalation complete, then the body's need for oxygen returns and evokes another inhalation. This process repeats itself consciously and unconsciously, and life depends on the resulting inhale-exhale oscillations. No one would question the life and death urgency of the breathing process.

Eastern wisdom traditions point to the heart as the seat of mind. Perhaps the primary internal oscillation center is the beating heart, the circulating blood that carries life-sustaining oxygen, a link and intimate connection that joins inner and outer through cycles of breath. Psychic, emotional, and spiritual breathing, despite their imperceptibility are similarly vital to sustain life. When interfered with, psychic deadness ensues. Intimacy with oxygen from the environment creates a connection with all life. In this sense, there is no inside and outside. The breath serves as a connection point and nexus for conscious and unconscious processes. The more one sits with this simple process, the more apparent these connections become.

Intellectual curiosity remains, albeit diminished by the long shadows cast by emotional pain. To truly suffer is to be human. Despite the negative connotations attributed to the word, suffering, when considered as permission, as Aitken suggests, engenders a deepening into life. We then can become open to suffer our pains and our pleasures, our terrors and our delights. Numbing or nulling out our capacity to suffer being human looms as an equally large problem as does the exquisiteness of felt suffering. Do oscillations engender balance points between insensate mindlessness and exquisite mindfulness where the impacts of life can be felt, experienced, permitted, endured, and allowed?

ENLIGHTENMENT

Enlightenment cuts through suffering, not by numbing it out or by mystical transcendence, which might provide temporary palliative relief, but by stripping away what it is that buffers or prevents suffering. Anna, for example, stays in bed. She attempts to avoid the fear and pain of being in the world. She avoids her pain and misses her passing life. Her depression functions to buffer what she might otherwise suffer so she keeps herself in a dreamless sleep. Anna lives at the perimeter of literal life and death, and she misses the wide-awake dream called life. Psychotherapy, for Anna, becomes a process of waking up to herself, her pains, and her joys.

Buddha literally means to be wide-awake. Being wide-awake means having the capacity to suffer. As seekers of Truth, we endeavor to tear away the psychic, emotional, and perceptual cocoons that we unconsciously spin in our misguided efforts to buffer suffering, to keep us dreaming, to keep us sleeping. From both the perspectives of Zen and psychoanalysis, being wide-awake, fully permitting the experience of life and enduring its impact fully remains a constant struggle. The poet Lucien Stryk points to this struggle by observing that " . . . awakened life is not a birthright but something to be won through, along a way beyond the self" (Stryk and Ikemoto 1991, xii). It would be a mistake to think otherwise. The Tibetan Buddhist, Chogyam Trungpa, makes this clear in the introduction to his influential book *The Myth of Freedom*. He writes:

> Many people respond to Buddhism as if it were a new cult which might save them, which might enable them to deal with the world in the manner of picking flowers in a beautiful garden. But if we wish to pick flowers from a tree, we must first cultivate the roots and trunk, which means we must work with our fears, frustrations, disappointments, and irritations, the painful aspects of life. (1976, 1)[3]

Suffering holds both violent and tender moments. Each wave of oscillation penetrates that much deeper and increases one's capacity to endure and permit what needs suffering and to see through the illusion and relinquish what need not be suffered. Scratching surfaces, digging deeper, hitting bedrock, one uncovers new surfaces to be scratched at, and then dug into if the pendulum had not swung back yet. The plunge into any spiritual practice that is supported by the formalized structure of a religious system contains both soft and rough edges, moments of equipoise and of chaos. Even solid bedrock can fragment into smithereens in the constant come-together break-apart life rhythms one inevitably encounters, whether suffered or not.

Accounts of literal and psychological violence, chaos, horror, and terror fill both the Zen and psychoanalytic literature. Maiming, dismemberment, and disfiguration appear as common Zen themes that express the intensity of desire for Truth (Suzuki 1949).

Here is a vignette from *Keitoku Dento-roku* (The Transmission of the Lamp) a classical collection of Zen koan that typifies this theme:

He [Shinko] went over there [Shorinji] and day and night beseeched Bodhidharma for instruction. The master always sat in zazen facing the wall and paid no attention to his entreaties. On the evening of December 9, heaven sent down a heavy snow. Shinko stood erect and unmoving. Toward daybreak the snow reached above his knees. The Master had pity on him and said, "You have been long standing in the snow. What are you seeking?" Shinko in bitter tears said, "I beseech you, O Master, with your compassion pray open your gate of Dharma and save all of us beings." The master said, "The incomparable Truth of the Buddha can only be attained by eternally striving, practicing what cannot be practiced and bearing the unbearable. How can you, with your little virtue, little wisdom, and with your easy and self-conceited mind, dare to aspire to attain the true teaching? It is only so much labor lost." Listening to the Master's admonition, Shinko secretly took out his sharp knife, himself cut off his own left arm, and placed it in front of the Master. The Master recognizing the Dharma[4] caliber told him, "Buddhas, when they first seek after the Truth, give no heed to their bodies for the sake of Dharma. You have now cut off your arm before me. I have seen the sincerity of your seeking." (Shibayama 1974, 287)

In his commentary to the text, Shibayama points out that "The above account is not in accordance with historically traceable facts. . . . But the painful and desperate struggle in seeking after the Truth, even at the risk of one's own life, is not a mythological fabrication by an old Zen Master. He who has experienced the same pain and hardship in really seeking the Truth cannot read just lightly as an old story" (287).

> The snow of Shorin is stained crimson,
> Let us dye our heart with it
> Humble though it may be

> (Shibayama, 287)

POETIC EXPRESSION

From a Christian perspective, Lynn Preston writes: "The artistic and poetic often provide the best handles for spiritual wisdom because they take us by surprise and break through our habitual expectancies" (2005, 208).

Indeed, consistent with Preston's observation, poetry constitutes an important aspect of the Zen religious literature. With regard to the spiritual force of Zen poetry, Lucian Stryk observes that "The point is that in Zen one must fathom more than the ordinary dualistic meaning of letters and words; that is, one must intuit Nothingness or Buddhahood, identifying oneself with it. This typical Zen experience is depicted more vigorously and succinctly in poetry than in prose. Appealing directly to one's feeling and volition, as poetry in general does, Zen poetry is more likely than Zen prose to enable one to make the leap to the ultimate Truth or, at least, deepen one's sense of Zen" (Stryk and Ikemoto 1973, xix). Needless to say, Zen poetry has increasingly become central to my practice and serves as a strong propellant for my oscillations.

Zen poets frequently speak of "void-splitting," "earth smashing to smithereens," "thunder and lightening," "ocean beds aflame," "leaping into the abyss," "letting go of one's hold on the precipice," and "swallowing molten iron balls, that cannot be vomited out" to describe the experience of Zen practice and awakening. The struggle involved in the stripping away of our self-imposed buffers to experience finds vivid expression in the following poem written by Muso, the thirteenth century Japanese Zen poet. He writes:

> Vainly I dug for a perfect sky,
> Piling a barrier all around.
> Then one black night, lifting a heavy
> Tile, I crushed the skeletal void![5]

Life and spiritual practice as an expression of life contains both sharp and soft aspects arising and falling in moments, lifetimes, and eternities. Soil encrusted seeds sprout, root, and give rise to thorny stems that support emerging roses.

Bion would say that effective practices create emotional turbulence and catastrophe (1965, 1970). However catastrophe and turbulence hold a necessary place in psycho-spiritual growth. Similarly, this theme asserts itself repeatedly and cogently in the Buddhist literature. Aitken, for example, notes that ". . . religious practice, no matter what the religion, is not necessarily joyous. People on the path commonly have a hard time with fear, terror, misery, and pain. One goes through this" (1994, 20). Light casts shadows and shadows cast light. Light and dark, day and night constitute oscillations of the clear sky that is neither dark nor light.

RESISTANCE

One might attribute the "out" aspect of the in and out oscillation of deepening involvement in psychoanalysis or Buddhist experience to resistance. Every opening becomes a closing to something else. A path taken becomes the many roads not taken. Resistance to what is known can become an opening to what remains unknown. Resistance as pure energy, accumulated, and stored, provides the force for smashing through the bedrock of reified states of self-deception. What we construct and hold up to be real protects us from the Real. Despite the choice of description, either as resistance, momentum building, or one of an infinite number of permutations of both, oscillations continue. Oscillating advances and retreats, ins and outs; a moment's movement spirals into infinity. One becomes lost in unfamiliar territory.

Time passes, with continued Buddhist practice and psychotherapy, perceptual alterations occur. Modes of being and relating to others in the world begin to shift. Both Buddhism and psychoanalysis converge, diverge, overlap, dovetail, dissolve, and intertwine. Practice engenders shifts in awareness and relatedness to self and other. Self might be taken more or less seriously, other more or less separately, depending on one's shifting perceptual vantage point.

AMBIVALENCE: LINEARITY—CIRCULARITY

The ghost moon
Pierced through by the oak branch
Bleeds snowflakes in the ink sky.

Ambivalence serves as an alternative explanation for resistance. Ambivalence contains both rough and soft edges from mild confusions to deep splits that cut through and divide the very core of being. Emotional splinters can magnify and evolve until they feel like stakes driven through the heart.

Ambivalence presents itself as a still-frame snapshot of imperceptibly slowed-down oscillations that at the extreme, freeze, and crack at fault lines. Cracks can expand into gaps of abysmal forbidding depth within the psyche. Melanie Klein speaks graphically of splits between internal and external reality, creative and destructive forces, joy, horror, love, and hate that derail natural movements. Bion adds the circular dimension of mystical experiencing to Klein's linear frame. He speaks of oscillations between being and knowing.[6] Bion also addresses relations between the medical and mystical points of view, the paranoid-schizoid and the depressive positions and between the container and contained, to name a few (1965, 1970).[7]

In my practice, psychoanalysis and Zen both further, become part of, and express natural rhythms. They are the warp and weft for weaving the seamless fabric for myriad oscillations. They form the structure and function that allows, encourages, restores, and sparks life. Like a haiku, they form a picture frame for whatever individual creativity might suggest. The movements charted by Zen/psychoanalytic oscillations weave together linear and circular elements, as the ongoing expanding and contracting infinity of the moment becomes significant—momentous.

Duality splits the universe and forces choices on us with both relinquishing and accumulating aspects. While on a retreat for psychotherapists organized by Cafh, a spiritual community near Tivoli, New York, the retreat participants were given the task of pruning fruit trees. This entailed examining clusters of young pears and snipping off the few smaller pears, leaving the remaining stronger fruits with better access to nutrients. Life and death decisions held in the palms of our hands. We live in a relative world. Subject and object discrimination gets one safely across busy streets.

Without disregarding the reality of ambivalence—caught between the reality of terror and the promise of delight, I find myself thinking about oscillations differently. They are inevitable, normal, necessary aspects of being when not derailed. From a linear model, the resistance function of ambivalence makes sense. Resistance inhibits growth, development, or progress. However, from a mystical perspective, resistance functions as a necessary aspect of oscillations. The natural circularity of life becomes revealed in oscillations. Many forms of circular movement exist. Spirals between definite and infinite express inner, outer, and in-between rhythms. Breathing, recurring thought patterns, transference generated repetition compulsions, seasons, tides. Macro and micro oscillations that circle inward and outward continue and are ever present unless derailed such as in derailment of introjective/projective cycles. The Zennist engages in endless rounds of chanting, bowing, and sitting meditation in the zendo. Patient and therapist participate together in recurring therapy sessions, transference and countertransference dynamic dramas, and emotional unfolding as they endure together the passing days, months, and years. Seeker, patient, and therapist alike begin again and again each term, year, week, day, and moment, in both real and phantasy time, that crystallize in both familiar and unfamiliar patterns and once again dissolve.

Fertility, lunar, solar, seasonal, and liturgical cycles continuously evolve. Young women with beating drums, rhythms pounding passionately, with abandon, refer to themselves collectively as "Seed." They sing songs that chronicle fertility, planting, sprouting, fullness, ripeness, and harvest around and around. In the fullness of raging passion, frenzy, they are alive, beautiful, beating drums and chanting lyrics until audience and performer distinctions dissolve, and the entire room becomes caught in the rhythm of one undulating oscillation. Together, we feel the Earth moving beneath us.

Rhythms intensify. Rhythms prime the ecstasy pump of orgasm—sexual, physical, emotional, artistic, psychic, and spiritual. Sufi whirling dervishes circle in and out of mystical union. Lovers circle in and out of climax . . . Molly Bloom screams "Yes!" It comes as no surprise that Bion chose "O" to represent the ineffable, unsayable, and unknowable ultimate Truth. In this respect, psychotherapy can be understood as igniting, reigniting, or rerailing oscillation processes; reshaping deformed oscillations, and finding balance points between diffusion and contraction.

Can linear and circular movements coexist? Perhaps lines are short arcs of wider circles with dimensions too vast to perceive. Perhaps circular movements flow along a linear plane. Perhaps lines and circles are natural rhythms that constitute oscillations. Despite one's speculations and conceptualizations, oscillations exist. Human beings: living/dying, loving/hating, working/ playing, asleep/awake, eating/shitting, bingeing/ purging, flesh and blood oscillation machines with heart.

THE ZENDO

One point along the oscillations of Zen practice that can up the intensity of involvement and practice to larger than life proportions occurs during *sesshin* (extended silent retreat). This point, when magnified, reveals micro oscillations within a frame not unlike the passing of day and night in the larger flow of changing seasons.

> Sesshin passes
> Bell by bell—
> What is the end?
>
> (Aitken 1978, 42)

Sesshin takes place in the zendo. This space is generally decorated with only the essential ritual items: a minimal altar adorned with a Buddha, arranged flowers, candle, and incense burner. The zendo feels clean, sparse, but not lacking. Round black zafus (cushions) in the center of larger square cushions line the hall or room in neat orderly rows for individuals to sit on. Many of the ritual items reflect a Spartan parsimony and efficiency of purposeful management. For example, a bell signals the ongoing beginnings and endings of silent sitting meditation periods. Wooden clappers signal the retreat participants to stand up, to walk, and to sit again. During the ninth century, the Chinese emperor Wu persecuted Zen Buddhism for economic reasons. Zen minimalism accounts for its survival during the time. Kenneth Ch'en points out that Zen's " . . . lack of dependence on the external paraphernalia of the religion, such as scriptures, images and so forth, enabled it to function and carry on even after the destruction of such externals."[8]

At first glance, Japanese ritual chanting feels magical, mystical, and occult. Chanting simultaneously clears the space, centers the practitioner, and invokes the strength and power of honored ancestors. Chanting reaffirms our commitment to Buddha, dharma (path), and sangha (spiritual community). Together, we celebrate life and the dependently arising circumstances that result in the auspicious nature of the present moment, the unfolding karmic circumstances that place us in a position to be exposed to the dharma, as a sangha.

Upon entering the zendo, I feel a twinge of anxiety. The structure of the zendo is something that I initially rebelled against, as it evoked many unpleasant memories regarding my early parochial school education. Perfectly lined up zafus remind me of elementary school seats nailed to the classroom floor, in neat orderly rows, preassigned, rigid overregimentation, corporal punishment, silence observed even at lunch. Stern grim-faced nuns monitor our every move. We eat without liquids and are punished for smiling. The lack of spontaneity in the classroom engenders deadness. I am ridiculed for drawing outside the lines and for mixing crayon colors in my vain efforts to capture reality. I try to obliterate the black outlines in the coloring book figures as black lines do not define us in the real world. My work is held up as an example of what not to do. Ridicule and humiliation douses my nascent creative sparks. Sadism, reigns in the form of excessive punishment witnessed by peers. Punishment, rationalized as sound discipline, engenders shame and destroys emerging glimpses of self. These long repressed memories return during extended periods of zazen. I begin to see how they color my present landscape.

During sitting periods, an assigned monk circles the room periodically offering to relieve tense muscles on the shoulders and back by striking the meditator with a hardwood stick. Initially, I wince and my body literally shakes to the cracking sound of the stick. The stick used to release tension from the meditator's backs and shoulders is so reminiscent of the stick used by the nuns for punishment. I then rationalize: "why would I put myself in this horrific situation?" Old coping mechanisms, that helped me survive the elementary school classroom become activated in the present and automatically go into operation. My mind shifts out of the present to passing time, fantasies, daydreams, and concerns of before and after. Dissociated mind states follow.

A warm, personable young monk in black robes, wearing a disarming smile just below his clean-shaven head provides unobtrusive, cryptic yet precise instructions for sitting zazen. His minimalism supports and reflects the teaching that one finds one's own way. I am told "Bring your attention down to the lower abdomen and simply follow the breath." Eventually, "count the breath." "Be the breath!" My rebelliousness becomes an obstacle. The fact that I was initially rebellious got worked through practice and deeper familiarity with the process and the structure. However, psychoanalytic formulations provide meaning for these dynamics detailing names and faces as internal object relations become conscious. My early experiences in the parochial school engendered stress, anxiety, and damage to self-esteem. Early anxieties become unconsciously reified and create fixation points that become activated along with associated self states in seemingly similar circumstances. I find myself feeling like the frightened boy of childhood anticipating a thrashing with a stick from an irate nun or parent. My body becomes tense, my posture rigid as I sense the monk slowly approaching. As he passes, I feel relief. Through deeper involvement these unconscious aspects can be exposed and named. Blind reactions, once revealed can be questioned. However, when not fully conscious of these processes, I become caught in a perceptual identity between the Zendo and the parochial grammar school. Black-robed monks, heads clean-shaven replace black-robed nuns—heads covered. I am caught and despite years of psychoanalysis, initially, I don't know it.

However, with continued practice and deepening familiarity with both inner experience and external structure juxtaposed, the zendo space and the discipline evolves into a holding environment that makes it possible for me to do everything I am there to do, as all incidentals and concerns are taken care of through the structure.

I am a spiritual fetus (seed) incubating (germinating) held safely in the room (womb) of the Zendo. I am planted in a place where I can grow from. Can I ripen and bloom forth at my own pace in my own time? Does the retreat provide a viable option to the suffering-resistant psychic cocoon wrapped tightly around my psychic skin? Sesshin remains highly defined and structured, yet simultaneously it also remains ambiguous enough to execute the necessary stripping away that I need to do in my own way. It eventually becomes clear to me that there is nothing parochial about it.

The booming predawn bell signals the approaching day. Time to wake up, wash, dress, and quickly find my way into the zendo to a preassigned seat on the zafu. Up for rapid *kinhin* (walking meditation). Almost at a run, kinhin at dawn gets the blood flowing, the body moving and warmed up. Morning prayers and settling into rounds of zazen interspersed with slow kinhin before breakfast. After breakfast, preassigned chores are done in silence. We then return to the zendo, at the sound of a bell, for more rounds of sitting, chanting, and walking until the lunch bell rings. After a short break, nap, and perhaps a walk outdoors, we then return to the zendo for rounds of sitting, walking, chanting, a dharma talk, dinner, after dinner zazen, walking, and an interview with the Roshi. Bedtime and then the cycle repeats. Cycles within cycles occur. Breathing, counting breaths, silent repetition of the sound Mu, heartbeats, temples pounding, bells clapped, passing moments, minutes, hours, days, eternities.

PASSION AND RAGE

Passion is primary, emerging from the heart center. Passion is the rhythm of the heart and the heartbeat of psychic life. Eastern wisdom depicts mind as residing in the heart, not the head. Buddhism, as an egalitarian reaction to Bramanic Indian caste structures renders passion universal, not just reserved for an enlightened elite. Buddhist cosmology describes both god realm and hell realm passions in both states of ecstasy and equipoise. However, for the most part, in my experience, Zen Buddhism does not deal fully with emotional life. For example, The *Cheng Tao Ke* (Song of Realization), asserts that "The Buddha's doctrine of directness/is not a matter of human emotion."[9] This lack of attention to emotional life in Zen practice and the interference it creates with regard to deepening involvement in Buddhist practice can be addressed by psychoanalysis.

The Buddhist belief is that overemphasis on emotional life will obscure the practitioner's realization of ultimate reality because the transient emotions such as anger, love, hurt, envy, for example, are aspects of the phenomenal world or relative reality. Commenting on the relation between emotions and realization, Robert Aitken writes that "Emotion is a condition; it comes and goes, and usually has no lasting importance or significance. Taking it upon ourselves, or projecting it upon others, obscures the fact with which we must work" (1978, 114). Despite the truth of this admonition, repression, denial, disavowal, or dissociation are not viable alternatives to overemphasis on emotional experience. Barry Magid (2002), who brings the nondualist philosophy of Zen into experiential terms points out that dissociation of emotional life functions as an internal form of dualistic thinking. The problem, as I see it, lies in an unhealthy avoidance or wholesale denial of emotions and their significance for the individual's internal world and with regard to one's relationship to self, others, and to practice. When not attended to, unconscious emotions become acted out and interfere with practice and with life in the way Aitken describes. The issue, however, becomes one of degree. That is, emotions need to be addressed, not obsessed about nor denied. Neither overindulgence nor denial are tenable.

In his monumental groundbreaking work *The Interpretation of Dreams* (1900), Sigmund Freud speaks of transference simply as the movement of pure energy from one psychic system to another. Energy manifests, crystallizing into form, oscillations of feeling and form, shape and perception in cycles of projection/introjection hurled from psychic location to psychic location, from person to person, body to body, psyche to psyche, and heart to heart. I will focus here on the anger/passion permutation, one current in the wider stream of flowing agony/ecstasy oscillations.

Passion/rage permutations mark an experiential converging point between time spent on the zafu and time spent on the analytic couch. Through Zen I become sensitized to both subtle and powerful energies. Buddhists often view anger as reflecting separation, unfulfilled longing. Sometimes separations are what we seek, especially during the experience of self-fragmentation such as in psychosis or when the oneness of mystical union is imminent. When approaching infinity, passion evolves into compassion. Dissolved subject and object distinctions close the you/me gap. The thirteenth century Zen master Dogen notes that "when I sit, the world sits, when I am Buddha, the world is Buddha." In Zen parlance, it occurs when the ten thousand things become the One. Similarly, from a psychoanalytic perspective, Matte-Blanco (1988) asserts that in the Alice in Wonderland logic of the unconscious, everything becomes everything else.

What is the psychic distance between the promise of something happening, (being innocently expected) being given and taken away? The promise of satori (enlightenment), teachings, connectedness, with self, with other, with what is beyond self and other distinctions, teachers, Buddha, waiting, sitting, and waiting. Zazen locates raw emotion, thought, and sensation. Mind then identifies the experience. With regard to emerging anger, through continued concentrated practice I feel the bubbling over, watch the volcanic eruption, watch self, selves, others, form, melt crystallize, shatter in permutations of liquid psychic lava, and emotional upsurge and outflow. Prolonged zazen increases the capacity for handling geometrically increasing intensities. However, in retrospect, I realize that it is psychoanalysis that gives meaning to bits and pieces of raw experience in terms of names and places, selves, and objects.[10] Continued sitting in the wider oscillations of both processes, as aspects of this one larger process, brings into the present situation an awareness of inner obstructions and dissolves anger, if suffered, which transforms into passion. Passion, longing for union with the divine, lover, universe, teachings, truth, life, death, moment, infinite moment, and intimate contact with the depths of one's own being, with what Zen describes as the face before I was born. Passion of forms and images swirling, spewing multicolored mind flowers, that blossom and melt away to the limits of what I can take and then back to breathing and sitting, the ringing bell. Up and slow walking once again.

I sit with rage and find myself opening into passion or perhaps passion opening into what I imagine is "the me." Rage, passion's seal and signpost, opening and/or closing—lock and key. Zen's gateless gate. "Mu" Barrier and entrance all in one. Can rage intensify and burn through enough of me to reveal itself as passion? Can one grow through rage, past rage's destructiveness until it burns itself into passion? From this zafu, if I embrace the horror and disturbance of felt rage, I can embrace the enlivening fires of passion. I swallow fire and dream rainbows. Fire—pure energy transforms into a multifaceted gem, a spring cornucopia of blossoming psychic flowers. Rage, passion's burning bush. The deadliness of rage can feed the aliveness of passion. Raging passions, passionate rages. The serpent swallows its own tail and dissolves into infinity. Rage feels tense, tight, constricted in my body, nerves, muscles, bones, and joints. The ache intensifies. Each heartbeat ripples through the body into the limbs, joints, and to the ends of my fingers and toes. Thoughts become simultaneously effusive and restricted. Tight oscillations spinning out from hurt, indignation, disappointment, failed grasping, tighter and tighter circles of thought and feeling continue spinning around repetitive motifs. Tightening qualities of rage conceal openings to passion. I am not referring to a love/hateand passion/rage dialectic tension. Beyond these posited dualities, I refer to the experience of pure energy, emerging from and permeating every cell and fiber of my being; the pure fluid energy with rage/passion aspects, rising in and out of form with varying proportions, with degrees of intensity and color. Yet, when the tail of rage's tiger is fully grasped, embraced, it *becomes* passion; passion, a multifaceted gem that crystallizes into form and action. Permutations of lived passion: for peace, creature comforts, foods, Eros, connectedness, aliveness, flesh pleasures, music, passion for writing, painting, creating and destroying, orgasmic passions, kitchen sink passions, dish washing, garbage collecting, and removing (All of it!) Psychoanalytic and Zen passions; passions for beginnings, becomings, and endings; passions that oscillate between work and play and love and hate mutually consumed and consuming. Play transforming to work, work becoming play. Love and hate passions that become split asunder, dissolve, and merge.

Passion energies can expand and crystallize into form, such as in religious dogma. Self and object separations engendered by splitting and concretization processes, for instance, manifest as competing dogmas that result in doctrinal disputes. Peace and turbulence passions raged on for centuries in debates between the mind-pacifying and insight engendering Zen schools culminating in the so-called Northern and Southern Schools. Death passions find an epitome of artistic and spiritual expression in the highly regarded death poems of the great Zen masters.

> Life's as we
> Find it—death too.
> A parting poem?
> Why insist?

(Date-Soko, 1089–1163)[11]

At the extreme, peace/turbulence evolve into life and death passions. The consequences can be far-reaching. The radical misguided Moslem Jihad represents a contemporary manifestation with horrific global life and death implications.

Rage expresses separation and subject and object disconnection but also functions to maintain self/other distinctions. Dualistic thinking splits rage/ passion, creating and perpetuating a seemingly unbridgeable gap between. Access to passion becomes lost. The multifaceted gem that life can be becomes flattened and one-dimensional.

Oscillating through the amorphous, global, and intuitive felt Zen experience to the specificity provided through the psychoanalytic encounter has me becoming the child who waits for his mother; the ideal mother who never comes, who promises to come, but fails. The too-far-gone mother never returns. The mother whose own mother descended from banished royalty. The idealized ancestral fantasy mother disowned and banished for living her passions with a common man. The mother who makes promises she wishes to but cannot ever keep. Failed promises and longings become bedrock and when shattered become pathways, concretized images that embody deeper unremembered longings, broken promises before promises were ever made. Womb promises, shattered by too soon birth, induced labors, and forced deliveries. What is Truth? Is it motherly love or reaction formation to hidden passion/rage that finds it impossible to hold her infant in her arms? Do oscillations circle between the fear of dropping and the wish to smash? The infant dropped too soon into labor bears the scar of the violence of forceps forced birth on his temple, an ever-present reminder to a pregnant mother that she let her son be torn away too soon. Too soon a relinquishing of the child from the womb. Does the broken unspoken promise of reward, gratification, and unavailable nourishment from a willing spirit with an unwilling breast become the palate from which present experience and expectations derive their color? Overlays of color obscure the moment's truth despite the suddenly emerging force of past memories, equally part of the same moment. When cut through by embrace, anger energies transform into passion energies. When pulling on the rage thread, passion unravels. When following the passion thread, what will one find? Fear can engender a full circle back to the safety of anger. Anger can exert itself to resist the fruits of passion.

> Anger, fear, passion, from this cushion
> where a hungry dawn
> swallows raging stars from an ink sky.

What is it like to be my pregnant mother, to be pregnant with me, her son? She knew—of course, a son—to be the son within her womb? Mother and son—one! What was it like to have the womb son ripped away too soon? Whose longings are these that I feel when plunging into abysmal emptiness and despair? Is it hers or mine? Both? The aged mother of my present, memory shattered by senility, but speaks with poignant intact passion of her son. "I miss my son, my son, my love." The mother whose own mother was taken away too soon, through poor health, leaving her daughter fragile, broken, in the care of older siblings and foster parents. Slipping away from womb, loins, arms, eyes, and life too short to realize her own passion now lived through me, her son, through my longings and passions. Passions become actualized and given form through my activity, Zen, analysis, work, writing, music, family, and children.

> from this zafu,
> just past the open window,
> between bare branches
> the rising dawn sun shimmers
> on a wind-rippled lake.

AARON'S JOURNEY

> You all look for a good teacher and try to speculate. Make no mistake, followers of the way, after all, you have a mother and a father. What else is there that you need to know?
>
> (Rinzai)[12]

While the great Zen master Rinzai was intending a somewhat different meaning, his comment holds relevance to the psychotherapeutic situation. Psychoanalysis conceptualizes oscillations through the notion of transference. Freud (1914) describes transference as an unconscious compulsion to repeat. Repetition functions as a closed circle, endlessly replaying. Psychotherapy can open such stagnant and closed circles and thus can restore the open-ended oscillations necessary for growth, for deepening into experience. However, as a closed circle, transference functions as a kind of bedrock.

Transference, or to state it differently, what an individual brings to and finds; what an individual looks for in terms of gratifications and disappointments; brings in terms of self-fulfilling expectations that can engender a vicious cycle in terms of unconsciously motivated enactments; that when they actualize are no longer unconscious (the meaning might remain so). What the individual brings to any situation in terms of old lenses to peer through will contribute to both erroneous and false perceptions. These false perceptions can then often be rationalized in idiosyncratic "understanding" of Buddhist principles and practices and in misinterpretations of personal experiences. These misinterpretations then result in responses to the situation based on unconscious organizing principles that color one's experiences and expectations of others such as the Zen teacher. Facing bedrock, psychotherapy can provide the names and faces and facilitate penetrating the illusions that might otherwise maintain transference repetitions and stifle life in general and Buddhist practice in particular. When understood psychoanalytically, the student can cut through idiosyncratic colorations, old unworkable organizing principles, projections and, as a result, develop a more accurate perception of Buddhist principles and practices and deepen one's participation during the retreat situation. The following case demonstrates these abstract principles.

Aaron, a serious, dedicated, long-term Zen practitioner and psychoanalytic candidate, unconsciously circles through unnamed repetitions that function as closed circles. Despite the unrelenting intensity of his Zen practice and his sensitivity to his emotional life, he has hit bedrock. He continuously drifts in and out of involvement with the Zen group and the teacher that he practices with. Aaron rationalizes his withdrawals, attributing them to professional and family commitments. The combined impact of both psychoanalysis and Zen practice facilitates Aaron's capacity for identifying and breaking out of closed circles and for engendering deepened involvement in his Zen discipline. This comes about through involvement in personal psychoanalysis and training analysis that engenders insight not available, in my opinion, exclusively, if at all, through Buddhist practice, despite the intensity of one's practice. Once internalized into a cognitive style of processing experience, psychoanalytically engendered insights can be exploited through further self-analysis and through conversations during the analytic sessions to identify the ways one creates obstacles and openings. Aaron's obstacles centered on the enactment of old transference repetitions that became activated in relation to the Roshi.

The Interview

While zazen, a form of concentrated meditation practice, commonly referred to as "sitting," constitutes the predominant activity, during sesshin, the core dialogue, dokusan, or one-to-one interview with the teacher facilitates the deepening of experience and insight.[13] In dokusan the student and teacher meet face-to-face. What occurs during this interview, which unlike the psychoanalytic session is rather brief, supports the student's otherwise solitary efforts.[14]

Obtaining an interview becomes seemingly difficult. However, sooner or later, everyone gets to speak with the Roshi periodically throughout the retreat. While there are realities to a teacher's restricted or limited availability, Aaron's internal processes, contribute significantly to his perception of the teacher's availability.

Aaron speaks of the difficulty associated with obtaining an interview with the Roshi. Certain ritualized procedures contribute to this difficulty in reality. However, for Aaron, the interview process becomes seemingly impossibly difficult due to the mobilization of his own early internal objects, associated feelings, and resulting perceptions. He has described his parents as unavailable both emotionally and physically. Aaron was a latchkey kid. He had to fend for himself. He spent long hours alone after school. Fear and loneliness remained his constant companions. He feared the onset of dusk, the encroaching chill of night. He imagined noises emanating from the basement. The parental mandate that he not invite others into the home when unsupervised further intensified his fear and feelings of isolation. Both parents worked long hours but were emotionally unavailable when home due to fatigue and frustration combined with their own emotional issues. This was particularly significant with Aaron's father whom Aaron described as schizoid and deeply depressed. Through a combination of fatigue, depression, and difficulties with intimacy, his father frequently left Aaron up to his own devices. Aaron's excitement engendered by the possibility of being with his father whom he loved and idealized was frequently crushed by rejecting comments, such as "don't you have something to do?" Aaron remembers withdrawing, feeling disappointed, alienated, and bewildered. His father perhaps did not know how to participate as an available father due to the lack of any model. His own father abandoned his family and died as a result of complications related to alcohol abuse when Aaron's father was in his early teens. Since he had lost his father during adolescence and was forced to fend for himself during the Depression, he saw no harm in demanding that Aaron "do things for himself." His refusal of support reflected this inner emotional state. In his words: "You will be stronger and the result will be that you will feel more valuable if you do it all for yourself without my help or guidance." Thus he became, in actuality, the unavailable father that he grew up with, despite any merit in his rationalization. He simply was not emotionally available for involvement with his son.

Unconsciously, for Aaron, the Roshi came to represent an emotionally unavailable father. To clarify this point further, had Aaron's father allowed himself to be emotionally available for his son, Aaron would have experienced his father's stance very differently, despite his long workday. He would have felt emotionally connected. This early relational dynamic now internalized as part of Aaron's inner object world colored his experience of the teacher. Thus he (mis)understood his teacher's admonishment as implied in the above quote from Rinzai "You need to find out for yourself" and "all the necessary resources are within" came to represent a tired, depressed, and withdrawn father's admonitions: "don't bother me," "stop pestering me," "find something to do." This was disappointing to the son who idealized his father and missed him during the long working hours of the workweek. The feelings were activated through long hours on the Zafu in-between brief interviews with the Roshi. Typically his father would be gone before Aaron would wake up in the morning and would return home after he was asleep. Alternatively, he would return home in such a tired and irritated condition that he would not be approachable. Aaron gradually withdrew into himself.

To further complicate matters, Aaron's mother, could be attentive to her son. However he served her narcissistic needs. That is, Aaron became a temporary stand-in for her absent husband. He described feeling "shelved" upon his father's arrival home, resulting in a double feeling of loss. She failed to respond to his uniqueness and to the fear, anxiety, and isolation he experienced during her absence. He gradually gave up and withdrew into himself. Thus, as Aaron said, as he related this to me during a post-retreat therapy session, "a conscious rationalized voice admonished me to not 'bother' the Roshi unless absolutely necessary." Not unlike dad, he must be much too tired to deal with the needs and demands of this entire group of people. The fact that the Roshi was suffering cold symptoms seriously curtailed his interview time, further strengthened Aaron's rationalization, and mobilized Aaron's internal imago of his unavailable father.

Aaron's erroneous reading of the Roshi's message blinded him to fact that the Roshi was also saying in many ways that "You need to discover for yourself *and* I [Roshi], we [sangha], zendo are all here to help you succeed through concern, support, one-to-one dialogue, understanding, and fellowship." While this was clearly articulated throughout the sesshin in many ways, none of this reached Aaron. So, he went back to his cushion after an interview of two minds. Consciously, the interview was energizing and positive and he thought to himself: "Wow, I am whole and complete just as I am."

Less consciously, this feeling of wholeness and completeness engendered an illusion of self-sufficiency, which took the form: "well, then, I don't need to speak with the Roshi, and I don't really need to be here, I can do this all at home, alone." Underneath the latter reaction was a strong feeling of talionic rage that eventually emerged as "If you are too busy, tired, sick to see me, if you are going to make it so difficult for us to talk, after all of the sacrifices I made to be here, then 'Fuck you too.'" "You are not giving me any attention; I won't give any to you. If you would rather be talking to someone else, the hell with it!" "I will show him, I will do it myself." "OK he is tired, I am too much for him, I will take care of myself."

Aaron's position on the interview line mobilized a paranoid structure. This requires some explanation. Aaron firmly believed that his preassigned seat in the Zendo, which he assumed was structured by the Roshi, had the sole intention of keeping him away. Legitimate prioritizing exacerbated Aaron's fantasy and associated anger. For example, monks running the retreat who could not compete for spaces in line were permitted to cut the line. The reality that monks assigned to run the retreat were given priority on the interview line so they could get back to their assignments, such as cooking and preparing meals in a timely manner, exacerbated Aaron's rage. Aaron became particularly upset when women were given priority. He interpreted this experience as being ignored by his parents. It was the initial lack of consciousness of this anger that facilitated a schizoid withdrawal (not unlike the childhood withdrawal described above). This withdrawal took the form of a wish to leave the zendo forever and to a loss of motivation to continue with interviews, to daydream during meditation periods, and at the extreme, to dissociate. This latter point will be come clear with some explanation of the interview process.

A striking bell signals that the interview line has just opened. A second bell is struck signaling the students to form a line. A mad rush ensues that is diametrically counter to the highly ritualized and controlled manner that every other aspect of the retreat is conducted. People are told there are no rules, etiquette, or manners to be observed to find one's place in the interview line. One's seat in the zendo, which is predetermined by the sesshin organizers, determines what one's chances are for reasonably expecting to actually have an interview in the time allocated for the interview period. Individuals at the end of the line are not likely to be granted an interview. However, they are given priority during the next interview period. A ringing bell signals priority students to find their places in the interview line before the mad rush ensues. Aaron had unconsciously blocked out this fact. Eventually, he realized that he was confused about the details of this procedure. He wondered about his confusion since this procedure was clearly and carefully explained to each retreat participant during a preretreat orientation. In retrospect, Aaron realized that he had blocked out this information, thinking, "I don't need advice, I will take care of myself." He recounted during his therapy session after the retreat that as he sat with the emerging awareness of confusion, he became increasingly aware of a deep fear. This fear was directed toward the nun assigned to monitor the line and who was available to answer questions. His fear was further exacerbated by memories of severe punishment for not paying attention in school. Further introspection stirred up old tapes relating again to cranky, critical, and unavailable parents. They would react negatively, even violently, should he express a problem usually related to school problems of both a social and academic nature upon their return from their long workday. As Aaron's awareness grew, his anxiety increased. The source of his anxiety rooted in these early memories gradually became clear though continued introspection. This awareness enabled Aaron to risk approaching the seemingly cold, stern, rigid nun. He was both surprised and relieved with the actuality of her gentle smile and warmth. Unlike his parents, or his childhood tormentors, she gave Aaron her full and patient attention. She slowly and carefully explained the procedure, took him under her wing, and guided him step-by-step through the process. Aaron was relieved and felt soothed by her warmth, compassion, and calming strength. This encounter also popped the bubble of his projection. His anger and anxiety evaporated. He approached the interview feeling somewhat embarrassed but with fortified confidence and renewed strength.

Aaron was then faced with his intellectual defense that he armed himself to approach the face-to-face interview with the Roshi. This took the form of an offense of a very clever and accurate wordplay based on his previous interview. His stance, which he was becoming aware of, reminded him of a familiar style of relatedness that operated consistently with me during his therapy sessions. We had worked on Aaron's relational style extensively. During the interview, Aaron made excellent and valid points related to the previous interview and the day's lecture. However, as the Roshi was in actuality *not* Aaron's father, actually a very different type of person, he perked up with keen interest when Aaron posed the questions. A lively banter ensued. Aaron was taken by surprise (unconsciously expecting a disinterested, disconnected, depressed and fatigued father). He gave Aaron terse, yet gentle specific answers to his questions. He was fully present with Aaron, despite Aaron's concerns that "I was taking up too much of his time." But more important, he worked through Aaron's resistance playfully and with a full sense of relatedness that resulted in a strong and heartfelt connection. Aaron left the interview feeling strength, energy, renewed vitality, and a sudden awareness of his own issue, which he became motivated to talk about with me during therapy. The ensuing weeks in analysis led to important discussions of how this dynamic extended beyond the retreat and inhibited Aaron's professional growth and personal life.

However, the point that begs stressing here is that Aaron was able to work out his projection during the retreat, as he was able to process his experience through the lens of his psychoanalytic training and through his psychotherapy. This is important. Prolonged sitting meditation releases blocks to unconscious processes and provides awareness of behaviors, feelings, and relations. However, the psychoanalytic understanding of how object relations become internalized gives specific "names" to these states and how they contribute to a false perception of experience and promote old cycles. The retreat becomes a place to work out these issues because of the heightened awareness, opening of primary process, and also because over a period of psychoanalysis, Aaron had internalized a cognitive processing style reflecting a new object relation with his analyst and reflecting the deepening free-associative inquiry and insights available through the psychoanalytic process. In other words, meaning comes to be attributed to experiences that were previously unconscious. Meaning engendered through self-introspection and through psychotherapy provides meaning to emerging pieces of raw experience and permits access to deeper and more productive involvement in Zen practice as Aaron was now able to make better use of his practice. This newly formed relationship with the Roshi was characterized by shared warmth, excitement, and a playful mutual curiosity. Through experiencing the genuine interest and the emotional availability of his analyst, Aaron was able to consolidate a sense of self, experienced as self-confident, creative, and articulate.

NOTES

1. Quoted in S. Mitchell (1989, p. 70).
2. Meditation hall.
3. Dorothy Yang discusses this issue of the American distortion of Buddhism in chapter 10, "Staying Honest."
4. Dharma: Buddhist doctrine, the law of cause and effect, phenomena and things.
5. In L. Stryk and T. Ikemoto, 1991, p. 24.
6. For a detailed discussion of being and knowing in Zen and psychoanalysis, see P. Cooper (2001a).
7. For a detailed discussion of Bion's container—contained dynamic in relation to Buddhist experience, see P. Cooper (2001b).
8. In John Wu (1996, p. 84).

9. In Robert Aitken, (1978, p. 114).

10. Jeffrey Rubin discusses the place of meaning in Buddhist practice in detail in chapter 7, "Through the Net."

11. In L. Stryk and T. Ikmoto (1991, p. 18).

12. Paraphrased from a talk given by Rev. Eido Shimano, Roshi, abbot of Dai Bosatsu Zendo, Livingston Manor, New York, December 2, 2001.

13. I am hesitant to say "facilitates progress or growth" despite the validity of such outcomes. They seem secondary to the deepening into one's capacity for awareness and involvement with the present moment as it is. Susan Rudnick explores the issue of presence in depth in chapter 2,"Coming Home to Wholeness."

14. The master does not teach in the didactic sense, although practical questions might be discussed and answered. Realization rests solely on the student's shoulders. In this sense the master can be said to "witness" the student's understanding.

REFERENCES

Aitken, R. (1978). *A Zen wave: Basho's haiku and Zen.* New York: Weatherhill.

———. (1991). *The gateless barrier: The Wu-men Kuan (Mumonkan).* New York: North Point Press.

———. (1994). *The practice of perfection: The paramitas from a Zen Buddhist perspective.* Washington, DC: Counterpoint, (1997).

Bion, W. (1965). *Transformations.* London: Karnac Books.

———. (1970). *Attention and Interpretation.* London: Karnac Books.

Cooper, P. (2001a). The gap between: Being and knowing in Zen Buddhism and psychoanalysis. *American Journal of Psychoanalysis,* 61(4), 341–62.

———. (2001b). Clouds into rain. *Journal of Religion and Health,* 40(1), 167–84.

———. (2004). Oscillations: Zen and psychoanalytic versions. *Journal of Religion and Health,* 43(3), 233–43.

Eigen, M. (1993). Breathing and identity. In *The electrified tightrope,* ed. A Phillips, 43–47. Northvale, NJ: Jason Aronson.

Freud, S. (1900). The interpretation of dreams. In *The standard edition of the complete psychological works of Sigmund Freud, IV,* ed. and trans. J. Strachey, 1–338. London: Hogarth Press (1953–1974).

———. (1914). Remembering, repeating, working through. In *The standard edition of the complete psychological works of Sigmund Freud, XII,* ed. and trans. J. Strachey, 145–56. London: Hogarth Press (1953–1974).

Joyce, V. (2005). Faith links. In *Psychotherapy and religion: Many paths, one journey,* ed. M. Bakur Weiner, P. Cooper, et al., 103–32. Montvale, NJ: Jason Aronson.

Magid, B. (2002). Ordinary mind. Boston: Wisdom Publications.

Matte-Blanco, I. (1988). Thinking, feeling, and being: Clinical reflections on the fundamental antinomy of human beings and world. New York: Routledge.

Mitchell, S. (1989). *The enlightened heart.* New York: Harper Collins.

Pfunder, J. (2005). Sufi meditations on psychotherapy. In *Psychotherapy and religion: Many paths, one journey,* ed. M. Bakur Weiner, P. Cooper, et al., 133–65. Montvale, NJ: Jason Aronson.

Preston, L. (2005). A Christian self psychological perspective. In *Psychotherapy and religion: Many paths, one journey*, ed. M. Bakur Weiner, P. Cooper, et al., 207–32. Montvale, NJ: Jason Aronson.

Shibayama, Z. (1974). *The gateless barrier: Zen comments on the Mumonkan.* Trans. S. Kudo. Boston, MA: Shambhala (2000).

Stryk, L., and T. Ikemoto, trans. (1973). *Zen poems of China and Japan: The crane's bill.* New York: Grove Press.

———. (1991). *Zen poetry: Let the spring breeze enter.* New York: Grove Press.

Suzuki, D. T. (1949). *Essays in Zen Buddhism: First series.* London: Rider & Co.

Trungpa, C. (1976). *The myth of freedom.* Boulder and London: Shambhala.

Wu, J. (1996). *The golden age of Zen.* New York: Image Books.

Chapter Ten

Staying Honest:
How Might Psychoanalysis
Benefit Buddhist Practitioners

Dorothy Yang

When Paul Cooper first approached me four years ago about writing a chapter for his book on psychoanalysis and Buddhism, I thought about a topic that has long captured my interest. How might psychoanalysis benefit Buddhist practitioners? As a practicing Buddhist and psychoanalyst, I have been curious about the possibilities of cross-fertilizations of the two traditions. Both disciplines share the same goal: to alleviate suffering. However, analysis deals with the suffering of one person, the patient, while Buddhism focuses on all sentient beings, including oneself. The two also differ in the methods and techniques of how to go about the practice of freeing oneself and others from suffering. There are many kinds of sufferings. In psychoanalysis, the focus is on the mental obscurations, what Buddhists call *kleshas*.[1] Before one can do something about these habitual patterns that cause suffering, one has to recognize them.

I was never more aware of my own habitual patterns than when I began to write this chapter. I experienced many of the obscuring emotions that underlie the experience of suffering. These emotions, known in Buddhism as the three poisons or three impediments include attachment (fixation on desires, benefits), aversion, and ignorance. I began this chapter full of excitement, ambition, and sense of grandiosity of how I might contribute to the actual benefit of Buddhist practitioners. As the writing progressed, doubts about my ability, skill, and motivation increased until they grew into mountainous proportions. Where do I begin? What do I include? Can I possibly cover everything that is important? Do I know enough about the topic to write about it? Fears of revealing my shortcomings and inadequacies periodically took over. Did I really want to expose "my self" to other people? My need for control made me feel even less in control. I took long breaks from writing to get back to what felt true to me. As the renowned Tibetan teacher, Chogyam Trungpa Rinpoche, wrote in his book *Cutting Through Spiritual Materialism*, the problem that comes up is that ego can convert anything to its own use, even spirituality. Ego is constantly trying to appropriate spirituality for its own benefit, to maintain a solid sense of self.[2] I considered quitting the project all together.

I began to do more Buddhist practice and visited my teachers at their monastery. In particular, both the practice of tranquility meditation (Tibetan: Shinay) and tonglen, a meditation in compassion, helped me to deal with attachment and clinging. For example, with continued practice, shinay calms down my mind and settles my ups and downs. Tonglen helped me to ease up on myself by diminishing my tendency toward self-judgment. One day, I read something that encouraged me to continue with the project. In her book, *Comfortable with Uncertainty* (2002), Pema Chodron reminded me of a basic Buddhist teaching, the importance of developing *maitri* or loving kindness toward others and toward *oneself*. The chapter will write itself. Yes, what I know is enough. I can put into use both my psychoanalytic training and Buddhist practice. More equanimous thoughts embraced my anxieties. I was inspired by what Rinpoche said in his book, *First Thought, Best Thought* (Trungpa 1983). He wrote, "Buddhism doesn't tell you what is false and what is true, but it encourages you to find out for yourself" (192). Is that not the spirit of psychoanalysis? Being curious and making inquiries?

To give a little background, I will say what first led me to Buddhism. During college, a course on Zen Buddhism stirred my interest in an effort to make sense of the upheavals in my life. Early life experiences included the loss of country, culture, and extended family while living in exile in Taiwan following the Communist takeover of China. Coming to another strange country seventeen years later and feeling foreign in American culture, I found Philip Kapleau's writings on Zen to be very liberating. Like a breath of fresh air, Buddhist teachings offered an authentic way to experience life, one that is not fixated on the past or future but focuses on living in the present. In 1974, after hearing the teachings of the Venerable Kalu Rinpoche, I took refuge in order to study and practice Buddhism in the Tibetan tradition. By taking refuge, one enters the Buddhist path and vows to develop *bodhichitta* or loving kindness toward all beings.

While the literature on Buddhism is vast and there are literally dozens of schools, my reference to Buddhist theory and practice in this chapter refers almost exclusively to Tibetan Buddhism. Space limitations in this chapter prevent me from describing the subtle and even not so subtle differences among the different Tibetan schools. For the interested reader, there is a burgeoning body of literature that can help to clarify these distinctions (Almaas 1996; Guenther

1971; Mipham 1999; Namgyal 1988; Nyinchay 1995; Thurman 1995). There is also a growing body of literature written by practicing Buddhists and psychotherapists and/or analysts that examines the relationship between psychotherapy and Buddhism (Almaas 1996; Cooper 1998; Epstein 2001, 1995; Finn 1998; Kornfield 1993; Rosenthal 1992, 1990; Safran 2003, Watson, Batchelor, and Claxton 2000; Welwood, 1983, 1979). Much of the available literature addresses the similarities and differences between Buddhism and psychoanalysis or how Buddhism can enhance the process of psychoanalysis. More recently, many distinguished analysts have started a dialogue to more precisely explore the similarities between the two processes by focusing on Buddhist and psychoanalytic terminology. These include such topics as the meaning of self, emptiness, compassion, alleviation of suffering, transference, and so on. Both psychoanalysis and Buddhism emphasize the expanded experience of the self. In Buddhism there is no enduring self (Safran 2003), just as psychoanalytic theory recognizes that there is no single immutable self that transcends different situations (Lionells et al. 1995). These dialogues are exciting and can only illuminate both the psychoanalytic as well as the Buddhist experience.

This chapter has a somewhat different focus; namely, to present arguments, personal experience, speculation, and case material to suggest that although psychoanalysis may not have as ultimate a set of ontological premises as Buddhism and may not offer as lofty claims such as the promise to end suffering, this venerable (and changing) Western discipline may be able to play a helpful role in freeing Buddhist practitioners from psychological fixations that may very well interfere with their Buddhist practice. The intention of this chapter is to invite people to think, contemplate, and inquire into this proposition, which falls within the realm of "Buddhist psychology."

My own experience both as a Buddhist practitioner and as a psychoanalyst informs this chapter and finds support through my conversations with colleagues, with fellow long-time Buddhist practitioners, and with Buddhist patients. There is a need, as I see it, for Buddhist practitioners to develop a basic psychological awareness so that they can work through their defenses, distortions, impatience, and magical thinking. Without that understanding, practitioners are susceptible to numerous generic and personal pitfalls and detours. For example, I have met many practitioners who enter the path by idealizing Buddhism and Buddhist teachers only to swing to devaluation, often resulting in eventually forsaking the practice altogether. This is a parallel process to psychoanalytic patients who are in a hurry to find a magical solution to their problems without having to develop the maturity and patience to ride through their discomfort.

I realize how sensitive this topic may be for practitioners, especially since they spent most of their adult lives committed to the practice of Buddhism and several of them even spent years in Buddhist retreat. I particularly value their insights as they went through the most difficult personal experience of facing their thoughts and emotions in a strict, disciplined manner. These practitioners were willing to discuss how their experiences were enhanced by psychotherapeutic accommodations. Each tradition's distinctive goals are that the Buddhist literature contains hundreds, if not thousands, of works on ontology—the nature of Being—while psychoanalysis was developed without any clearly stated ontological premises. Contemporary psychoanalysis is just beginning to engage in a serious, focused examination of its own onto-premises (for example, see Wilner 1998, 1999).

So the goals of the two disciplines flow directly from their approach to the nature of reality. For Buddhism, all experience that is grounded in dualistic subjective experience will lead to suffering. Therefore, all of the techniques of Tibetan Buddhism, in one way or another, are meant to lead the practitioner to a direct, nonconceptual realization that transcends all dualism and, thus, to freedom from suffering. Such nondual experience is said to liberate all potential personal qualities that previously had become dimmed, diminished in the context of fixation on "self" and (or, vs.) "other." This is consistent with the eminent scholar Herbert Guenther's (1976) rendering of the Tibetan term *marigpa*, the fundamental context for fixation, as "the loss of the optimum level of excitation [or] 'energetic charge'" (253, n. 9). Just remember and reflect from your own experience how tiring it is to try to drive so-called negative thoughts and feelings out of consciousness. The consciousness of an individual's mind is tricky, though, functioning 24/7 as they say. So what happens to someone's "upset" is usually that it does not disappear but may emerge in, for instance, passive-aggressive ways, out of the person's awareness. For example, a young man who feels hurt and slighted by his father's apparent lack of interest in his recent promotion may *unconsciously* "forget" this upset while finding himself more impatient with his father. The effort needed to repress and become critical will likely diminish his range of options regarding his father and all the "fathers" he encounters.

As noted above, the goals of psychoanalysis are typically symptom reduction and, more recently, that the analysand "becomes" herself more fully, thus leading to a more happy and productive life. Psychoanalysis does not appear to concern itself with the nature of mind/reality but rather with the idiosyncratic ways in which individuals either block or facilitate personal happiness. As we shall see, in this lies the rub.

Externally, the two disciplines also look very different. A fly on the wall of a Buddhist's practice place would likely see a person just sitting quietly cross-legged on a cushion. The same proverbial fly would witness a dramatic encounter between two persons, psychoanalyst and patient, if they were to observe a therapy session.

So, how are they the same? What they appear to share is a conviction that nonfixation is a process worth moving toward. Both cultivate the capacity for nonfixation, albeit in different ways, and both view this process as "curative." The difference is that Buddhism focuses its fixation-busting awareness back on the one who is aware, always moving toward more and more subtle levels of fixation until the ultimate fixation has been transcended.[3] The methods are more generic rather than personal and idiosyncratic to the practitioner, while in the psychoanalytic conversation the focus of fixation-busting awareness is targeted specifically on the analysand's idiosyncratic defensive processes, such as rejection of particular "parts" of the personality or projection onto others of feelings, thoughts, and behaviors that do not conform to a person's version of oneself. A common fixation amongst Buddhists is the clinging to self-definitions, self-image, and self-concepts that can become further complicated by the additional identification of being a Buddhist. For reasons of security and cohesiveness, the self is mistakenly viewed as continuous, always the same. In fact, what is more accurate experience is that we think, feel, and behave differently moment to moment. We even feel differently at different times with the same other person. What an analyst does is to help the patient develop a healthy ability to respond to new situations, to participate in increasingly complex interactions with others, and to be able to behave in ways that do not rigidly adhere to one's view of oneself (Lionells et al. 1995). This multiplicity of self is a perspective central to current theories formulated by interpersonal psychoanalysts. The point here is that, without working through some particularly significant and powerful personal fixations, it is possible that a Buddhist practitioner could practice meditation for a hundred years without result.

What we do in psychoanalysis is to talk about our feelings and to note the reenactment of old primary relationships. Emotions are often difficult for us to accept because we feel like we may be overtaken by forces beyond our control, beyond what seems to fit our identity. Disturbances to our self-image are particularly powerful during times of stress and upheaval. Sometimes these emotions may feel threatening to us because we fear experiencing them will cause us to fall to pieces or go crazy, leaving us unable to function at all. According to the basic tenets of psychoanalysis, the reality is just the opposite. If we allow ourselves to face, explore, and accept all our emotions, we can transcend fear and learn to cope with our feelings in a more skillful way. We can experience seeing them more as a challenge and an opportunity.

Life does present us with painful and difficult feelings. What if we were to move toward them, face them, and, in a sense, become friends with them instead of feeling they are separate from us and are harmful to us, which causes us to resist them, condemn them, and suppress them as "other" and "alien" from ourselves? Regarding them as demons, these alienating feelings bring up a strong response to get rid of them. In reacting to our fears with fear, our anger with rage, and our sadness with depression, we turn against ourselves. Such reactions can often lead to a cycle of these feelings, increasing in intensity and frequency until our minds become cloudy and the feelings dominate our attention to the point where we either explode or become claustrophobic. Through the process of personal, idiosyncratic fixation-busting, psychoanalytic inquiry can lead to the discovery and integration of underlying emotions, conflicts, and rigidified defenses. Thus the individual can become free of the accompanying emotional maelstrom. The following case vignette exemplifies this process.

Case Vignette

Alice, age forty-five, came to therapy because she had suffered a major depressive episode after the rejection from a young man she perceived to be interested in her. She reported a significant loss of weight and difficulty in focusing. Alice secretly felt she was still in her twenties and fantasized about relationships with younger men nearly half her age. She could not understand why her family and the rest of the world did not recognize her for her exceptional kindness and compassion toward others. When asked how she felt about that, Alice replied that she did not feel angry. In fact, she did not feel anything negative. An animal lover, she once paid for an expensive surgery to save the life of a dog that belonged to a stranger.

Upon further exploration, Alice revealed she was the remaining "child" in her family, still going home weekly to be with her aging parents and living in a space they provided for her rent-free. Her family frequently gave her advice to improve herself but did not seem to really "see" her. After many temporary jobs that did not challenge her, Alice went back to school and struggled to begin writing her PhD dissertation. Years had passed, and her committee was pressuring her to finish. Alice could not then see the continuing construction of herself as a child, nor could she admit she expected everyone else to provide for her.

As she came to realize that her siblings had married, started families, and had become successful in their careers, she felt as if she had been victimized. Terrified that she would be left all alone in the world with no one to take care of her, she asked, "What's the use?" and she admitted that she was very angry. What Alice was enraged and depressed about was that she did not know what to do with her life, how to deal with finding a home on her own, find satisfaction in a job, or seek out relationships. She finally acknowledged her unconscious yearning to remain a child and her fears about the responsibilities of being an adult. After years of being stuck with feeling helpless, Alice began to recognize and discriminate between *fixations* about real or imagined limitations on the one hand and the real resources she possessed all along on the other.

In freeing up deeply rooted beliefs about oneself and one's patterns of behavior, fears of being inadequate and unable to cope with life, as it is, can be dealt with more directly. Sometimes the process can continue as an endless exploration of emotions, as an end in itself. If the psychoanalyst is well trained and attentive, however, she will also inquire into her own psychological processes or what we call countertransference. Without such an inquiry, there is always the possibility of the analyst's fixations distorting the therapeutic exchange.

For example, my own anxiety when hidden and left unresolved caused me to get ahead of both myself and my patient who was grieving over her lost youth. My wish for my patient to be free from her pain was partly motivated by genuine bodhichitta and partly by my anxiety. My own self-analysis helped me to work through my feelings in order to be more present with her. Over the course of treatment, Alice came to connect with herself and her family in a new and healthier way.

While Buddhist meditation may help us to expand and experience our senses, feelings, and thoughts as simply the energy of Being with no hypothesized "self," the psychoanalytic dialogue can help both the patient and analyst to discover a much wider range of meanings and responses than general emotion. Psychoanalysis helps us to understand the specific meaning of our particular emotions. Emotions cannot be speculated to be the same in all patients even if they suffer from the same basic feelings. The psychoanalytic process may very well become an important factor in a person's capacity to remain clear regarding personal feelings and motivations. Alice, for example, may recognize she becomes angry both when she is not taken care of *and* when she is treated like a child rather than the adult she is. The young man in our previous example may become genuinely aware of his anger when he feels slighted.

SUSCEPTIBILITY OF BUDDHIST PRACTITIONERS
TO SPECIFIC DEFENSIVE FIXATED POSITIONS

In the 1970s when the great Tibetan Buddhist teachers first came to the United States, there were very few people who attended their teachings. Few of their teachings were published and very little literature on Buddhism and psychotherapy was available. Today, nearly thirty years later, so many more resources are available. It is very inspiring to see how the analytic world has responded to this influence from the East and also to spiritual disciplines. To stay remote, unaffected, and intact would be stultifying, and the analytic world needs to broaden its scope and incorporate and integrate what has existed as a source of wisdom for many years in the history of Asia. As Buddhism flourishes in the mainstream culture, the number of Buddhists has grown tremendously.

Unfortunately, there is a downside to this development. It's considered "cool" to be a Buddhist or to be interested in Buddhism, even if only intellectually. This is understandable. Everyone wants to feel "special," but that need for specialness can only contribute to the narcissistic defense that is at the core of our suffering (Almaas 1996). While people may fear that experience of their soft spot may destroy them, to be able to be vulnerable with their therapist may lead them to realize that they don't have to hide themselves behind a cloak of goodness and perfection, what Rinpoche (Trungpa 1973) termed "spiritual materialism." This point may be particularly applicable to practitioners of spiritual disciplines and to analysts, not just to patients.

In analysis, as in basic Buddhist meditation, patients experience feelings and thoughts that come and go. In fact, impermanence is a basic fact of life. When people can relax and realize that they need not hang onto labels, references, and evaluations of themselves, they eventually fear the unknown less. In both disciplines this letting go and letting be is a gradual process, which may begin with some unsettling questions. Who would we be without all this solidifying of our identity?

During our therapy sessions together, Adam, for example, talked about his constant search for something better. After a few months at a new position as graphic artist, he became bored and thought of going to interviews for a "better job," one that would allow him to sculpt, a dream he could not allow himself to pursue after his father's death. The job changes always entailed exhaustive obsessional struggles. Now Adam was thinking of waiting tables to devote himself completely to his art. When we explored his dissatisfaction, he would respond with, "You know how I am. I am not going to leave my current job that easily. I am cautious and pragmatic."

What Adam called "cautious and pragmatic" was really a cover for terror when faced with change. Seven years before, his father had died from a heart attack at age forty when Adam was seventeen years old. Adam got caught in the battle between his long divorced parents about who was going to pay for his education at a private college. His father had promised many years before to sell his beach house, his most prized position. A few days after a heated argument over how he had failed to adequately provide for his children, Adams father died. His father's family blamed him for the death and cut off all relations. Adam's life in the ensuing years was filled with pain, confusion, and self-numbing. Despite all the changes he had gone through over the past three years in therapy, he still clings to his solidified identity as overcautious and pragmatic. For example, Adam's wish for increasingly bigger challenges so that he can feel more productive prevents him from being happy. Thus his solidified identity fosters his depression. The unending pursuit for "the perfect job" kept Adam continually frustrated and hid the real issue: to face his guilt and self-condemnation for his father's death. Until he faced his painful loss and sadness, Adam could not allow himself to accept what he had always wanted and could now have, a career in sculpting.

Adam's search for a quick and magical alternative solution manifested in his job hunt is much like the search for a quick Enlightenment experience in that many new practitioners bring to their first encounters with Buddhism. In contrast, when patients and practitioners can let go of their "identity"—ordinary with a lot of suffering or special because they are practitioners—they realize freedom in simply being.

In analysis as in daily life, loving and hateful feelings come and go; they don't stay forever. Freud's concept of "evenly hovering attention" has contributed much to the psychoanalysts' openness to meditation and provides a stance from which to experience impermanence. He describes this foundational technique as follows:

> The technique, is a very simple one . . . and simply consists in making no effort to concentrate the attention on anything in particular, and in maintaining in regard to all that one hears the same measure of calm, quiet attentiveness of "evenly-hovering attention, . . ." [And] All conscious exertion is to be withheld from the capacity for attention, and one's "unconscious memory" is to be given full play; or to express it in terms of technique, pure and simple; One has simply to listen and not to trouble to keep in mind anything in particular. (Freud 1912, 112)

A major difference between Freud's "hovering attention" and the awareness developed in Buddhist practice is that in Buddhist meditation, we always begin our practice by focusing on a physical or mental object. After our meditation stabilizes over a substantial period of time, we can then meditate without an object.

Similar to Freud's technique, when Buddhists practice sitting meditation, we notice a continuous flow of changing sensations, emotions, and thoughts. We often experience long periods of discomfort. Our backs ache, our legs become numb, and all kinds of other discomforts come up, including the arising of our emotional "soft spots." We keep adjusting our postures and positions (both physical and psychological) to find some sinecure of comfort. Both traditions, therefore, introduce us to the possibility that discomfort will evaporate, become something different, or disappear naturally if we were to stop fighting it.

Two years ago I attended a ten-day retreat. I had sustained a back injury that made sitting up and taking notes without back support impossible. I wanted, however, to continue my habit of "missing nothing," part of being the good student. I sat right in front of the Lama, on a meditation cushion without any back support. In less than a day, I was in terrible pain, and I had to lie on the floor in the back of the meditation hall for the rest of the retreat. My back would simply not allow me to maintain my stance. I was now not only a failure but "exposed." This feeling of shame of being "less than perfect" was so intense that the reality of three herniated disks and chronic pain did not relieve me. I needed to relinquish my solidified identity as the "ardent and perfect practitioner," my self-ideal. It was only after an examination of my embarrassment and practicing compassion toward myself that I was able to relax into my new and different position.

SOME THOUGHTS ON ELEMENTS OF A COMMON BUDDHIST DEFENSIVE STANCE

Idealization, as a defense mechanism, occurs when certain exaggerated superlative qualities are ascribed to oneself or to others. These qualities may be a realistic part of the person's actual makeup and become exaggerated, or they may be fabricated out of whole cloth. Either way, they may become part and parcel of the practitioner's defense against the First Noble Truth of Buddhism, namely, that suffering is inherent in human life.

Practitioners may imagine that no matter what happens, "everything is wonderful" or happening according to their idealized spiritual teacher's "plan" for them. What then happens when stressful events occur that would normally elicit a range of intense emotional responses? What happens to these emotions? How do practitioners reconcile their idealized worldview with their very genuine visceral and meaning-creating responses to these stressful events?

My explorations, as well as my own training and experience as a therapist, indicate that all too often, when emotions are viewed as "anti-Buddhist," they often go underground, only to appear indirectly in the practitioner's life and, ironically, increase the possibility of creating additional negative karma[4] but out of the practitioner's awareness. Psychoanalysis, a method that I see as a means, par excellence, for eliciting unconscious process, could have the potential to make conscious the idealization defense as well as recover an awareness of a broader range of genuine feelings, thus allowing the patient/practitioner to actually remain more true to her Buddhist values through conscious choice.

Reification of "Goodness"

In Buddhist practice, true goodness, or what Trungpa describes as "Basic Goodness," (1984), arises when we let go. What is it that we let go of? We let go of baggage from the past, expectations for the future, and even the construct of an identifiable present moment. Mostly, we let go of any and all reified versions of who we are, including being a "good" Buddhist. An example might illustrate some aspects of this.

You are at a Buddhist retreat and you perceive someone to be insulting you. You, attempting to act as a "good" Buddhist, begin, perhaps somewhat unconsciously, to drive out any negative feelings, such as shame or anger. The next time you see the person, you find yourself inquiring as to the state of their health because they don't "look well" or jokingly say, "you don't look a day over eighty."

Many people who study Buddhism have a misconception that when we start to meditate, we think that we are going to improve. Pema Chodron (2002) says there is a subtle aggression about who we are. If I meditate, I'll be a better person. Meditation is not about throwing ourselves away in order to get a better self-image but rather simply befriending ourselves.

Concretization of Self-Image

The Buddhist teachings exhort practitioners to transcend self-image. The irony is that if we don't work through our defenses, we may unwittingly concretize an idealized version of selflessness or a good self-image. The realization of selflessness is a virtue worthy of aspiration. However, a lack of awareness of unconscious emotions and processes may ironically contribute to the very opposite of that worthy goal—the concretization of identity that inhibits the experience of the energy and fullness of Being and self-valuing.

A psychoanalyst could enhance the Buddhist's practice by "skillful means," that is, skillfully evoking the flow of underlying feelings. The process of psychoanalysis can elicit the ways and whys of a practitioner's avoidance of the truth of her genuine feelings, thus freeing her up to let go.

According to Neil Altman (2003), the Winnicottian tradition in psychoanalysis deals with resolving paradoxes. Can a practitioner be only a

compassionate adult all the time? Or can he or she allow assertion of infantile needs? Paradoxes are particularly difficult in spiritual communities
where virtuous qualities may be the only ones that are allowed to surface.
This is not what loving kindness is about. I have seen people who drive
themselves relentlessly while working at dharma centers until they burn out
physically and mentally. When that happens, the only recourse appears to be
to isolate, to get aggressive, or to leave. This one-dimensional self-image is
a false self-hiding of other needs. Through psychoanalytic work, the practitioner may allow herself to feel needy as well as other uncomfortable feelings. She may recognize that the need to be always compassionate and effi-
cient creates a false self that can lead to more serious problems.

PSYCHOANALYSIS AS A
CATALYST FOR BUDDHIST PRACTICE

In general, we are considering how the process of psychoanalysis might serve
as a means by which Buddhist practitioners may develop awareness of unconscious experience that may run counter to their conscious objectives as a
Buddhist practitioner. Buddhist practitioners, who lack any substantial experience of psychological exploration of their inner self, may carry their lack of
psychological acumen into their practice. In exploring the unconscious in
psychoanalytic work, they may learn about that part of themselves that is usually out of their awareness, which could affect their real motivations in practice. For example, people may be generous in their material offerings to a
Buddhist teacher or dharma center with a conscious intention of contributing
but an unconscious egocentric motivation, for example, "I am a generous person gathering 'merit.'"

Clearly, Buddhism itself offers powerful generic antidotes for all types of
fixation associated with spiritual practice (Namgyal 1988). In the previous example, the Tibetan Buddhist tradition might counsel the practitioner to view
the three aspects of the situation (giver, gift, and act of giving) as "empty,"
that is, without inherent existence. This is a supremely powerful antidote for
those few who have actually directly experienced even a glimpse of the
"empty" nature of all things and events. I must confess I believe the rest of us
may be partially fooling ourselves, mistaking a conceptual understanding for
direct perception. This is where the more individualized practice of psychoanalytic psychotherapy could play a significant role. In the process of self-
exploration that is at the heart of analytic work, we may at least become aware
of any narcissistic yearnings associated with such a "meritorious" act. Such
awareness may dissolve one's fixations concerning one's own generosity.

TONGLEN

I believe that such awareness of one's "true" motivations becomes even more important as one becomes a more "accomplished" practitioner. For example, practitioners who have established a modicum of stability in their meditation practice are typically taught a particularly sublime method for developing compassion—the Tibetan technique called *tonglen*, or "sending and taking."

In tonglen practice, the meditator imagines that she is breathing in all the suffering of all beings (taking) and breathing out all the wisdom, clarity, freedom, and joy of nonfixated awakened experience (sending) so that all beings may benefit from this radiance. Although Buddhist teachers go to great lengths to emphasize that a practitioner must be prepared for such a practice, that is, has some experience of *emptiness*[5] and some degree of stabilized concentration, the practice is taught widely. Instructions for tonglen practice are readily available in several popular Buddhist books (Berzin 1998; Chodron 1994; Trungpa 1993).

Let me be clear. For those who are properly prepared and motivated, tonglen can truly be a transformative practice. Our focus here, however, is on the pitfalls that may arise, which are probably already obvious to the reader. For those not adequately prepared (possibly the majority of those exposed to this teaching), there is a very strong possibility of becoming engulfed in a kind of narcissistic fog while doing this practice. For example it is typical to imagine that "I am able to take on the suffering of all beings." I have caught myself in this state of delusional grandiosity, which only created more obstacles to my practice. The psychoanalytic process with its individualized approach to fixation may be uniquely suited to reveal such a potentially harmful detour from the true purpose of the practice. For example, over time, I learned not to take my Tonglen practice quite so literally. Rather, the wish and commitment to save all sentient beings is more an attitude that one cultivates. As Khenpo Karther, the abbot of the monastery where I practice said to me "we are not that powerful." I was able, through my own analysis, to gradually get a more realistic sense of both my strengths and limitations, which has strengthened both my Buddhist practice and my capacity to work more effectively with my patients.

In Tibetan Buddhism, it is said that one moment of anger can destroy eons of good works. What does that mean? Anger can operate both consciously and unconsciously. Would it be better for a person to know that he is angry and be able to deal with it or just to say, "oh, one moment of anger, I better get rid of this anger " and have the anger come out in passive aggressive ways for months and months? I raise this question in the spirit of inquiry that is so essential to both Buddhism and psychoanalysis. The following case vignette exemplifies this point.

Case Vignette

Nancy, age forty-seven, has been a Buddhist practitioner for a long time. The only child in her family, she experienced her father's rage, devaluation, and verbal abuse. Her mother, who also bore the brunt of her husband's anger, did not intervene on her daughter's behalf. Nancy could not allow herself to feel her own feelings toward her father, since her mother, her role model, did not. She developed a high tolerance for mistreatment. Actually she had difficulty in discriminating what was a normal reaction from what was harmful. She married several times. Each husband betrayed her, financially or sexually. She tried to be the compassionate Buddhist that she aspired to be, avoiding conflict, forgiving her husbands. Nancy stated that without analysis, she would not have recognized the connection between the pattern of abuse from her husbands with her father's harshness and taking out his anger at her. When her father was dying, she spent a great deal of time with him. She was as compassionate a daughter as she could be. However, she also felt a great deal of anger toward him. When she did prayers and practices for him, she questioned her own motivation. In doing tonglen, when she practiced taking on her father's sufferings and sending her good merit to him, she wondered if she was doing it out of compassion or out of her wish to gain good merit and good karma.

Having spent time in analysis, she grew to understand how her fixation on being good, loyal, and tolerant irregardless of the abuse from the other left her with few options. As a child, Nancy encountered severe anxiety from her harsh and restrictive environment (Lionells et al. 1995). That anxiety as well as certain accompanying interpersonal patterns had to be split off, sent out of her awareness. The abuse later reappeared in a different form in her relationships with men. After many years of practicing awareness in meditation and focusing on her fixations in psychoanalysis, Nancy was able to allow herself to experience other emotions, those that did not conform to her self-image of a loving and compassionate person. By the time her father was dying, Nancy was able to move from feelings of anger to those of genuine sadness and empathy.

SUMMARY AND CONCLUSIONS

In this chapter, I have sought to interest the reader in exploring the potential of psychoanalysis and psychotherapy to facilitate the practice of Buddhism. Friends and colleagues seeped in both traditions have been forthcoming and helpful. Their experiences, as well as my own, lend confirmation to my strong belief that Buddhist practitioners are susceptible to the same range of defensive mechanisms as nonpractitioners. These defensive mechanisms, moreover, can create serious obstacles for the Buddhist practitioner in her pursuit of awakening.

In conclusion, I have found, in my own experience that psychoanalysis and psychotherapy can benefit Buddhists caught in a web of self-deception. Psychoanalytic therapies are uniquely designed to address defenses idiosyncratic to the individual while Tibetan Buddhism provides a more generic approach to the habit of fixation. (This may be especially the case for students of teachers that are renowned and responsible for teaching hundreds or thousands of practitioners.)

It is my hope that the examination in this chapter will be of benefit to serious students of Buddhist practice as well as therapists and analysts working with practicing Buddhist patients. I also hope that this chapter will stimulate others to examine and research these basic issues more precisely and systematically. There needs to be a constant questioning and going over what we do in staying honest that can cut through the false belief of many Buddhist practitioners that "things will" happen or that suffering will disappear simply because one has "faith." We live in the ordinary world with other people. This includes the psychological terrain of thoughts and emotions. While it is easy to dismiss uncomfortable feelings and eject them by labeling them as samsara or suffering, these very same uncomfortable feelings may provide the fuel for our awakening.

NOTES

1. Mental agitations.

2. For Trungpa, "ego" refers to the process or ". . . struggle to maintain the sense of a solid and continuous self." (1973, p. 5).

3. M. L. Weiner (1975) provides an interesting Western formulation that has some similarity in theory to Buddhist depth psychology.

4. Karma literally means action. "The unerring law of cause and effect, eg.: Positive actions bring happiness and negative actions bring suffering." K. Thrangu (2002, p. 160).

5. Emptiness: "The true nature of phenomena, which is empty of the self of the individual sentient being, empty of true existence, and ultimately empty of any conceptual notion of what it might be, including the notion of emptiness itself." K. T. Gyamtso (2003, p. 210).

REFERENCES

Almaas, A. H. (1996). *The point of existence*. Berkeley, CA: Diamond Books.

Altman, N. (2003). Psychoanalysis as a spiritual quest. In *Psychoanalysis and Buddhism,* ed. J. Safran, (115–22). Boston: Wisdom.

Berzin, A. (1998). *Developing balanced sensitivity*. Ithaca, NY: Snow Lion.

Chodron, P. (1994). *Start where you are*. Boston: Shambhala.

——. (1996). *Awakening loving kindness*. Boston: Shambhala.

——. (2002). *Comfortable with uncertainty*. Boston: Shambhala.

Cooper, P. (1998). The disavowal of the self: Integration and wholeness in Buddhism and psychoanalysis. In *The couch and the tree: Dialogues in psychoanalysis and Buddhism*, ed. A. Molino. New York: North Point Press.

Epstein, M. (1995). *Thoughts without a thinker*. New York: Basic Books.

——. (2001). *Going on being*. New York: Broadway Books.

Finn, M. (1998). Tibetan Buddhism and comparative psychoanalysis. In *The couch and the tree: Dialogues in psychoanalysis and Buddhism*, ed. A. Molino, NewYork: North Point Press.

Freud, S. (1912). Recommendations to physicians practicing psycho-analysis. In *The standard edition of the complete psychological works of Sigmund Freud*, ed. and trans J. Strachey, 12, 109–20. London: Hogarth Press (1953–1974).

Gill, M. (1982). *Analysis of transference*. NewYork: International Universities Press.

Guenther, H. (1971). *Buddhist philosophy in theory and practice*. Boulder: Shambhala.

——. (1976). *The tantric view of life*. Boulder: Shambhala.

Gyamtso, K. T. (2003). *The sun of wisdom*. Boston: Shambhala.

Khenchen, T. (2003). *Teachings on the practice of meditation*. Auckland: Zhyisil Chokyi Ghatsal Publications.

Khenchen, T. R. (2003). *Crystal clear*. Hong Kong: Rangjung Yeshe Publications.

Kongtrul, J. (1987). *The great path of awakening*. Trans. K. McCleod. Boston: Shambhala.

Kornfield, J. (1993). *A path with heart*. New York: Bantam Books.

Lionells, M., J. Fiscalini, C. Mann, and D. Stern. (1995). *Handbook of interpersonal psychoanalysis*. Hillsdale: Analytic Press, Inc.

Mipham, L. (1999). *Beacon of certainty*. Boston: Wisdom.

Mitchell, S. A., and L. Aron. (1999). Relational psychoanalysis. Hillsdale: Analytic Press.

Namgyal, T. D. (1988). *Mahamudra: the quintessence of mind and meditation*. Trans. L. P. Lhalungpa. Boston: Shambhala.

Nyinchay, T. (1995). Mahamudra teachings of the supreme siddhas. Trans. S. Dorje. Ithaca, NY: Snow Lion.

Rosenthal, J. (1990). The meditative therapist. *The family therapy networker*, September–October, 38–71.

——. (1992) The bodhi-therapist. *Journal of couples therapy,* I(1) 27–52.

Safran, J. (2003). *Psychoanalysis and Buddhism*. Boston: Wisdom.

Sogyal, R. (1992). *The Tibetan book of living and dying*. San Francisco: HarperCollins.

Thrangu, K. (2002). *The life of Tilopa and the Ganges mahamudra*. Auckland: Namo Buddha Pub.

Thurman, R. (1995). *Essential Tibetan Buddhism*. San Francisco: HarperCollins.

Trungpa, C. (1973). *Cutting through spiritual materialism*. Berkeley, CA: Shambhala.

——. (1983). *First thought, best thought*. Boulder and London: Shambhala.

——. (1984). *Shambhala: The sacred path of the warrior*. Boston: Shambhala.

——. (1993). *Training the mind and cultivating loving-kindness*. Boston: Shambhala.

Watson, G., S. Batchelor, and G. Claxton. (2000). *The psychology of awakening*. York Beach, ME: Samuel Weiser.

Weiner, M. L. (1975). *The cognitive unconscious: A Piagetian approach to psychotherapy*. Davis, CA: International Psychological Press.

———. (1979). *The meeting of the ways. Explorations in East/West psychology*. New York: Schocken.

Welwood, J. (1983). *Awakening the heart: East/West approaches to psychotherapy and the healing relationship*. Boulder, CO: Shambhala.

Wilner, W. (1999). The un-consciousing of awareness in psychoanalytic therapy. *Contemporary psychoanalysis,* 35(4), 617–28.

———. (1998). Experience, metaphor, and the crucial nature of the analyst's expressive participation. *Contemporary Psychoanalysis,* 34(3), 413–43.

Chapter Eleven

Bringing Practice Home

Joan H. Hoeberichts

Barefoot and naked of breast, I mingle with the people of the world.
My clothes are ragged and dust-laden, and I am ever blissful.
I use no magic to extend my life;
Now, before me, the dead trees become alive.
Master Kakuan, picture 10 of The Zen Oxherding Pictures

(Bercholz and Kohn 1993, 222)

The practice of sitting meditation often provides the meditator with a profound sense of connection to everything in the universe. There comes a moment when body and mind drop off, and the meditator experiences herself as one with the universe and everything in it. This feeling of connection is so strong that in post-meditation life, the memory of these numinous moments is continuous in the person's sense of being in the world. Such experience of my own interconnection with the universe and all things within it permeates my life with my family and my practice as a psychotherapist. It is my personal truth; it is who I am and it infuses my values as a therapist. It is through our connection to others and to life itself that we live a life that satisfies us. This is the interface of my Buddhist practice and my life.

Both psychoanalysis and Buddhism have a history in which being an autonomous, independent individual was treated as more important than being in relationship. Jung, for example, stressed the importance of separation and individuation, not connection, for growth. Freud was primarily concerned with the individual and how to resolve inner conflicts that developed in childhood. In Buddhism, I have always been uncomfortable with the story that the Buddha left his wife and infant son and went off to the woods to pursue nirvana. "What about his family?" I found myself asking in dismay. The model of implicit conflict between practice and family responsibility is still embedded in Buddhist practice. Traditional Buddhists generally regard monastic practice as the better, more rigorous, more devoted practice because monks can dedicate themselves to their teacher's care and concentrate completely on study and practice. There remains today in much of the world, a hierarchy between Buddhist monks and nuns on the one hand and lay practitioners or householders on the other hand, with monks holding the higher rank. Tung-shan Liang-chieh (Chinese) or Tozan (Japanese), the thirty-eighth Zen patriarch and a founder of the Soto school of Zen, reportedly abandoned his old mother to extreme poverty in going off to "acquire the dharma." In 1300, Zen Master Keizan tells this story of Tung-Shan:

> Eventually, he completed his study and later went to live on Mt. Tung. Since his mother was alone and had no one else to depend on, she looked for him every day, finally wandering around with some beggars. When she heard that her son was on Mt. Tung she yearned to go and see him, but Tung-shan avoided her, barring the [entrance to the] room so she could not enter. It was because he didn't want to meet her. Consequently, his mother died of grief outside his room. After she died, Tung-shan went personally and took the small amount of rice she had collected as a beggar and he mixed it with the community's morning rice gruel. By offering it to the whole community of monks, he made a funerary offering to assist her on her journey [to future enlightenment]. Not long after, she told Tung-shan [in a dream], "Because you firmly maintained your resolve and did not meet me, I severed the delusive feelings of love and attachment. As a result of the power of these good roots, I was reborn in the Realm of the Satisfied Celestials." (Keizan 1991, 175)

Attachment to family is often misunderstood to be an obstacle to enlightenment because in the instant of dropping off body and mind, all attachments dissolve. This is sometimes misunderstood to mean that attachments to family are an ongoing obstacle to living an enlightened life. And what is enlightenment? Enlightenment is letting go of the sense of self as separate and fixed, and experiencing life moment to moment. Such an experience may result in a sense of liberation beyond the personal ego and may also integrate a transcendental awareness into everyday life. What could be more important than that sense of liberation in family connection? During my own years as a Buddhist practitioner, the tension between practice and family has been my greatest obstacle, my greatest source of inspiration, and my truest place of growth.

In psychoanalytic thinking in the last half of the twentieth century, the importance of connection in human relationships has become more salient than it was in the days of Freud and Jung. Beginning with the object relations school in England in the first half of the twentieth century, the relationship between the mother (or primary caregiver) and the child began to be seen by advocates of the object relations school as the key to future mental health in adulthood.

Fairbairn (1952) departed radically from Freud by stating that the primary psychic drive was not toward pleasure or a sexual partner as Freud posited, but, instead, toward a love object. He believed that it is disturbances in the object relationship (parent/child) that cause all psychopathological conditions. For Fairbairn, the primary drive was toward relationship. He identified relational problems in adulthood that could be traced back to the childhood relationship with the mother. For example, a mother who was distant and inconsistent in her attentions to her child would leave her child with a longing for an alluring, but distant partner. Such a child would often marry someone who was perpetually unavailable.

Winnicott (1965) believed that it was the reexperiencing of "good-enough mothering" in the therapy that provided the facilitating environment to allow the patient to let go of her false self and become her "true self." According to Winnicott, the therapist must be the good parent that the patient lacked in childhood and be readily available to meet the patient's needs as they are presented. The psychoanalyst creates a holding environment that accepts the patient as she is, thus creating connection. The patient, in this safe environment, can differentiate herself from her therapist, thus releasing the false compliant self she created to please her parent and become more authentic. The healing occurs as the patient begins to internalize the therapist and the facilitating environment. For Winnicott, the essence of the "good-enough" mother was this quality of accepting the child as she is. This offers the child the inner strength to follow her own inner guide into adulthood. With Julie, an acting out fourteen-year-old whose family life was filled with bitter conflict, I allowed her to do as much "relaxation," a form of meditation, in our therapy hour as she needed. She responded positively to the lack of demand on her to perform or to be pleasing. She just relaxed lying on the couch with her hands on her abdomen as it rose and fell, following her breath. For those minutes where she knew I was present and approving of her doing "nothing," she could accept herself just as she was. Often, halfway through a session, she would ask if we could do the "relaxation" and leave feeling just a little bit better.

Guntrip (1995), following Winnicott, wrote further that it was the relationship with the therapist that cures. By providing herself as a "good object," a parental figure that cares about the patient, who tolerantly sustains the patient's attempts at growth despite the patient's many failures, the therapist allows the patient to let go of the internalized bad objects from childhood and replace them with the internalization of the good therapist, a nonpossessive, noncritical good parent. For example, Peter, a forty-year-old patient, had never had an intimate relationship with a woman. His mother was a highly anxious, extremely volatile woman throughout his childhood. In the beginning of his treatment, he sat on the edge of the couch in my consulting room, waiting "for the explosion." It was not until he'd actually expressed his own volatility and anger toward me and experienced my calm, nonreactive response that he was able to sit back and feel safe with me. Following his slowly developing trust through being with me, his relationship with his mother began to improve and he began to form relationships with other women.

More recently, Stephen Mitchell has expanded the importance of the relationship between the psychoanalyst and patient to relationships in general. He has explored a model in which the human psyche is formed through relational interactions between self and other. He writes, "The state of psychoanalytic knowledge is not anchored in enduring truths or proof, but rather in its use value for making sense of a life, deepening relationships with others, and expanding and enriching the texture of experience" (1993, 65). With Mitchell we begin to see psychoanalytic thinking pay serious attention to how relationships may enhance happiness and mental health. My own objective, as a clinician, is to facilitate patients building relationships in their life, experiencing their authentic self in relationship, and living their lives moment by moment. Furthermore, as a Buddhist, I would like to see the value of family life and personal human relationships come to be more openly appreciated in the Buddhist world.

In the Oxherding Pictures, the ancient story of a spiritual journey told in pictures, a monk begins his journey by looking for something outside himself to salve his anguish. Slowly he realizes that what he seeks is within him. He was always enlightened, but he didn't see it. There is nothing to search for. He integrates his understanding and returns to the marketplace of ordinary life, but his anguish is resolved. He brings his new insight and his awakened mind into his ordinary life. For practitioners with families, coming home from a retreat is like coming down from the mountaintop and entering into the marketplace of family transaction. In the subsequent sections, using composite profiles of patients, I pursue my interest in relationships and family life as a path to mental health and a home to enlightened experience. The intimacy of a relationship with ourselves, with another, and within family provides a container that may enable us to let go of our fixed sense of self.

INTIMACY

To study the Buddha way is to study the self.
To study the self is to forget the self.
To forget the self is to be enlightened by ten thousand dharmas.

To be enlightened by ten thousand dharmas
Is to free one's body and mind and those of others.
Dogen, Genjokoan

(Bercholz and Kohn 1993, 206)

We usually think of intimacy as the revealing of self to other. It is through our interaction with others that we reveal who we are by what we say and do. We are often threatened by it. If we are not acceptable to ourselves, we certainly do not wish to be seen by another. Fear of intimacy encompasses both fear of being known and fear of losing oneself. Nonetheless, the experience of intimacy is enriching and validating and removes, for a moment at least, the sense of alienation and loneliness that pervades our culture. However, the prerequisite for intimacy with another is a mature level of honest self-awareness.

It is difficult, if not impossible, to be intimate with oneself in isolation. We need others to mirror and engage us through relationship in order to see ourselves. Thus revealing ourselves and being intimate with another are mutually reinforcing and supportive. Intimate relationships are great partners in the path of meditation practice. Meditation practice lowers our defenses and allows us to see and feel aspects of ourselves we might not have access to otherwise.

"In your daily life, please accept yourself as you are and your life as it is. Be intimate with yourself," Maezumi Roshi instructed.

Once, I said to him, presenting a koan, "I feel so stupid."

"Ahhh," he said, "If you feel stupid, be stupid. That's the most intimate."[1]

Admitting to myself my feeling of stupidity was being most intimate with myself. It was stepping into not knowing. Allowing myself to look and feel stupid in front of someone else is, indeed, most intimate in relationship. But in the face of another, I prefer to look and feel smart, competent, and on top of things. And even with myself, I would prefer to deny the feeling of stupidity, but being in relationship makes it impossible.

It's at home with my family that I am seen with the least pretense. I just can't keep the pretense up. Following a fight with my husband where I can't get what I want, I sit in meditation with boiling anger. Following a day of impatience and irritability with my family, I sit with my own aggression. No place to hide. Frankly, it's not a pretty sight. Being intimate with myself is not a warm, cozy, transcendent experience. I would much prefer to ignore these aspects of myself. Living in an intimate relationship with my husband forces me into an intimate relationship with myself because I can't ignore all these darker aspects of myself. But seeing myself as I am, not as I would like to think I am (and as I would like everyone else to think I am), I can sometimes accept my own imperfection.

Anna

It is less threatening to allow oneself to be seen by another if we have already seen and opened to our own imperfections. People who secretly hate themselves will not allow another to get close. Consider a psychotherapy patient of mine named Anna, a serious Zen student, who is very lovely looking and very intelligent and who first came to see me when she was twenty-nine.

Anna couldn't seem to hold on to relationships and felt she somehow sabotaged them. She had just begun a new relationship with a man she thought she could care about. She wanted help at understanding what went on within her when she was in a relationship. She tended toward an eating disorder, exercising madly and feeling "disgustingly fat" whenever she thought a man was interested in her. As we reviewed her history, she talked about her parents with apparent fondness, but over time it began to appear that her mother was an unrelenting critic, who consistently destroyed Anna's self-esteem. Although Anna denied her mother's comments affected her, my dismay at what she reported gradually allowed Anna to see that remarks such as "You'll never be able to keep a man—if you don't dump them first, they'll dump you" left her depleted and insecure. Her mother was toxic; leaving her feeling that at her core she wasn't OK. Sitting meditation was difficult for her because she couldn't sit with the corrosive anxiety that ate away her inadequate self. She felt empty.

I encouraged her to be with both her emptiness and anxiety on the cushion and in the consulting room. Her habit was to keep very busy as a defense against being present to herself. She very slowly began to reveal the inner terror of being known by another. Revealing herself entailed that she had to face that which she hid so well. She pretended to herself that she was fine; that she was her pretty, intelligent exterior self. But in permitting me to see the terror, inadequacy, and shame, she, herself, faced her own interior. If she could allow herself to be seen by me, she might be able to allow a man to see her as well. She is now thirty-four, and she still hides from me in a pattern not unlike the one in which she engages men. She cancels many appointments but works diligently when she appears. Following an intense session, she may miss the following session. There is a limit to how much intimacy with herself and another (me) she can endure. Meanwhile, in a parallel process in her current relationship, she approaches and leaves her boyfriend, circling closer and moving out again and again. Her meditation pattern is similar. She can rarely stay a whole sesshin (a week-long period of practice) because it is so painful for her to sit with herself. She usually leaves early. Anna has an intense desire to be viewed as "spiritual and good." There's a fragile grandiosity in her goodness that is not uncommon among religious practitioners. Being present and seeing herself honestly is intensely painful and disturbs her self-view of her goodness. Like many people on a spiritual path or like those involved in social action and doing good for others, she relates only to the part of herself that is loving and kind, and denies, even to herself, her angry, hating, darker aspect. Deep spiritual practice demands the integration and acceptance of our own darkest selves. When we can acknowledge and accept our own shadows, our negative self-judgment lightens. When our negative self-judgment lightens, our negative judgment of others lightens simultaneously, and compassion for the pain of others arises. Anna still struggles with her own negative self-judgment, coming of course, from her harsh and critical mother, but she continues to move toward self-acceptance in slow but conscious steps.

I see signs of improvement in her relationship to herself and the people she wishes to be close to. Anna has women friends now, and she sees them regularly. Her present relationship with a man is one she's been in and out of over a period of four years, but she's never let him go entirely and he seems to wait patiently or impatiently, struggling with his own similar issues, I presume. Anna is much more aware of how her mother brings her down with her toxic remarks, and she fights back instead of swallowing the poison. She demands less perfection of herself and projects less criticism onto others. She risks being herself in her life. Her relationship is slowly maturing. As she becomes more intimate with herself, she can allow another more fully into her life.

COUPLING

Let no one deceive another or despise any being in any state,
Let none by anger or hatred wish harm to another.
As a mother watches over her child, willing to risk her
Own life to protect her only child, so with a boundless
Heart should one cherish all living beings, suffusing the
Whole world with unobstructed loving-kindness.

—The Metta Sutta
(Bercholz and Kohn 1993, 142)

Couples represent a large proportion of my psychotherapy practice. Much of my work with couples is to help them let go of their fixed mind and move into a more fluid connection with each other. Learning to disagree and, at the same time, remain connected to one another can be an awakening. They come to understand that the other's point of view holds validity from the other's world, and it need not threaten them. They need not feel judged or criticized by the other's lack of agreement. Hendrix writes:

> When you accept the limited nature of your own perceptions and become more receptive to the truth of your partner's perceptions, a whole world opens up to you. Instead of seeing your partner's differing views as a source of conflict, you find them a source of knowledge. "What are you seeing that I am not seeing?" "What have you learned that I have yet to learn?" Marriage gives you the opportunity to be schooled in your own reality and in the reality of another person. (1988, 136–37)

Terry and Joe

Terry and Joe recently appeared in my office in a significant amount of pain. They were both lawyers, and they viewed marital conflict as they viewed court cases. There had to be a winner and a loser. Every argument was a competition. They could not grasp that they could both be right but just in disagreement. They had two small children and a newborn infant. The conflict they presented was over their second child, a two-year-old girl who was not happy about the recent arrival of a new baby in the family. Terry had elected to stay home with her children and was no longer working. She had been at the lake with the children for summer vacation, and Joe had arrived one Friday night to spend the weekend with his family. He had bought a present for his oldest child but nothing for the middle one because he hadn't thought that a Knicks jersey—his present for the oldest—was appropriate for a two-year-old girl. However, the two-year-old was inconsolable that her Daddy had nothing for her, and Terry was very angry that Joe had not anticipated her distress—nor did he seem disturbed by the child's hurt. In Terry's pain she lashed out at Joe, who responded by becoming more fixed in his position that he was right. His view was he hadn't done anything wrong, and their disagreement was Terry's fault because she couldn't contain her anger.

In the treatment process, I wanted the couple to experience each other's world and maintain a connection despite holding their different viewpoints. My objective was that they stay in process until they could come to understand the other's pain, respect the other's viewpoint, and let go of the rigidity of "I am right and you are wrong."

In the work with Terry and Joe, they struggled for several weeks with just listening and mirroring[2] what the other said. Their own emotions would get in the way, and they would interrupt one another and not be able to follow what the other was saying because their own feelings were so strong. Maintaining the connection was impossible for them those first weeks because they could not understand how to take in the other's point of view and respect it without feeling like they were betraying their own viewpoint.

At first, Joe refused to say Terry's position made sense to him because he needed her to be wrong. He insisted that if he said her position made sense to him, he would himself be wrong. He could not grasp that it was possible to hear and understand her position without agreeing with it. At first grudgingly, then more willingly, he would acknowledge that the position made sense when viewed from within her world. And then one day, he was able to say, "I imagine you must be feeling hurt and angry with me for being so stubborn." At this Terry's whole demeanor softened and her eyes glistened. The connection between them was palpable. They were disagreeing and maintaining the connection between them. Suddenly the content of the argument was much less important. Terry, in turn, was able to understand how hurtful her angry attacks were for Joe and said, "I imagine you must be feeling hurt and judged inadequate as a dad by my reaction." Joe, in turn, softened and responded by saying how much he loved the children.

Such intimacy with another can push us toward the letting go of a fixed sense of self, which is intrinsic to awakening. As we let go of the necessity of being right and of clinging to our viewpoint, we open to a larger universe. It is living meditation, the awakened mind in daily family life.

John Wellwood (1996) captured the pleasure of connection in an enlightened loving relationship:

> Love inspires us to relax into the blessed flow of our being. That is why we value it so. What we most cherish with our loved ones are experiences of *just being* together. All our deepest, intimate moments are those in which we're simply present—being ourselves, and sharing the richness of that with someone we love. Not so much *together* as *being together*. . . . Beyond all the particular things two people *have* or *do* together, their deepest connection is the quality of being they experience in each other's presence.
>
> Only in this still point of presence can we really appreciate our life. Indeed, the things we most enjoy—lovemaking, natural beauty, creative challenges, sports or strenuous exercise—are those that bring us alive and fully here. And when we are fully here, we taste our true nature-that quality of open presence, which is homeground, the source of all joy and fulfillment." (1996, 5)

Rebecca and Joel

In a mature relationship, it is the ability to accept each other despite differing viewpoints that allows the connection to flow into the kind of lovely intimacy described above by Wellwood. It is this acceptance that permits the deepest satisfaction in relationship with others. It does not, however, provide any guarantees that there will never be conflict, as we see in the following case.

Rebecca and Joel had been married almost twenty-five years when they entered my office the first time. They had two grown sons who had finished college and were working in other cities. Rebecca, of Jewish roots, had been a Buddhist for twenty years. Joel had been interested in Buddhism from a philosophical point of view, but he was not a meditator. He had been raised a Catholic, but was not church-going. He was deeply spiritual in his own untraditional, unorthodox way. They seemed comfortable, respectful and accepting of one another, but they were engaged in a conflict that had already been going on for a number of years. Rebecca wanted to be ordained as a Zen Buddhist priest. Joel was thoroughly opposed and said he was "out of there" were she to go ahead.

As we explored their dilemma it seemed that not much had shifted in the years they'd been talking about it. Rebecca went on three or four week-long retreats each year and had a meditation group that met in their house. Joel had never become fully reconciled to Rebecca's absence when she went on retreats, but he tolerated the group that met in the house on Sunday mornings. On the whole he was supportive of her practice and felt that she had benefited from it and so had their marriage. He felt she had become more patient and less ambitious, and more accepting of him. However, he adamantly did not want to be married to a priest. They both felt stuck and did not know how to move forward. They felt locked into position and could not see how they could possibly resolve this struggle.

We agreed that their process would be to stay in dialogue about the conflict until it would begin to clarify for them. I explained that when couples felt they were at total loggerheads about an issue, if they could continue talking about it without giving up, eventually something would soften and it would resolve. Even if they felt they were saying the same thing over and over, being in dialogue allowed them to stay connected throughout the process. It was important not to put a time limit on this. For Rebecca, that meant giving up the idea that ordination would happen within a specified amount of time. She thought she could agree to that.

We agreed to examine what ordaining meant to Rebecca and what Rebecca's becoming a priest meant to Joel. Rebecca shared that, for her, ordination was essentially a private spiritual matter, and she did not see that her relationship with Joel would be affected. She already had the meditation group in the house that he tolerated, and she did not imagine a significant increase in time or energy. When I pressed her to clarify why, in that case, she wished to be ordained; she said it had to do with making something very private more public. It was about revealing herself as someone whose spiritual life really defined her. She explained that for many years she had been a closet Buddhist, not letting anyone at work know where she was when she was away on retreats.

Rebecca had always been on a spiritual quest and had eventually landed in Buddhism. Rebecca's deepening connection to Buddhist practice had led her to leave a high level corporate position to become a therapist. When I met them she was in graduate school. She was no longer a closet Buddhist but was out and enjoying a new sense of fuller union with herself. She felt she had lived most of her life with a compartmentalized self, one compartment for her family, one for work, and one for spiritual practice. Rebecca regarded becoming a therapist as something of a calling and a good fit for her Buddhist practice, making work and spiritual practice one. Ordaining seemed like a next step. She said she was beginning to live from her own spiritual source and letting it lead her. As Joel listened and mirrored, he did not dismiss her desire. She felt he heard her and she relaxed. Her sense of urgency was reduced, and she became patient with the process.

For his part, Joel felt that he could not be married to a priest. Specters from his Catholic childhood arose of authoritarian figures cloaked in black. They were unmarried and masculine. Their first priority was their parish. Furthermore, he rejected the hierarchy implicit in organized religion where priests claim to have a higher authority than the congregation. For Joel, priests were separated from the community in which they lived by their priesthood. That violated his democratic instincts. He feared that by becoming a Buddhist priest, Rebecca would likewise become separated from their marriage. The issue for him was that he would lose her in spirit. He feared they would not share a spiritual life since his path was still a work in progress and her path was now going to receive official sanction. He liked her spirituality and was glad that that was important to her, but he wanted her to remain who she was. He was afraid that, by ordaining, Rebecca would change and so would their relationship. For many weeks he refused to budge.

, Over time, as Rebecca mirrored Joel, and stayed in process expressing clearly her understanding of his pain and fear, he began to relax his fear of losing her. He could take in how important this was to her and how committed she was to him and their relationship. Rebecca had never intended to distance herself from the marriage or to be any less present than she already was. She was able to express to Joel that being with him was her practice. She wanted to model how to live both a family life and a committed Zen practice. She felt she would always be a wife first and that there was no conflict in the two roles for her. From this point they slowly moved forward in their process.

Joel became less obstinate, and Rebecca more open and patient. Joel felt cared about, Rebecca felt respected. He acknowledged that her desire to ordain was important to her and, feeling loved himself, he could love her and allow her to do what she wanted without a break in their connection.

FAMILY

> Sit upon your meditation seat in a comfortable posture and visualize your mother of this life sitting before you. Contemplate how she carried you in her womb for almost ten months, and how during this time she experienced much suffering and inconvenience for you. At your actual birth her pain was as intense as that of being crushed to death. Yet she did not mind undergoing all this misery for you, no matter how great it was; and, when you finally emerged from her womb, looking like a naked and helpless worm covered in blood and mucus, she took you lovingly in her arms and placed you to her soft flesh to give you warmth, gave you milk from
> Her own breast . . .
>
> Exchanging Oneself for Others
(Bercholz and Kohn 1993, 159–60)

The bond between a baby and its mother is an experience of deep connection. Giving birth is a miracle experienced daily everywhere in the world. It is an entrance into mystery. There is a profound sense of connection with all those ancestors who went before and all the future progeny yet to come. The mother and child in an instant are no longer one, but two, and yet not two either, as they are yet deeply intertwined. The baby cries, and the mother's milk begins to flow. Out of a sound sleep a mother is awakened by the whimpers no one else in the house hears.

Not One, Not Two

Infant cries,
Dark night
Cold floor
Baby, warm, soft.
Seeking mouth turns towards mother's hand,
Pants with urgency.
Tiny mouth moves over neck, shoulder, breast, searching, searching,
Seizes nipple, sucks
Mother's milk releases
Small body sighs with satisfaction.

All eyes close, lost in mutual feeding.
Infant hand caresses mother's breast, strokes so gentle.
Tenderness deeper than pleasure.
Two bodies one body, nothing else exists.

(Joan Hoeberichts)

The ease of that early connection seems to break down these days, as childhood progresses. The naturalness of the parents being in charge and in control, keeping the child safe, often seems to rupture as children become more independent. Parents have difficulty with children who do not match the unconscious template of parental expectation. If the parents were good students, they assume their child will be a good student. If that doesn't happen, family struggle ensues. If they were popular extroverts or athletes, they feel a sense of failure or shame at their child's introversion or nerdiness. If they viewed themselves as failures in adolescence, they need their child to be successful where they failed. Parents do not realize they are forcing their child into the mold of their own needs and desires. They think they only want what is best for their child. It is so hard for them to see their child for himself or herself.

Family work is the most complex, difficult work I do. I limit the number of families I can work with in the same period of time to no more than three because it is so demanding. I try, instead, to facilitate the family working things out their own way through better communication and better understanding. As a therapist, I find it demanding because it is hard to hold three or more different, usually conflicting viewpoints, in a neutral and empathic state of mind. Being a parent is a very difficult job that most of us are poorly prepared for, so I try to hold the parents from a nonjudgmental, supportive stance. However, often the parents are at odds, which complicates the dynamic and requires that I hold both views with equal understanding. The child or children usually want to be heard, respected, and understood so I try to facilitate the parents listening, respecting, and understanding them. This requires from the therapist a high level of concentration and attention to every minute family interaction, including body language, silence, eye contact, and lack of eye contact.

Family work usually begins with an adolescent or child coming in for treatment because the parents feel the child needs it. Once I feel I have built a therapeutic alliance with the child, I will begin, with the child's agreement, to get the family involved.

Our American culture seems to foster disconnection in families. Everyone is so busy; no time or importance is given to connection. Leaving all the family theory behind, when I see a family together I get them talking to each other. Families don't seem to realize how little they talk to each other about themselves, about what's important or going on for each person. Their daily conversations seem to be limited to organizational issues, such as how to manage time, chores, schoolwork, transportation, and so on. Unfortunately, this problem is not limited to families in therapy but is widespread. The paradigm of staying connected without entering into an enmeshed or merged relationship creates constant tension. This paradigm seems so clear in theory, but in life it's muddy and full of conflict. Parents want their children to be good, obedient, compliant and independent, autonomous, creative, and successful. For the most part these are opposing sets of desires. A child cannot be compliant and independent at the same moment. Of course, adolescence is about separation from parents, and conflict is inevitable and even makes the separation process easier to bear. However, it is possible, if difficult, to stay connected throughout the separation process and the difficult adolescent years. The key is listening to each other carefully and with respect, even while disagreeing.

Ken

His parents brought Ken, a depressed sixteen-year-old, to therapy. Ken's parents were worried about their inability to communicate with him except through terrible arguments. Furthermore, they worried, Ken lied whenever it was more convenient than telling the truth. Following our third visit, by which time I had barely established an alliance, Ken made a suicidal gesture and was subsequently hospitalized for a week at an adolescent residential psychiatric hospital. He loved it there and said it was like a "family." He didn't want to come home. Why, I wondered, was the hospital more like a family than home? He said he could be "real" there, and people talked about what was really going on for them.

At the first family visit, Ken began to tell his parents how he was feeling about school. He was miserable. He could do the work, but if he kept up the standard he had set himself, he had no time for his friends. His friends were the most important aspect of his life. He was in all advanced placement courses. Both parents insisted they were not invested in his academic achievement. His dad announced, much to Ken's surprise, that he himself had been a poor student. Ken could not believe it. Dad had gone on to graduate school and held a very important job in industry, so Ken assumed his success was due to his having been a very good student. Dad insisted he had been very disinterested in high school and gotten mostly Cs. His mother realized as the session progressed, that she was indeed, invested in Ken's academic performance. She had been a very good student and had subsequently earned a PhD in economics. It was hard for her not to encourage Ken to extend himself the utmost academically, and she kept a close eye on how Ken did—or rather didn't—organize his time.

Observing the family dynamic, I noticed the mother constantly attempting to interrupt the lovely conversation that was taking place between father and son. It was really hard for Mom to hold back and just allow the connection between Dad and Ken to develop. Dad's job took him away from home often, and he rarely had an opportunity to talk to his son, and when he did have that chance he didn't know where to start. Mom was so used to running the home show that she did not realize she had inadvertently helped to sever the father-son connection. Her own connection with her son was marred by the constant conflict they engaged in over all the things Ken was "supposed to do." They regularly had screaming battles and barely heard one another. Ken was isolated in his own family.

In a subsequent visit, mother and son dialogued about all the things that caused conflict. Ken wanted to be trusted to manage his own time and did not want his mother telling him when to do his homework and when to go to sleep. Mom was concerned that he was not getting enough sleep and was letting his homework go until the last moment. This resulted in Ken's feeling highly stressed because the homework wasn't done or wasn't good enough. I did not see it as my job to negotiate this process or to set rules, although separately with the parents I encouraged them to maintain clear rules and to set consequences for Ken when he broke the rules. In the family session, I saw my task as one of coach, managing the dialogue so that they could fully express to each other all their feelings and thus connect. I suspected Ken was not ready to manage his time fully independently, but I thought it would not be so bad if his mom could back off a bit and let him try. However, I did not offer any opinion. I just insisted that Mom listen carefully and mirror Ken. As Ken felt fully heard, he began to listen more carefully himself to what his mother was saying and what she was feeling. When his mother felt heard and respected, she softened and spoke more warmly and less anxiously.

There was no doubt in my mind that this family cared about each other. The task was to rebuild the connections among them all. The parents had a severe rupture in their relationship. They had never been able to talk about problems in their own relationship. Ken habitually kept secrets from both parents. He struggled with trying to look to them from what they wanted in a son, but he wanted most to just be himself. My goal was to help them talk about the things they couldn't talk about on their own and help them allow each other to be "real" in the family. As parents, most of the dialogue directed at their son, was around guidance and "shoulds." The parents seemed not to allow themselves to just enjoy this intelligent and lively son.

Working with them separately and together as a family, I noticed real communication slowly but steadily beginning to take place. As Ken felt he could express himself more fully with his parents and trusted that they would listen with less judgment, he began to feel the connection with them for which he was unconsciously yearning. His mother worked hard to restrain her tendency to be overly directive and to interject herself in his interactions with his dad. Ken's father made an effort to connect with Ken by teaching him golf and then spending time golfing with him on a fairly regular basis. There was nothing dramatic in this family therapy. There were only subtle shifts taking place as they leaned toward each other in more gentle ways, tentatively at first and later with relaxed laughter as they began to find their natural connection. This tenuous renewed connection allowed them to be more genuine with one another.

The connection between family members is constantly being challenged. How far to go toward satisfying oneself and how far to compromise our own desires when they conflict with what is best for others, is a constant tension in family relationships. However, it is often possible to stay in that tension without pressing for an immediate resolution. When that can be done, even intractable problems may resolve themselves given patience, time, and trust. The key is maintaining that sense of caring, mutual respect, and connection while the dialogue takes place and, most important, staying in dialogue. Dialogue itself maintains connection and keeps relationships vital. We are interdependent beings. Our notion of total independence is illusion. Managing our relationships is the greatest challenge we have as human beings but staying in relationship is also the most rewarding.

Of course, this tension between what is best for me and what is best for others brings me full circle to my own Zen practice. How to be present with my family and participate fully in my Zen practice? That question remains my practice as I continue to experience occasional conflict between my desire to be with my family and my desire to practice.

CONCLUDING THOUGHTS

In the beginning mind is like a turbulent river.
In the middle it is like the river Ganges, flowing slowly.
In the end it is like the confluence of all rivers, like the meeting of son and
    mother.
Tilopa,

—The Union of Joy and Happiness
(Bercholz and Kohn 1993, 270)

I have a meditation group that sits at my house every week. One morning recently, the sangha arrived when my house was full of visiting adult children and grandchildren. I introduced a couple of early arrivals to my family and then we went to sit. Later, as we did walking meditation outside, my two-year-old grandson raked the leaves in the backyard. "Hi Steve," he called happily to one of the silent walking meditators he had met that morning. Steve waved back. As I reflected on this with amusement, I thought that, in fact, I had come a long way toward integrating practice with my family. Our sangha's practice doesn't look a bit monastic, and we lack the lovely precision of a formal temple. We sit amidst the messy chaos of undressed grandchildren and unmade beds. When we do sesshins, my husband will often enter the kitchen and strike up a conversation forgetting that a silent retreat is in progress. And yet, this is my life, and it is full and satisfying.

NOTES

1. Personal communication, Zen Center of Los Angeles, (1993).
2. Mirroring is a therapeutic technique in which the therapist, or in this case, the partner, repeats the speaker's words. In Hendricks' model, the mirroring process permits the speaker to feel fully listened to and provides the partner an opportunity to practice containing her emotions while listening until the speaker is finished.

REFERENCES

Bercholz, S., and S. Kohn. (1993). *Entering the stream*. Boston: Shambhala.

Fairbairn, W. R. D. (1952). *Psychoanalytic studies of the personality*. London: Routledge Press.

Guntrip, H. (1995). *Schizoid phenomena, object relations and the self*. Madison, CT: International Universities Press, Inc.

Hendrix, H. (1988). *Getting the love you want*. New York: Harper Perennial.

Keizan, Z. (1991). *The record of transmitting the light*. Trans. F. H. Cook. Los Angeles: Center Publications. (Original work circa 1300).

Miller, J., and I. Stiver. (1997). *The healing connection*. Boston: Beacon Press.

Mitchell, S. (1993). *Hope and dread in psychoanalysis*. New York: Basic Books.

Wellwood, J. (1996). *Love and awakening: Discovering the sacred path of intimate relationships*. New York: HarperCollins.

Winnicott, D.W. (1965). *Maturational processes and the facilitating environment: Studies in the theory of emotional development*. Madison, CT: International Universities Press.

Chapter Twelve

A Transformational Moment

Susan Flynn

I would like to describe the experience I had that prompted me to write a chapter on "A Transformational Moment," then discuss the questions this experience has stimulated.[1] One of the things I have worried about in writing this chapter was whether this experience was only personal—that the questions I've been living these past months would not be of interest to others. I worried that it was too personal. After all, what if I cried in a room full of people I don't even know. I felt embarrassed as I thought about trying to write as I feel so vulnerable these days, and this paper would make that an obvious shared reality. I then was reminded of the kind of writing that seems to me most worth reading. It's the kind where people write about the most personal of experiences and somehow manage to make that experience ours, or like ours enough to help us remember. So, I decided it was worth a try, even though I've always been frustrated with the limitations of language to convey emotional experience. I believe I'm writing this because I have to. The desire to come to terms with the personal power of the experience is very compelling, but I do believe the questions this experience has raised in addition to being of the utmost personal import, are questions that are embedded in human experience.

I found the flier announcing the conference on my desk late last April, two days before I visited my sister who was dying of cancer. It seems sychronistic, now in retrospect, to have found the flier and to have decided based on my immediate response to the theme of "the Transformational Experience" that I wanted to write something. Something. About what something? I didn't know. The something I was on the edge of, as it turned out.

My sister and I had not seen each other for ten months. The last time I saw her was at a family wedding in Chicago, in June. She seemed healthy.

In November, a sizable tumor was discovered in her lung; it was irradiated and she had chemotherapy to shrink the tumor so it could be surgically removed. She had the surgery done in January and proceeded on a very difficult recuperative process (she had three ribs removed) and a significant reactive depression, in addition to the assault of major surgery. The scans done months after the surgery were clear, and she was pronounced "free and clear of cancer." She and her husband went to Florida in gratitude for the beginning of the next phase of their life, and while there she began having seizures, and upon diagnostic investigation, it was discovered she had ten little brain tumors and had a very short anticipated life span.

I wrote the proposal for the conference presentation right after I returned from that first visit to my sister. This was in early May. My sister died August 30. I would like to talk about my experience of her death, and the transformations involved for me, for her, and for the relationship. I would also like to discuss my understanding of how my being a student and practitioner of both meditation and psychoanalysis made possible my capacity to stay with the intensity of this experience more fully.

My sister lived in Chicago, where I grew up, and I live in California, where I have lived since my mid-twenties. This visit in May was a visit I anticipated with much anxiety. The sister whom I had seen in apparently good health nine months before was now clearly dying. How would she look, how would I respond, what would I say, how would she feel, how would I feel? All these unanswerable and relentless anxiety-driven questions.

I was well aware that, although I would not call this a "bad relationship," my relationship with my sister was more of a "nonexistent relationship." Seven years in early childhood can be a lifetime, and she is my "big sister" by seven years, and we coped with our family difficulties differently. Her path included getting out early and often, including starting her own family when I was twelve and she was nineteen. The sister whom I was going to visit in the hospital last May (I was seeing her in the hospital because she had fallen the weekend before and broken her hip, and had just had a hip replacement) was someone I was aware I felt like I never knew. And she was dying. And she would probably die with my having the feeling we never knew each other. Not really. It added greatly to my sadness and anxiety.

As I walked into the hospital room, I saw my completely bald sister, whom I barely recognized physically because of the ravages of the cancer and the treatment. As I looked at her, I experienced what I now consider a transformative moment—all that was there in that moment was love. No history, no other people in the room (there were actually five), just the experience of knowing, and being known, loving, and being loved. Later I would like to talk about, and think about, the transformative power of that moment. I think that moment has implications for our clinical understanding of what can happen between two people, and in certain circumstances, more than two people, when they are completely present in the moment.

This was all I planned to focus on when I wrote the proposal, that particular transformative moment. But the experience that I have come to consider transformative continued until and through her death, as did my questions.

After this visit, I returned to California and was surprised to see how constantly my sister was in my thoughts. How was she? Was she in pain? Could I do anything to help? How would I want someone to be with me if I were dying? How would I want her to be with me if I were dying? I sent her cards often, called her often, but we have never had much phone contact, and the truth is we had no context for conversation established. The fact that she was dying of cancer made it hard to feel like anything else was worth talking about. As she continued to rapidly fail, she understandably wanted less phone contact. It took energy, and it was awkward. I thought about my sister more in those four months than I'm sure I thought about her during her whole life. I started to get anxious that she would just slip away. My husband and I had planned a visit to see her in early August; I was afraid she would be dead by then. I wrote her a letter telling her everything I wish I had told her during her life. The conversations I had wished we had, the questions I'd wished I had answered, like "What happened to your first marriage—why did you divorce?" I answered that question with an understanding and honesty I was incapable of at the time. I told her how glad I was that she had been my big sister. I had never called her my big sister before, nor had she ever called me little sister. It was a letter that was enormously relieving to write. It supposedly touched her deeply, and she asked it to be read often; she also shared it with our other sister.

During this visit, the one after she received the letter, I had about ten minutes alone with her—the only minutes alone with her between that first visit in May and her death. There are different ways to explain this, our individual defenses, a family emotional system that does not support verbal communication about painful experiences, and her husband, six children, seventeen grandchildren, in-laws, and other sister, who wanted to be around her as much as I did. After the recuperation from the broken hip in May, she was at home, with no more visits to the hospital through her death. This visit in early August, the one I thought would be the last, was of course very emotional, both in anticipation, and in actuality. She and I both thought that was to be our last time to see each other. My husband and I visited her often for the three days we were there, and on the last day before we were to leave to fly back to California, I didn't think I could say good-bye to her. She was resting on the couch, and as I went to say good-bye, everybody else left, my husband, her husband, and her two daughters who were there. We then had quite a wonderful, albeit confusing interchange; confusing on a verbal content level but a deep emotional communication. The first thing she asked me was if our mother knew? I wasn't quite sure what to do with that question, for many reasons, not the least of which being our mother died three years ago. I answered what I felt to be the truth, "Yes, Mom knows what's happening with you, and she is waiting for you." She looked deeply into my eyes, teared up, and said, quite intently, "That's good to know." She said something again about our mom, was she OK; Judy seemed to have considerable anxiety about something she was calling "our mom," so I tried to see if I could just address the anxiety without understanding it—or the meaning of it—and I said that my sense of our mom from my dreams about her was that she was fine, and she was much more peaceful and less anxious than she had been before, and that she was waiting for Judy. She was right there waiting for her. What I remember feeling was enormous amounts of love, very peaceful, and so grateful for a real human contact with my sister. Time was very different than usual linear time. Everything seemed to be happening very slowly, or better said: time didn't seem to be happening at all. I was holding her hands—she tried to say something else to me and got very frustrated and said how much she hated what was going on—and I said how hard it was she couldn't find the words sometimes anymore—and she cried, then looked at me intently, and asked, "Does Sue know what is happening?" and I said, "Yes, she does," because at this point, I wasn't sure who I was to her, and I knew that wasn't the most important thing. What was important was that she knew we all knew what she was going through. I remember thinking as I watched her effort, how much dying felt like giving birth; how similar the struggle of the baby leaving the womb, is to the struggle of the life leaving the body. Then I told her I thought it was really important that she knew we would all miss her very much when she left, but that we all wanted her to go when it was the right time for her. That we all had each other, we would take care of each other, we would all be OK, and that our mom, and I sensed, our dad, was right there waiting for her when it was the right time for her to leave. She looked at me again, for a very long and serious moment, and said, again, "That's good to know." We were quiet for quite awhile, in that timeless time. I told her I loved her very much. She said she knew that, and that she also loved me. I sat very close, holding her, this sister I had seldom touched. In some intuitive way I knew that I needed to stay until she told me to go. We were quiet, and then she looked away for a split second before she said the words I anticipated, "You have to go now." I said, "I know," kissed her, held her close, then left.

I felt in a completely different state of consciousness. It wasn't quite euphoria, and I don't believe it was mania. I think I had the privilege of being in some liminal space with her. By that I mean some in-between space between life and death, between separateness and oneness. I wrote the experience down as soon as I got in the car because I knew my conscious mind would lose it, like a dream.

We returned to California: I continued to feel like the recipient of a gift, and also that I had been able to give Judy a gift—or perhaps the real gift was to see the gift going back and forth. As August continued, so did Judy's march toward death. I more than ever just wanted to be with her. She wasn't talking on the phone anymore. I wrote her often but had no satisfaction in that the words on paper seemed so unreal compared to the experience I had in her presence. My husband and I had planned a trip to Hawaii for a conference and vacation before we knew of Judy's metastasis. The trip was planned for the end of August. I suffered with the questions should I go, should we go, should I just take a leave from my practice and go be with my sister, why would I do that, what good would that do anybody? Would it make any difference to her? Could I just do it for myself, etc. etc. etc.? Right before we left for Hawaii, I struck a bargain with myself. If Judy made it through the week we were gone to Hawaii, I would fly to see her the morning we got back—simply because I wanted to see her again. It might not make too much difference to her at that point because she was in and out of consciousness, but no one seemed to have a sense of how long she would live. The nurse said she could die tomorrow or in two months, so I didn't know how to plan. But I realized that I just wanted to see her. Once I made that decision, my mind quieted, and we went to Hawaii and returned to Sacramento at midnight on Friday night, August 29. I got on the plane to Chicago, Saturday morning August 30, at 10 a.m. and arrived in Chicago at 5. My other sister picked me up from the airport, and we drove directly to Judy's home, where we arrived at 6:15. She died at 7:30 that evening. I was so deeply grateful I had let myself go see her. It was a privilege to be with her, her family, four of her six kids, their spouses, her husband, my sister and me. I was sitting right next to her for most of that hour before she died, able to touch her and care for her. Now, maybe it was just luck that I got there. But I felt she called me, and I went. I felt completely drawn to be with her, and my mind would not stop thinking about her until I decided to go. She knew I was coming and knew *when* I was coming. It doesn't seem quite right to say she waited for me. I think the way I would describe it that seems most real is that we had to give each other something and that we had to be together to do it. I think I helped her die in some way I can't use words to explain, and I think she's helping me live, wake up, be transformed in the experience.

In a way it is too early to have to write a paper about this because she died less than a month ago. I'm aware that this is a very raw experience—unmetabolized, unmentalized—to a great degree, hanging around in me in a visceral way. I dream about Judy and her death often.

But in a very real way, it is still worth talking about. And after all, the conference is in early November, so reality wins again. So is this what I would write with the perspective of time? No, but it is what I can write now. Anyway, questions are more compelling than answers.

What happened between my sister and me? What did we break out of in that moment in the hospital room? What are the implications for our clinical work as psychotherapists where we can also get frozen in time and thought about our patients, as we can get frozen in their time and thoughts? Was it as simple as cancer had so humbled her, and dismantled her defenses, that I saw for the first time my sister's vulnerability? I know I felt in that moment that I had seen her for the first time. What about me? What happened to me in that moment? It was like these two people, life-long sisters, had just met and fell in love, in a certain way. The best word for that moment is startling. I remember being very anxious, in anticipating seeing her. But I also remember being surprised how deeply disturbed I was by what was happening to her. I remember thinking I had no idea I loved her that much. I've always been closer to my other sister. If it had been Sharon, my overwhelming response would have made sense. It didn't fit with how I thought I felt about Judy.

What does death have to do with this transformation? There is nothing like the end of the line to make things more urgent, more real, and more precious. Why can't we/why can't I be that awake all the time? What would it take? Could she and I have awoken to each other without her dying pushing us to it? I think so, but I'm not sure how. It wasn't that we were different people. We were just who we had always been, underneath all the ways we had developed to "be sisters"—we were finally just who we are with each other. What a relief.

Why did she talk so much about our mother? Perhaps that seems like a strange question, but my sister and my mother, as far as I know, never achieved closeness before my mother's death, and early on it had been a painful and stormy relationship for both. When I shared the first draft of this paper with my consultation group, one of my friends/colleagues associated to a Wallace Stevens's poem "Sunday Morning," which I include with gratitude to Dr. Barbara Brandes for her association and Stevens for the beauty of language that succinctly expresses the ineffable.

> Death is the mother of beauty, mystical
> Within whose burning bosom we devise
> Our earthly mother's waiting, sleeplessly.

> (Stevens 1971, 7)

Yes, Judy was talking about our shared mothers, biological and mystical; birth mother and death mother. I knew we were having a big conversation about more than I could understand at the time; I remember having a split second thought, "I have no idea what we're talking about," then I just tried to stay connected and not lose either of us. There were also my thoughts during that earlier visit watching Judy labor, of how much the work of dying is like the work of giving birth. How similar the struggle of the baby leaving the body is like the struggle of the life, the soul, leaving the body. The baby wants to stay inside the known womb-mother as much as our life wants to stay inside our known earthly body; and the baby also wants to be allowed to be free, to be unconstricted, as much as our spirit wants to be freed. Of course by the time of delivery, the mother is very well ready to have the baby outside, and gone, at least gone from inside her; as our earthly body is well ready to have our life, our spirit gone, from inside it. I felt like I was cheering for Judy to die at the end, to let go, just let go, let it happen. Such work, such labor. Perhaps like a mother who has just delivered, the peaceful look I saw on Judy's face after her death spoke to her awareness of her job well done, her life delivered, as clearly as she had delivered the life of her six children.

Why did this relationship with my sister, four months, and in a particular way ten personal minutes, transform my relationship to my family and to my early experience? I don't know how, but it has, as my dream life has attested. I have revisited family life with a depth of insight I have never had before. I am seeing things I couldn't see before. Much of it is painful. I think that I can see it because of the contrast with the very good experience I had with my sister. Like when our patients feel held in a better and safer way, they can reach more deeply for their as yet unexperienced terror or pain.

I think that we needed each other. She needed me to be with her as she died, and I needed her to continue to live in a different way. She gave me an enormous gift, as I did her, and I don't know how to talk about it, but I can feel it, and I know it changed me and my life.

My death is more real now—not as what will happen at the end of my life but that my death is just as much a part of my life as the living, alive part of my life. Maybe what I'm trying to say is this experience of being so deeply involved in my sister's dying has made me more alive and opened the possibility to be more completely alive in the moment of death, like Lester in the movie *American Beauty*, who, as he was dying and was as alive as he had ever been, was grateful for every single moment of his "stupid little life."

Judy was alive when she died. Maybe just for a split second—but right before she took her last breath her eyes opened, and she saw something—we all talk about it differently. My brother-in-law says that she looked around and saw each of us in the room. One of her daughters said she looked like she was looking for something. I thought she saw something—but it wasn't in the room—it seemed to startle her as her eyes got very big and then, last breath, and she was gone.

Who knows, perhaps my mother was waiting, or perhaps she was looking for something, or perhaps . . . well, either way, she's gone—and has left me with a beautiful something in my hand, that I appreciate the opportunity to look at with you. Two days after I started to put this experience into words, I had one of the dreams about Judy—she gave me a beautiful gift as she was leading a meditation group I was attending. It was a cut glass bowl, a translucent amber color that matched something she was wearing. I felt our giving and receiving this gift.

Now, Judy doesn't, or I should say, didn't lead a meditation group. But I do. I coordinate the Sacramento Satsang in my home for the Blue Mountain Meditation Community in Tomales, California. Judy did not know that, bit it's not Judy's dream, it's mine, alluding to the centrality of my understanding of the centrality of my meditation practice to my capacity to stay with the experience of her death, of *dying*. Also, my dream says that Judy and I were in a meditation group that she was leading and that I was attending. Exactly right. The deep source of my gratitude toward my sister stems from my awareness that Judy allowed me to participate in one of the mysteries of life, that of dying, of her dying. I doubt if it is possible to learn about death in an impersonal way. She let me learn from, and with her, as we do in meditation, about some truth far bigger than us, or our capacity to understand.

I couldn't successfully stay with my meditation practice until I completed my psychoanalysis eight years ago. Before that, meditation was a "good idea" that I could not endure. I had attempted participation in several different meditation communities and practices and discontinued each, feeling discouraged. Psychoanalysis deepened my capacity to stay with myself, to ride the waves of personal, primarily emotional, experience, which allowed me to sit with myself no matter what happened or didn't happen. At the end of my analysis I could also play the piano again, something that I desired but could not stay with before that time. I think that all of this, the meditation, the analysis, playing the piano, participating in Judy's death have one thing in common—the simple art of staying present, and the only thing simple about that is writing the previous sentence.

I have always felt that psychoanalysis saved my emotional life; well, actually, always is not quite true. In fact, my personal analysis felt life-threatening as I experienced it in a certain way that meditation feels life-threatening. There are certain aspects of our character, of our life experience that we are very identified with, and it feels like a "little death" to transcend these attachments. However, there are moments of what feel like "pure reward"; of validation of the worth of the discipline and of commitment to processes like psychoanalysis and meditation. When you know beyond a shadow of a shadow of a doubt, that every session—be it analysis or meditation—was past being well worth it. Being with Judy during her death was just such a moment.

NOTE

1. This chapter is an expanded version of a paper that I originally presented at the International Federation for Psychoanalytic Education Conference held in Pasadena, California, in November 2003.

REFERENCE

Stevens, W. (1971). *The palm at the end of the mind: Selected poems and a play by Wallace Stevens*. Ed. Holly Stevens. New York: Knopf.

Index

About the Contributors

Paul C. Cooper is a training analyst, a clinical supervisor, and on the faculty of the National Psychological Association for Psychoanalysis. He is a former board member and faculty member at the Center for Spirituality and Psychotherapy. He is also on the faculty and is a supervisor at the Institute for Expressive Analysis. In addition, Dr. Cooper is on the editorial board of *Groundwater: Journal of Buddhism and Psychotherapy* and the *Psychoanalytic Review*. He is the author of numerous award-winning poems and articles, including the Ernest Angel Award for "Affects and Self States: A Case Study on the Integration of Buddhist Analytic Meditation and Psychoanalysis." He coedited *Religion and Psychotherapy: Many Paths, One Journey*. Dr. Cooper maintains a private psychotherapy practice in New York City.

Jeffrey L. Eaton is a full member of the Northwestern Psychoanalytic Society in Seattle and a fellow of the International Psychoanalytic Association. He is a clinical faculty member of the department of psychiatry at the University of Washington Medical School. He is cofounder and chair of the steering committee of the Alliance Community Psychotherapy Clinic and in private practice in Seattle. His essays have appeared in the *Journal of Melanie Klein and Object Relations* and *Psychoanalytic Review.*

Mark Finn is a psychologist and psychoanalyst who has been active in the conversation between Buddhism and psychoanalysis for the past twenty years. He coordinated a series of large conferences on Buddhism and psychotherapy and for eleven years presented on these issues for the Cape Cod Institute of Albert Einstein College of Medicine. He has been on the faculty of Cornell Medical College and the Albert Einstein College of Medicine. Dr.

Finn has lectured in New Zealand and Finland and is the author of numerous chapters, essays, and book reviews on the relationship between spiritual issues and psychoanalysis, including contributions to *Psychoanalysis and Buddhism: An Unfolding Dialogue* (2003) and *The Couch and the Tree: Dialogues in Psychoanalysis and Buddhism* (1998). He coedited *Object Relations and Religion: Clinical Applications* (1992).

Susan Flynn is a psychoanalyst and clinical psychologist in private practice in Sacramento. She is a training and supervising analyst at the Psychoanalytic Institute of Northern California and a graduate and member of the Psychoanalytic Center of California in Los Angeles. She currently teaches and supervises in the psychiatry department at UC Davis. She has been a meditator for ten years and is coordinator of a Satsang for the Blue Mountain Center of Meditation, a member of the San Francisco Psychoanalytic Institute, and a participant in the New Directions Writing Program, affiliated with the Washington Psychoanalytic Society.

Joan H. Hoeberichts is a psychoanalytic psychotherapist in private practice in New York City and Montclair, New Jersey. Formerly on the faculty of Blanton-Peale Graduate Institute where she taught and supervised, she is a Zen teacher in the White Plum Asangha, a lineage founded by Maezumi Roshi. She leads the Heart Circle Sangha in Ridgewood, New Jersey (www.heartcirclesangha.org). Ms. Hoeberichts initiated the U.S. involvement in the Sarvodaya Psycho-Spiritual Healing Program in Sri Lanka following the tsunami in December 2004. This project provides therapeutic healing processes within a spiritual context to tsunami survivors. She has previously published in *Tricycle: The Buddhist Review;* the *Journal of Religion and Health;* and the *Journal of Sandplay Therapy.*

Robert A. Jonas is director of the Empty Bell, a contemplative sanctuary (www.emptybell.org). Trained as a psychotherapist, he is now a retreat leader, author and musician. A Christian in the Carmelite tradition, he has also received spiritual formation with Buddhist teachers. He is the author of *Rebecca* (1996), *Henri Nouwen* (1998), and many articles. He is a student of *Sui-Zen,* the Japanese bamboo flute (*shakuhachi*). His CDs, *Blowing Bamboo, New Life from Ruins* and *Many Paths, One Joy* are available at: www.cdfreedom.com/robertjonas.

Barry Magid is a training and supervising analyst at the Postgraduate Center for Mental Health in New York City, where he completed his psychoanalytic training in 1981. He has published numerous articles within the psychoanalytic field of self psychology and is the editor of *Freud's Case Studies: Self Psychological Perspectives* (1993), his own translation of Diogenes Laertius, *Life of Zeno* (1996), and *Ordinary Mind: Exploring the Common Ground of Zen and Psychotherapy* (2002). In October 1996, Charlotte Joko Beck gave him permission to establish *The Ordinary Mind Zendo* as an affiliate of the San Diego Zen Center and to serve as its Zen reacher. He received Dharma Transmission from Joko in 1999.

Jeffrey B. Rubin practices psychoanalysis and psychoanalytically informed psychotherapy in New York City and Bedford Hills, New York. He has taught at various psychoanalytic institutes and universities, including the Postgraduate Center of Mental Health, the Object Relations Institute, the C. G. Jung Foundation, the Harlem Family Institute, Union Theological Seminary, and Yeshiva University. He is the author of *Psychotherapy and Buddhism: Toward an Integration* (1996), *A Psychoanalysis for Our Time: Exploring the Blindness of the Seeing I* (1998), and *The Good Life: Psychoanalytic Reflections on Love, Ethics, Creativity and Spirituality* (2004). A long-term student of meditation and yoga, Dr. Rubin is interested in how they each might enrich the psychotherapeutic process.

Susan Rudnick has had a private practice of psychoanalysis and psychotherapy in Manhattan for over thirty years. She has been a training and supervising analyst at the American Institute for Psychoanalysis and is a Certified Focusing Oriented Psychotherapist. For the last twenty years, she has also studied Zen Buddhism. Her work integrates these three related practices, and she is currently working in the area of sleep disorders. Ms. Rudnick was guest editor for a special issue of the *American Journal of Psychoanalysis, Special Issue: Buddhism and Psychoanalysis*, and she is the coauthor of *"A Glimpse of Zen Practice in the Realm of Countertransference"* appearing in that issue.

Marjorie Schuman is a clinical psychologist and psychoanalyst in private practice. She is the program director at the Center for Mindfulness and Psychotherapy in Los Angeles and a member of the faculty of the Los Angeles Institute and Society for Clinical Studies. Along with her Vipassana practice of more than twenty-five years, Dr. Schuman has presented original thinking on the psychophysiology of meditation, eastern and western concept of self, and the evolution of subjectivity. Dr. Schuman's work in this area has been published in *Psychoanalysis and Contemporary Thought* and in *The Psychobiology of Consciousness*, edited by R. J. Davidson.

Tony Stern is a student of Zen Buddhism and other spiritual traditions for the last thirty years. He was educated at Harvard College and Mount Sinai School of Medicine and trained in psychiatry at Cornell. He is a clinical associate professor of psychiatry at New York Medical College and, in addition to private practice, works as an attending psychiatrist at the Westchester mobile crisis team and the assertive community treatment team of the Mental Health Association of Westchester. Dr. Stern has presented widely on psychotherapy and spirituality; settings have included the World Psychiatric Association, the New York Open Center, the American Academy of Psychoanalysis, Pendle Hill Quaker Retreat Center, the American Psychiatric Association, the American Museum of Natural History, and Sarah Lawrence College. Dr. Stern's publications include "Faith and Denial" in the *Journal of the American Academy of Psychoanalysis* (1996) and "Psychosis and Religious Conversion" and *Academy Forum* (2002). He edited *Everything Starts from Prayer: Mother Teresa's Meditations on Spiritual Life for People of All Faiths* (1998) and contributed a chapter to *The Power of Prayer* edited by Dale Salwak (1998) and "The Narrow Ridge: Insights from Zen, Judaism, and Psychoanalysis" in the *Academy Forum* (2006).

Dorothy Yang is a psychoanalytic psychotherapist in private practice in New York City and is a member of the Manhattan Institute for Psychoanalysis. Ms. Yang has treated Mandarin-speaking families as a social worker at Bellevue Hospital's Asian Unit In-Patient Psychiatry. She has worked intensively with HIV-affected families at Bronx Lebanon Hospital. Ms. Yang's current writing focuses on innovative strategies for psychotherapy with Asian individuals and families. She has presented her work with Asian individuals and families in various venues, including Mt. Sinai Hospital in New York City, at the National Psychological Association for Psychoanalysis Discussion Group for Asian-American Mental Health Professionals, and at the NYU School of Social Work. Her article "Cultural Implications in Working With Asian Patients" appeared in *The Participant Observer* (2002). Ms. Yang has practiced Buddhism under the guidance of many of the major highly accomplished Tibetan lamas since 1974.